DENİZ ERTEN

SIGN 1

Qiyamat

Author: Deniz Erten

Translator: Fatma Güler Özşahin

First Edition 2022

ISBN: 9798354225071

DENİZ ERTEN

SIGN 1

Qiyamat

To my dear Allah … to my beautiful Allah …

To my dear Prophet Hazrat Muhammed (pbuh) who shed light on all of us on this path with his noor and to Hazrat Ali, Hazrat Umar, Hazrat Abu Bakr, Hazrat Uthman, Hazrat Hasan, Hazrat Hussein, and the whole Ahl al-Bayt and companions of the Prophet … to Abdal Qadr Gilani, my dear teacher Hazrat Ibn Arabi, Rumi, and Shams … To all beautiful friends of my beautiful Allah …

To my dear family granted to me by my Allah, particularly to my mother Tülay, my aunt Şenay, my sister Mira Şeniz, and to dear Mehmet Ali Bulut. To Dursun and Neslihan … To my dear grandmother Servet who passed away as I was writing these books …

To my precious friend Azra who inspired me to write these books … To my editor and friend Arzu Çağlayan who provided full support … To Kezban who strove with me day and night …

To all my sisters and brothers whom we have been walking together since Sign 1, to all the readers of the Sign …

To everyone whose hearts are beating for Allah and who wants to be an ambassador of charity …

Thank you with all my heart. I owe you a debt of gratitude.

My dear Allah … We are pleased with You … Please treat us with Your grace and mercy … May You make things easier for us …

And …

Please, my dear Allah …

Even if we do not deserve it … May You be pleased with us …

I know …

The beginning and the end of all my words and contemplations in the Series of Sign is

"Only Allah knows the truth of everything …"

Wallahu a'lam bi muradihi bihi …

For our loved ones to forget the promises they gave us, perhaps it is the price for forgetting our promise to Allah.

NEVER GIVE UP

She was one of my sister's friends ...l met her when l came back home from the studio after an exhausting day. They were having dinner and chatting when I arrived, she was enthusiastically telling my sister about something. My sister called me over as soon as I walked through the door.

"Have you finally arrived? Look who I want to introduce you to. Come."

l smiled and left my belongings on the table at the entrance and went right inside.

"Gülnur... this is my sister Deniz," said my sister.

"Hello…"

"Hello Deniz, I was very eager to meet you."

"Thank you."

Under the veil of a harsh nature, I sensed that she housed a fragile and wounded child. She gave me the feeling of a child who closed her eyes to avoid her fear of the dark … She was actually like most of us.

A naive child who tries to cover his/her fragility by trying to prove that he/she is growing and strong. That night, the conversation lasted for several hours, and from that day onwards she would call me from time to time. We worked in the same industry. She had some troubles. She would call and pour out her grief to me. Every time we spoke she would express her disapprovals and complaints about the world, and I would suggest that she should try not to see what is apparent, not what is visible, but what is hidden deep down. However, she would somehow evade this topic, saying that she did not want to think and that she was not yet ready for her life to change.

One day, Gülnur called me, she was crying so much that she was struggling to speak.

"Deniz, why are people like that?" At that moment l became deeply saddened.

"What happened? Where are you? Shall l come to you?" l asked.

"No, that won't be necessary. My friend fetched me I'm going to my grandmother."

She avoided expressing her weaknesses. Like every human being... I could not understand people/why people behaved in a certain way. To personalize this life and one's experiences so much has always meant that you miss the big picture. And life was just an experience, anything could happen to all of us. There was nothing to be ashamed of or to hide from in this... Everything was for human beings ... However, Gülnur could not express herself comfortably on these issues and was unable to realize that her overwhelming grief was from suppressing her feelings...

She had lost her mother at a young age and was subsequently raised by her grandmother. She had a very difficult upbringing and was now making a living for her beloved grandmother and brother. Life has never been easy for her. Although she failed to notice, Allah was always with her and by her side. The injustices she had suffered at the hands of others and the tribulations she did not "deserve" in life led her to question Allah and His system. And in her words, this caused her to only believe in her existence with a perception far away from Allah.

When we spoke over the phone, she started to tell me about being unfairly dismissed from her job and began to list all the injustices she had suffered. She was right... The sector she was in was actually riddled with injustice and twists and turns like all other sectors.

Actually, this is what the whole world is like.

From that day forth, she was unable to understand how the people whom she knew as friends and those who never left her side while she was at her office ran away from her as soon as she lost her strong position!

She called me every few days during her period of unemployment. Gülnur was disappointed. We chatted for hours. She began to understand that Allah was revealing the truths for her benefit, her spiritual growth, and for her salvation in this way.

Sometime later after one of our conversations, which always left her feeling peaceful, she would send me messages saying, "I started performing salah today" or "I started fasting today". These messages that she sent me over several months as well as the conversations we had began to show that she now had a completely different comprehension and true power. She had begun to feel, even live the fact that Allah accompanied her in her migration from her ego to her soul.

When those that had to go were gone and she was reborn into a true resurrection after that rebirth, everything she lost returned to her. But now she had changed. The "Universe Television" that she perceived at another frequency offered her tremendous beauties and broadcasts with the change in her destiny.

Just a year after the day she started losing everything, her life was improving and was better than it was before.

A year passed by... One day, my phone rang... Gülnur was on the other end, her voice trembled with excitement, and she said the following words, "You did not leave me when my so-called friends left me; you, your sister, and even your mother... You held my hand when everyone turned away. Now I have received a better job offer and I got the job. You can ask anything from me."

I cannot explain how my heart began to palpitate...

What could l want? I said, "I did not do anything. It is my Allah who molds and does everything. Just pray for me. Allah bless you for these beautiful words".

A day later she called me again. "Deniz, I wanted to ask yesterday, but I couldn't ask. I have a problem ..."

"What happened?" I asked.

"Look, I am doing this job as a person who has a university degree and has worked in this sector for years ... but how can I say it? There is a lot of unfairness in this business. I see a lot of injustice and relations based on self-interest. Is it right to stay in this sector when I have just established such a nice relationship with my Allah and found peace for the first time in my life? What if my Allah gets away from me when I'm struggling with such things?"

"Don't think like that. People like you, righteous and fair people, should stay in every sector contaminated by unfairness and fight so that our numbers can increase. The concept of humanity is now on vacation indefinitely."

"I don't know, I have such fear in me, fear of falling away from my Allah."

"Gülnur… Who am I? Just a humble servant who tries to communicate between her limited intellect and her heart. Allah is the Knower and the Wise… Don't ask me, ask Allah. He will show you what you have to do and will provide the answer to your question. Do you know what?"

"What?"

"Tomorrow morning before going to work, during the morning salah, ask Allah and say, "My Allah, My dear Allah… Should I quit this job, or should I continue? Give me a SIGN, show me a SIGN of what will happen. Please!" And keep me posted. My Allah will reach you."

"Ok. I will let you know."

She did not call me all day. Then, at seven o'clock in the evening, my phone rang, Gülnur was calling.

"Deniz, I couldn't call you before because I have been crying and shaking for hours."

"What happened?"

"I got out of work, recuperated, and was finally able to call you. I couldn't talk to you earlier because I was crying all day."

I became really worried. "What happened? Please tell me," I said.

"I performed my salah in the morning. I talked to Allah. I told Him everything. You always say, 'Although Allah knows everything, we think He doesn't, so you can talk to Him as if you were talking to your mother or friend,' and I did so. When I finished my salah, I opened my hands and said, My Allah, My dear Allah... You know the situation. Please give me a SIGN. Should I quit this job or should I continue? Please my Allah, I can't decide what I should do, send me a sign. Should I quit or continue? Then I dressed and got into the company transport service. My eyes were closed, I begged Allah like there was a phone line from my heart to Him, holding on to that line every moment. Should I quit or go on, please help me? I was calling out to my Allah, who is closer to me than my jugular vein.

Another company employee got into the staff transport at that time. As I internally repeated my question, I saw him out of the corner of my eye. As soon as he got in, he shouted "laa laaa laa viva Fenerbahçe (a Turkish football team). Fenerbahçe had a match on that day.

He came and sat in the seat in front of me. He took off his Fenerbahçe jersey and put it on the seat. I saw what happened with my eyes half closed.

I asked my Allah for the last time: My Allah please give me a SIGN. Should I quit this job or continue? Then I started to open my eyes slowly. The Fenerbahçe jersey draped on the seat in front of me, was at my eye level. As I slowly opened my eyes, I started to see the jersey clearly. The number 9 was written on it."

I curiously asked her to continue.

"And right above the number 9 the following words were written, "NEVER GIVE UP...""

INTRODUCTION

"The true beloved is Allah, the rest causes wounds."
Rumi

You have a feeling of loss, right? Luck, for example, has never been on your side in this life. Everything you started is ruined. Or your family? Your problems with your family never end…. You gave and gave, but you were always met with ingratitude... Maybe your father or some of your family members passed away when you were very young, like me. I do not know, maybe you have never laughed. People you love and rely on have deceived you. You are having problems with your child, or with your husband or wife whom you trust the most. You look at some people, and think that their lives are going very well without any outstanding achievements or efforts, although they don't deserve it at all, right? But heaven knows why everything happens to you. Financial problems and impossibilities always find you, right?

What did I do to whom that I have experienced these things? Why am I in this situation when everyone's life is just fine?

If these questions that were echoing inside you started to be reflected on the outside, if it has reached an unbearable point, then I won't say that I have more bad news for you.

On the contrary… relax…

The sun begins to shine immediately after the darkest moment of the night. Your sun is about to rise. What matters is the rest and what you will experience from now on.

So, good news for you: Your "Qiyamah" (the Last Judgment Day) is about to come, but this is not a kind of end that you know. This dream, which is actually a "nightmare" for you, is about to end. Just "wake up" and be at "Qiyam" (the standing position during salah).

The days are coming when your "suitable" fate will smile at you again thanks to you.

The days where you will become independent from the past and the future to catch the "MOMENT"…I am telling you that I am also coming from there, and ever since the day I started striving to ESTABLISH my MOMENT, I realized that I was given a big slice of the chance to write the destiny that is considered "written."

And everything has changed since that day…

I started to re-establish my moment with the Quran…

Are you unfortunate?

Or is it YOU that is the fortune?

Everything can change if we can understand this without wasting any more time.

"The person who does not get out of the water will drown, not falling into the water," said Rumi

Don't do this to yourself…

Until now, you have wronged yourself because you could not grasp the truth…

Do not torture your nafs anymore… You are both the heaven and the hell...

And whichever one you take from here; you will live with it forever…

Because YOU are the fortune.

WE ARE ALL ORPHANS

If only you knew when I fell in love with Him…

I lost my father at a very young age; too young to remember what kind of person he was, what he liked, what he thought about life… I always felt a constant loneliness in life. In a crowded solitude… Among people but still all alone… I only had my Allah with me. When I had problems at school or with my friends, I would try to deal with them in my own way.

You know you feel the need to lean on someone, you wish that someone would make life easier for you, but I've never had such a feeling in my life.

I used to listen to my friends in primary and secondary school telling me how their fathers would handle their problems, and how their fathers were looking over their shoulders.

My best friend's father had so much affection for her that it wouldn't have been "human" if I didn't feel like I had a broken wing. I cannot say that I was jealous, but I admit that I was envious. I admired my friends' relationships with their fathers.

When you meet with Allah and Islam, you can be thankful for all the pain you suffered. How strange, isn't it?

For example, I am glad that I am an orphan…

That doesn't mean it's good that my father passed away, don't get me wrong. If the time for him to leave hadn't arrived for his own good, for our good, and for the good of the whole system, he would never have been able to go anyway. The concept called "wisdom" in Islam is hidden in here.

It was the night my father passed away ... "Our father is dead," said my sister. I asked, "What do you mean he died?" She said, "I mean, he won't be able to come back again."

I am not going to deny the fact that, I remained hopeful each time there was a knock at the door. I believed that he would walk in and say, "I'm back!". So, from that day forth, I designated myself to the duty of opening the door every time there was a knock.

But he never came...

The night my father passed away, my sister said these precise words, "Do not cry Deniz, don't cry. Let's do something for our father."

Do something for him?

"What will we do?" I asked.

"People who die go to Allah. We need to pray for them. Come on, let's pray for our father," she said. I said okay in tears.

"My friend taught me this today. Now repeat after me, our father will hear us."

"Really?"

"Yes, really," she said.

And she began to recite Surah Al-Fatiha. I don't remember exactly how she recited it.

She opened her little hands and gestured for me to open mine too.

So, I opened my hands, I cannot recall our pronunciation of the words but together we recited our first Arabic prayer.

Life is not cruel, but people are.

You can experience or be exposed to such things that sometimes you want to give up. Everyone's pain is too great for them, and everyone is equally insensitive to someone else's pain.

With each passing day, I began to believe that my father would not return.

One day my grandmother told me that Allah is the father of us all and He protects and looks after the orphan children even more. The words uttered by both my sister and grandmother initiated those first days of my conversations with my Allah… I cannot explain this.

You know He never broke me.

Whatever we spoke about, He was sending me a sign related to it. He seemed to be saying, "I'm with you, don't worry."

I was out one day. My friends suggested that we go to the breakwater and play. But I lost them along the way, I got lost. The evening came, and at that moment I was overcome by a shiver, and I became frightened …

As I walked, I realized that I was lost, and I thought it would be better to sit on a bench and wait.

I sat down on a roadside bench and began looking at the stars. This is how I started watching them.

"I'm with you, don't be afraid," said a voice inside me. I said, "My Allah…"

He was with me…

"Come on, your mother is worried about you, let's go back," He said. I said, "Okay."

He said, "Don't be afraid, I'll show you the way."

It was not me finding the way home, but my feet acting as if they had received instructions...

l arrived home and knocked on the door. There were voices from inside. I realized everyone was in a state of panic.

Our neighbor Aunty Nermin opened the door and she shouted, "Deniz!"

She began crying.

My mother came running, and she said, "my girl", whilst looking at me through her eyes that had swollen from crying, and she hugged me.

"Where were you? What happened? We were in such despair looking for you," she said. I replied, "I was lost, mom."

If this was any other circumstance, I would have bitten my lip and began crying, but "He" was with me.

"Weren't you scared, my girl?" my mother asked.

"I was not afraid, mom, don't worry. I was not alone; Allah was with me."

Aunty Nermin, my mom, and everybody in the house looked at me. l said as I smiled, "We returned together, don't worry." My "remembering" of Allah was when I lost my father. I can never deny this.

People do not question before they suffer, they do not need shelter before they feel weak, and they do not turn to Him before they realize their helplessness.

In fact, the saying "Allah will distress His beloved servants" stems from the fact that people do not bother to seek the truth unless they are suffering, or they are hurt. However, besides turning this world of people into a paradise, the truth is the only real key to happiness.

Just as people connect to each other through pain rather than happiness, they also attach to/connect to Allah through pain.

Unfortunately, this situation stems from the nature of people being prone to forgetfulness and ingratitude.

They say that Allah alienates His beloved servants from the world. They even tell the story of the Pharaoh.

The Pharaoh had teeth that were tightly locked together like those of a donkey So much so that if something got in between his teeth, it would cause him excruciating pain. However, Allah did not even inflict him with an iota of pain, not even a headache.

We sometimes see people who have inflicted so much harm on others, but still, nothing happens to them.

In fact, what should come to our minds here is the story of Allah giving respite to the devil who did not submit to Adam.

The fact that you don't immediately get a response for the mistake you make in the system is because Allah does not want to lose you. In fact, this is called a "compassion slap" in Sufism.

Do not allow the delay granted by Allah or people saying "Okay, go on, never mind. Nothing happens to the bad," mislead you.

The sooner you are warned, the more loved you are. Remember this...

Years after my father passed away, I met him while I was still carrying my pain inside.

That magnificent man.

The thing that caught my attention about him was his love and affection. Do you know why I fell for him?

One day, there were children playing in the street and his children were among them. The people who saw him said that he did not hug his children, thinking that there might be orphans among those children. Who knows, one of them might have been upset.

I thought no one could have known that heartbreak better than I did.

Then, I wept profusely upon learning that when a bird that was fed by a local boy died he went to visit the boy to offer his condolences.

What a beautiful person he was. I had to find him. I wanted to be one of his beloved orphans.

That luminous person was Hazrat Muhammed (PBUH), and he was also an orphan...

And even the Arabs called the Messenger of Allah "Durri Yateem" (the pearl-like orphan, unique). Due to the invaluableness of the pearl, he was named "Durri (unique) Yateem" which means the one and unique pearl.

The pearl, which is also a symbol of the science of truth, has a very deep meaning ... The pearl is a "living" stone that takes the color of the wearer, heals, reproduces, and darkens itself if it fails to harmonize with the wearer...

An orphan is also like a pearl. It is born from a grain of sand under the sea, and some say that it is, from the tear of an oyster or a raindrop... The oyster patiently keeps it and waits for it to mature... And one day, when that grain of sand and tears become pearls, they become precious, priceless... And immortal...The day comes when the oyster opens its shell, the mother of pearl inside shines so brightly that the fish that see it fall in love with its beauty and begin to swim towards it...

Just like us swimming in the sea of Allah and drawn to the light of our Prophet...

He embellishes and beautifies hearts with his uniqueness... Like a unique pearl...

Even thinking about the art and elegance in these metaphors draws one to the path of Allah and His Messenger...

Years later, while I was working on the verse (ayah) "Protect the orphan", I realized this...

We have come to a completely different realm from our real home. We have been missing our home, we have been missing Allah. We were cut adrift from heaven.

Actually, we are all just trying to get back to where we came from. Whether or not we know where that is... Whether or not we remember...

We have all been in our homelands. We are all orphans...

On that day, I realized that there is a kind of orphanhood that is beyond being fatherless and that orphanhood is related to the meaning of Allah's "protection."

Because otherwise, only the orphans who do not have fathers would benefit …We should always remember that real orphans are those who comprehend that they do not truly have anyone or anything except for Allah even if they are members of a large family or a tribe and they have great amounts of properties, it is those who are aware of this, and who absolutely rely on and surrender to Allah…

Those who rely only on Allah, trust in Allah, surrender to Allah, and ask for whatever they need from Allah alone are orphans in the real sense. They are and will be always under the protection of Allah. Whether they have fathers, a crowded family, or a dynasty …

This is how the justice and mercy of Allah is.

Just like people who are orphans in the sense of fatherlessness or homelessness, there are orphans in ESSENCE, who come from such big families and to whom Allah brings the realization that they are essentially orphans.

If you have felt lonely all your life, if you could not completely rely on anyone or if those you relied on betrayed you, if you have always struggled and succeeded if your life has never been easy, then you live the verse, "There is ease in every difficulty...."

Because when you thought you were alone, Allah was always with you...

Allah is always with you when you think you are not understood...

Whoever relies only on Allah, He will never allow them to depend on anyone else. People do not see what is happening around them, just because they only look at what is in front of their eyes.

People may fail to understand or realize because they are in a hurry but once they slow down and think thoroughly, they begin to understand the truth...

My grandfather, who grew up as an orphan, witnessed the murder of his family when he was five years old, grew up in an orphanage after being brought to Turkey from his homeland, and who was one of the most compassionate people I know, used to say when we were children;

"Don't lean against the wall, it can collapse. Don't lean on people, they die. Only lean on Allah, my darlings!"

People sometimes think how unlucky they are because they consider the happenings with "virtual" values in the world...

However, when the values in the world go out of the world, they lose their validity.

Even the concept of night and day disappears upon going beyond the atmosphere, leaving an endless darkness and emptiness...

In this human-made world system, although we think that the values such as being rich, powerful, or famous provide us with a superior status, after passing to an order where the laws of truth apply and when everything is explicitly set forth, we will likely wish to be poor and to live a rather modest life.

If we go to a world where money has no use and where people with "knowledge and morals" constitute a higher class, then maybe we will be humiliated when showing off with our latest car models.

While classifying events and people as lucky or unlucky, do not make the mistake of deciding according to the apparent perception of the worldly justice system.

For example, it is said that the way to heaven opens for a mother who loses a small child…

How painful it will be for that mother, right?

But if she knows that this great pain she is suffering in her short life will bestow both her and her child a reward in their eternal lives that will be envied by everyone else, perhaps this reversed life may completely turn into something different.

The world is our mirror…

When we look in the mirror, we raise our right arm, but the reflection we see is that we raise our left arm…

We throw our elderly into the street and worship our children. However, just as a beloved servant of Allah became a neighbor to Moses in heaven through his mother's prayer, another servant was sentenced to Hell because she raised a bad son…

Our children, with whom we experience an egoistic sense of ownership and love, become a test for us. As we continue to be overly devoted to them, they lead us to our own hell. We voluntarily accept it, but we don't even notice it…

We see and live this world from the reverse side. When we approach death, we seek Allah and begin worshiping…

However, worship is required to start living; it is not possible to live without truly "living" ...

They are the LIVING DEAD…[1]

---

1 They asked Huzeyfet'ubnu Yeman: "Who are those considered dead although they are alive?" Huzeyfet'ubnu Yeman answered, "Those are the ones who do not hinder an evil that they witness with their hands and tongues or who do not hate it with their hearts."

TO BEGIN WITH

Do not identify the truth with the standards of people, but
identify people with the standard of the truth
-Hazrat Ali

As there are within yourselves. Can you not see?
-Surah adh-Dhariyat 21 [2]

Life is created so intelligently that the same substance either gives life or takes life because of its amount... Nothing else... The same substance. The story of the poison and the antidote is a summary of life...

They call this world the "mirror" of the true world that we will go to later...

I thought about it a great deal and one day, my Creator made me realize the truth and I wept...

This world is the mirror of the real world, yes and you know what the result is?

In this world, everything but everything is seen and lived in reverse according to the original...If Hazrat Muhammed (PBUH), the prophet of Allah to whom He presented the world and whom He referred

---

2 Dhariyat: The state of the winds that scatter and raise clouds of dust. The verse "scattered by the wind" (Surah al-Kahf 18:45) supports this. As an explanation of this verse, Hazrat Ali also mentions the meaning "that erupts the volcanos, destroys the creatures." It is possible to consider explosives in this category.

to as " My Beloved," chose to accept what was happening, to needlessly bear all the suffering and defamation even when he knew that Allah could destroy those who tried to harm him with a single word, and if he chose "faqr," unnecessary poverty, although the reign of the universe was offered to him. Did he, the possessor of the profound knowledge granted by Allah, go through all these adversities for no reason?

-No… There was great wisdom and knowledge underlying all these. A pearl of wisdom that most of us cannot see when we look with these physical eyes. And the truth and reflection of this world is the underlying secret of that wisdom.

Your reflection in the mirror is called "your opposite." Your opposite is also your reverse.

You see your truth in reverse.

Every time you are lost, every time you are hurt… just look in the mirror…

And raise your right hand … When you see in the "opposite" image in front of you that you have your left hand raised, not right, realize that you misunderstood the message… SMILE…

Realize that you were treated with "grace," not "pain" and SMILE…
And BE GRATEFUL…

Everything you lose is your gain … Remember, medicine is said to taste bitter, but it also brings healing to people.

This story belongs to YESTERDAY.

The setting of this story is called the "WORLD". In His sight, everything has come to pass. …

The reverse was actually the front, and the front was actually the reverse…"Nafs (ego)" is a delightful hypocrisy…

You think "you are living, " but tell me what do you do on the day you realize this? You realize that everything is just a DREAM.

Both have existed and never existed…

Everything happened yesterday and ended. That's why the only comment about life is "I'm watching…"

Watch…

If you're holding this book in your hands and still haven't understood the SIGNS after all that has happened to you, it's time to "wake up".

Stop searching outside to find the treasure you were given…The treasure is buried in you. Dig through the soil towards your heart…

When you get there, you'll feel like you're in the sky…You will ascend as you descend into your heart…

You will see that each of us, each child of Allah, who loves you so much more than your mother does, is indiscriminately endowed with genius, with happiness, and with art, and raised in the cradle of this world rocking back and forth.

When each caterpillar leaves its cocoon, it becomes a butterfly and begins to fly…

Unless it finds the treasure inside and comes out of the cocoon, nobody can get it out…

Each person's lack is another person's surplus. When you see this, you will understand unlimited justice…

Those who change their past change their future…

The world is a game
Life is a toy
The one who understands this has salvation
The one who does not understand this will burn
-Deniz Erten

"All praise is due to Allah, the Lord of all Worlds…"

Another word we have uttered many times but have never thought enough about …

"Realm" (ālam in Arabic) is a word derived from the same root as the words "scholar" (Alīm in Arabic) and "omens" (ālamāt in Arabic) …

What does "omens" mean?

Omens; SIGNS showing people their way in deserts (trace, symbol, mark…).

See the beauty of the description…

My beautiful Allah, who summarizes the entire existence and what each of us has lived in one word…

"Signs showing people their way in deserts…"

We, lost children of Islam, are lost in this desert-equivalent world…

We were unable to READ the signs that Allah gave us… We were lost in a burning desert like the blind.

The sight of the eyes is not enough, the heart must see. And the Quran also points to this…. The Quran gives signs, it guides, but for it to become useful, one must contemplate …One has to comprehend and practice.

The person who follows the tracks and signs reaches the main road sooner or later…To the path of salvation… Yet, we cannot see the light of Allah although we are all surrounded by Him and His signs and by the divine light of our Prophet… We are the children of crowded loneliness...

We are the children who are under the illusion of the apparent knowledge ... And we are lost in the realms...

Realm means "symbol, sign, trace, starboard, flag, and mountain..." The mountain... Yes, this realm is like a mountain... Whatever you say, it will echo back to you...

And this realm and each of us with our internal individual realms are also signs… Each of us is one of the highest signs bearing the meanings of Allah's names and attributes as "Ayat al-Kursi" (the Throne Verse) …

And Allah is also the Lord of those realms, that are, the "signs".

"Realm", "omens" … All these words and signs are related to the word KNOWLEDGE (ilm in Arabic) … What does this Signify to us?

Knowledge means "knew and understood the knowledge and science, and reached the knowledge by interpreting the TRACES AND SIGNS..."

Each of us carries the meaning of Allah's names and attributes... Each of us also carries His name the All-Knowing to a certain extent.

Each of us will proceed towards our truth only if we try to reach knowledge by reading Allah's verses, which are the signs and traces. This is not what Allah needs. This is our need to move forward to our fullness as we migrate to the real world from this virtual world where we came as incomplete ...

Allah says He will give knowledge to anyone who wants it... What we are talking about here is the knowledge of Allah. That is the only knowledge that encompasses all the knowledge...

And whoever has knowledge has everything... And understands that there is nothing else...

Everyone's book differs from one another but remains the same...

Everyone's communication with Him depends on the "wireless network" strength of their own heart and brain... This communication is different for each of us...

As long as we want to communicate, as long as we say, "My Allah, are you there?"

At that moment, we see that Allah has embraced us there, in ourselves, and everywhere...

At that moment, we realize that this has always been the case, but "we" have not seen it nor made any effort to see it...

Such heartbreak! The only true friend in life, the only true love, the only real support... Living for years in a state of oblivion while Allah is with you in every way and anytime, watching you and talking to you in every moment...

Being unable to see how the day we realize these truths inside ourselves, not the solutions we are looking for outside, will beautify and change everything...

If your problems do not end, if the "same kind of" lessons do not end, then you haven't learned... You have not been able to give the correct answers to the exams you are taking... It means there is a communication problem between you and your teacher...

It means the time has come...

The time is now...

The moment of establishing a "real" dialogue with Allah by feeling it deep in your heart instead of a "memorized one without knowing the meaning", starting to talk to Him, to share your grief with Him sincerely, and to start asking only from Him...

Actually, this is His advice to us... Seeing Him in ourselves and everywhere... Realizing that He is always in dialogue with us... Trying to see what He shows us in terms of our own deficiencies and reach Him, meet Him...

Everything we rely on "other than" Him will turn its back on us and will be our test.

Just like our shadows, which are always with us, abandon us in the dark... Because darkness is being away from Him.

I was going to a meeting, but I was worried about whether or not it was good, "My Allah, I don't know, but you know. If this is not good for me, only put red traffic lights in my way and if it is good, open my way..."

Do you know that all the lights on the road were red on that day? When I looked at this business meeting which I could not find the line between trade and justice and which might have been beneficial for my nafs (ego) and for my worldly life, the content itself was not problematic. Mentally, it was okay, but in terms of sense, no, there was something else repelling me... I thought to myself, "What are you doing, Deniz? You cannot see and know the truth... Ask your Allah... " and I asked...

Allah was enough for His servant... I had my answer and after a short time, He showed me that the answer was good for my spirit, not my nafs (ego) ...

Beginning to understand with knowledge of Allah seems like something that turns life upside down at first... There are meanings that seem incomprehensible and contradictory to the worldly view... Money is valuable in the world, objects are precious ... If it is in the way of Allah, knowledge, and prayer... While some ask for prayers and others want to earn money, the signs tell us which ones we keep in our pockets in the world of truth ...

Here, the scholars and the wise who guide us to read the signs presented to us show their directions to people like road signs or a compass... They put up signs like flags on the areas of the meaning and draw borders...The concept of "mountain", which is used in the Quran to refer to the perfect and accomplished guide (murshid al-kamil), also includes the scholars who have this knowledge. The scholars who hammer the pieces of land into the earth with mountains, lead the lost children on the path of Allah to reach their destination in a sheltered way, without getting lost any further...

We are the beings who are stuck between those who live far from Allah and those who claim that there is only one way to talk to Allah or otherwise it will be impossible to contact Him. Yet we are beings who know in their hearts that there is no one but Allah...

We have been convinced of the correctness of false teachings on so many issues that we have become unable to know where to take shelter like a "needy", and feel like we are unprotected...

There are numerous realms equal to the number of living beings, and Allah talks to us using the language that we understand...

As long as we open up the "access networks" that we have closed due to worldly concerns...

Whether or not we realize it, there are other things happening behind the apparent world system...

When we start to talk about Allah, religion, or our prophet, people who are distant from this subject immediately start to tell a thousand different stories... What is told is based on, "interpretation and channelization" or "what they heard from here and there". Whereas the only book that has been written and not tampered with is the Quran, and when you can understand it as soon as you take it in your hands, what else can a person rely on?

I experience this very often, and I interestingly realize that those who deny Allah, religion, and the prophet do not even know what they deny, and they are stuck in their own concepts with their presumptions... It is really sad to realize with a few answers given and a few questions asked that people do not even know what they deny...

It hurts one's heart to "forget" that even the breath you take is not under your control, and to realize the pain of not being able to experience the "power of knowing your neediness" or not being "predestined" to this...

When you do not come to the point they want in this matter, this time, it is upsetting that they try to portray themselves as victims, this time with claims that they are alienated from religion due to false religious interpretations and other similar expressions...

Our taking shelter in a mentality such as victimization is nothing more than our own laziness... Because it has never been seen that Allah turns His back on a person who takes the Quran by themselves with a clean heart and comprehension, or who says, "my Allah, teach me Your knowledge" even without making much effort... The Quran is such a book that by trying to get to the root of the words and understand the real meanings of the words, it conquers you and you get such a divine attraction (jadhb) that everything remains undefined. On the one hand, it tells you of the past, the whole history of humanity, and on the other hand, tomorrow, and the future while telling you about the present in the same line or even in the same word...

The endless knowledge, hidden in the extraordinary poetic and artistic nature of the words used, gradually draws you in as you turn to it. When you take a closer look at the mystery of the numbers used, the planets, and the chosen words, "hidden truths" begin to gradually unfold for you…. When you start to understand some truths, you realize that you are faced with a "poetic" expression of a scientific determination or determinations in every word of Allah's friends, and you are astonished…

The fact that the Quran is not a "human word" can be understood by its interactive communication with any reader…

All that is needed is to try to communicate with a heart that is "cleansed of worldly intellect and conditioning" and is directed towards Allah…So, the situation here is not like in the "world" order… If you try to reach the deputy governor, who knows when you will successfully reach the deputy governor, or you might need someone who knows him. You need a contact to consult a senior manager of a bank… This book has nothing to do with the impossible…

You don't need an intermediary to talk to the owner of the infinite might. That majestic door is always open to you with infinite generosity and mercy. As long as you know how to knock on that door and read the signs sent to you…

This book is written so that every servant who turns to Allah can understand… It is not Arabic, but a-RABB-ic (an expression I heard from Terzibaba/Necdet Ardıç.)

If you say that you don't know how to read, remember the Prophet … and if so, "Recite in the name of your Allah…" Try to understand this verse, that is the "sign" …

If you make your heart dumb and deaf to the virtual voices of this world, then you will see that Allah is communicating with you in "sign language…" That's when the signs turn into sound and the voice of Allah starts to echo in your heart and you become deaf and dumb to worldly deceits…

Only then you will understand who is actually ignorant in "reality" and not "in appearance," who is a scholar, who is high, who is low, who is rich, who is poor, and who is lucky or unlucky…

You actually understand who is the Master and who is the servant…

CUSTOM

You think everything is in your hands
You set the stage
Life will play...
As you continue to make mistakes thinking that you know, your spirit
will burn down in the fire you set...
Have you ever loved more than I have loved with passion? Have you
overflown and gone beyond?
Did you approach your presumed masters for rental?
Even if you change, the world is the same, the eternal custom won't
change
Nobody really knows who is the master and who is the slave
You wanted what you lived
The costs are according to the awards ...
Nobody really knows who is the master who is the slave

-Deniz Erten

We live in reverse...

We are even evaluating heaven as a mansion or a houri.

Although we have a genderless spirit and even though the concept of "houri" also means "magnificent beauties" and the ego that has turned into a magnificent beauty. We perceive a houri as a "girl", and we are STILL trapped in the perception of a heaven that we have reduced to our current understanding of it based on the criteria and concepts related to a virtual world that we have yet to see regardless of the fact that we will be transferred to a realm where the concept of material will have a different state...

We are evaluating everything MATERIALLY, so, we are still looking for mansions and houris in heaven! We are not concerned about the love of Allah in our intentions and understanding! We are still concerned about "buying a place" in heaven where matter turns into meaning!

Yes, Allah is so great that if we perceive it this way, He says, "I am as My servant thinks I am..." and He says that He will give mansions and houris to those who perceive heaven as so. But this is nothing more than pursuing possessions by leaving the true treasure because of our ignorance...

My Allah! What kind of materialism trickery is this? What an addiction this is to a body that turns into soil and decays although it is equipped with a spirit of unlimited power!

We have lost our concept of justice. We obey the unfair but powerful. We throw the afterlife into the fire with our own hands for the sake of a world that doesn't exist!

We are setting our eternity on fire with our own hands in this world that lasts a MOMENT. We brag about doing a favor for someone. We are unaware that we are doing ourselves a favor through that person. We should be the ones who are thankful... We are unaware...

We live the world in reverse...

Because this world is the reflection of the original...

This realm, which is a reflection, is a minus, and its original is a plus... Therefore, the matter that we deem worthy here will leave its place to its original meaning with recourse...

If you are poor here, infinite wealth awaits you, if you are oppressed, eternal happiness awaits you ...

Some people describe another person as "unlucky" according to worldly values. However, the one who seems "lucky" in this world although undeserving and who always seems strong despite their cruelties, will live in the opposite position in the other world ...While materialism is dominant here, meaning is dominant in the hereafter; while there is evil here, there is good in the hereafter...

Our humanity lost in the reflection of its twin and humanity which sees the opposite in the reflection in the mirror ...

If we read the universe from right to left like the Quran, perhaps we can be cognizant of the true direction to read from...

If we flowed from right to left as in circumambulation, we would understand that both the world, the Sun, and everything is circumambulating on the path to Allah...

Not from left to right like time tricks us to and runs towards the opposite direction...

We are all pained.
We are from elsewhere.
We do not think, we are wrong.
We are ordinary, just ordinary...

-Deniz Erten

I.
DESTINY

"All the world's a stage.
And all the men and women merely players.
They have their exits and their entrances..."
-William Shakespeare

"We have bound every human's deeds (or destiny) to their neck".
-Surah Al-Isra, Verse 13

"And that there is not for man except that [good] for which he strives".
-Surah An-Najm, Verse 39

"And whatever strikes you of disaster - it is for what your hands have earned, but God pardons much".
-Surah Ash-Shuraa, Verse 30

The Concept of Time and Destiny

Have you heard these verses before?

Maybe you have, but just recited them from your memory without understanding their meanings, and they most probably fell through the cracks among the verses we have only read and muttered to ourselves...

For a person, to get to know themselves, they, have to first try to know Allah. Of course, none of us have the capacity to get to know Allah thoroughly since it is impossible "to comprehend an infinite mind with a finite one," yet the role of Islam whose foremost meaning and philosophy is "submission" starts here. When an infinite mind cannot be understood through a finite one, you must first "remove" and "give up" your mindset and patterns.

People put on clothes made of conditions and judgments one on top of another. Therefore, this causes them to evaluate the "big picture" before them "in parts, in units" and to interpret the "truth" differently, causing them to bypass the "truth" ....

Islamic teachings, in fact, invite us to the most essential concept of "reflection" by making a kind of comparison with our worships that we call supererogatory (beneficial). It is said that a moment of reflection is superior to a thousand supererogatory salahs (prayers)."

Almost one out of every three verses asks, "Don't you ever reflect?" "Why don't people use their minds?" So, what is reflection?

The verb reflect refers to "tafakkur" in Arabic originating from the verb "fakara." It means producing ideas on a matter and to comprehend that matter... As you know, this ability is intrinsic to human beings, and this is what distinguishes them from other living beings.

Actually, this verse discredits those who attempt to turn religion into a kind of system of fear to ensure that people serve the interests of a different system which is basically distant from the essence of religion by "covering" the real system of Allah by deceiving them as if Allah expects unquestioned obedience and by claiming to act under the name of religion. Moreover, the Arabic word "kafir" does not mean sinner, unbeliever, etc. as most of us think. Kafir originates from the word "kufr" and is generally misused and misunderstood in our language.

Kufr means "to cover, veil, conceal the truth and be ungrateful to blessings." In fact, the night is also called kafir in Arabic, as it covers and veils everything with its darkness. Thus, in essence, one "knows" the truth, yet "covers and rejects" it.

Allah wants us to use our intellect, but what should be considered is, which "intellect" should it be? Is it our "artificial, relative intellect" that has been shaped by ourselves or our circle, or is it the intellect that belongs to the One and Only?

We will discuss this issue in the following chapters and try to explain how our "individual self-intellect" which we are all bragging about, is in fact artificial, and what really needs to be achieved is "to be equipped with the intellect of Allah" and thus to look with the intellect of the One who has a grasp of the big picture.

Now, let's get back to our previous subject.

The fact that we have bypassed the real meanings and essence of the above verses related to destiny among the other verses that we recite one by one; without understanding, even without bothering to understand their meanings, only makes us the objects of our lives and not the subjects.

Thinking and living with an insight of a person who has always been "bedeviled" or "victimized" from an active structure to a passive structure makes both our highly important "worldly lives" which are the means to pass to eternity and "our eternal lives" after we change dimension unbearable…,

And we are the ones who are responsible for it….

Every person is their own killer and victim…

This situation is emphasized repeatedly in many verses of the Quran.

"Whatever good reaches you is from Allah. Whatever ill comes to you is from yourself" (Surah an-Nisa, Verse 79).

"The response (reward) for good is good, the response (penalty) for evil is evil" (Surah Ar-Rahman, Verse 60).

"Whoever comes with a good deed will be rewarded tenfold. But whoever comes with a bad deed will be punished for only one." None will be wronged." (Surah al- An'am, Verse 160)

"So, whoever does an atom's weight of good will see it. And whoever does an atom's weight of evil will see it." (Surah az-Zalzalah, Verses 7-8)

Accepting one's being the victim of their own doings is a bitter self-criticism for an undisciplined[3] person. Because for the ego/nafs, it is always others who are guilty. Somebody else is always responsible or is always to blame, hence we want to convince ourselves that it is their fault that we committed those actions.

In the absence of the other parties to accuse, the guilt is cast upon "destiny."

Even if we think that destiny hurts us, making destiny a notorious "scapegoat" because of our own mistakes, misunderstandings, and weaknesses is basically the only relief for us to continue loving ourselves.

We are always right and innocent because we indemnify ourselves first, even if we do not admit it, then those whom we idolize beyond love and our egos...

If we are all innocent according to ourselves in a world full of crime where everybody claims and thinks themselves to be "innocent," then who commits all the crimes? This is interesting, isn't it?

I was at a Sufi sohbat (spiritual gathering) where the discussion was about the science/knowledge of truth.

A woman in the audience asked that inevitable question that was also lingering in our minds, and which we hadn't been able to understand or which we avoided understanding:

"Master!, I am 55 years old. I have got two sons. I lived a normal

---

3 There is no worse condemnation in this world than of those who have to live with themselves although they dislike themselves. Like a criminal serving a life sentence, who is executed every day...

life, until one day my husband and son fought for no reason…"

Everybody was waiting for the rest of the story with bated breath. Tears were welling up in her eyes. Her voice started trembling.

She was trying to speak, whilst struggling to breathe….

"My husband threw a crystal ashtray at my son… in a moment of anger. The ashtray hit my son's forehead and he fell on the floor hitting the back of his head hard on a marble coffee table. Consequently, he had a brain hemorrhage due to the blows he sustained…"

Everybody who was in attendance that day was looking at her with tears in their eyes, deep sadness, and compassion for her. They saw their own pain reflected in her. She kept her head bowed down as she spoke, avoiding eye contact with anyone.

Now, trembling, she could hardly speak…

"Unfortunately, we lost my son… And my husband was convicted for his murder…"

She started crying like everyone else in the hall. Then wiped her nose and sighed deeply…

"But…" she said, "If Allah didn't want it, it wouldn't have happened right, Master? This wouldn't have happened unless Allah willed it…"

She was asking her question between her sighs, trembling….

"So, it is fate then, is this not fate Master?" "That is… what was bound to happen inevitably?" she asked…

The question of destiny in the essence of this story is a question that occupies each of our minds regarding the experiences and happenings we or our loved ones have been through, whether or not with such tragic consequences.

"If Allah DIDN'T WILL it, it wouldn't happen after all, right?" "So, it is destiny then…"

"That means Allah willed it…"

Unfortunately, even if we don't know about it, the biggest difference between humankind and the devil lies behind this.

As Satan was being cast out of heaven because of his wrongdoings he said to Allah: "You caused me to go astray! If it weren't for You, I would not have gone astray!"

Whereas Adam, as he erred, he said, "My Lord, I victimized my own ego/nafs!" He acknowledged his own mistake. Therefore, he was bestowed the mercy and grace of Allah again.

Actually, we should have understood this very important message about the essence of our lives and destiny from this anecdote that is cited in Quran... However, because we read Quran as if it is an old "storybook" talking about past events experienced in previous centuries by those who lived in that ancient era, we failed to determine with this frame of mind that we acquired the attributes of the devil which has meanings such as "the deceiver" rather than assuming the attributes of Adam. That is why we were cast out of heaven and fell from the grace of Allah like the devil himself, and exiled to unhappiness...

If we had searched for the ways of returning to heaven or looked for the ways of turning our destiny into heaven instead of making our exile harder than it is with our own deeds, then maybe, history and the sufferings in history would not have repeated themselves.

Yet, unfortunately, neither blame nor guilt can be placed on destiny ... I wish we could get away with it that easily, right?

I wish we could take the easy way out...

"Allah will send me to hell in any case. So? Why should I make any effort? I'll go to hell anyway."

"Allah won't predestine me for that. So? Am I crazy to fervently fight and strive in vain?"

"It is destiny, destiny. Let me sit and wait. Is this not what patience is? Well, let's hope for the best!"

To get the answers to all these questions, you should first be ready to face yourselves... ready to have a look inward not outward...

Everything outside you is nothing but a reflection of what is happening inside you...

Shams said, "I cannot explain what destiny is, but I can say what it is not..."

"Destiny does not mean that your life is predestined. For this reason, it is a sign of ignorance to bow down by saying, 'What shall we do, this is our destiny...' Destiny does not give the whole road, but only the crossroads. The route is determined, but all turns, and bends belong to the traveler. So, you are neither the ruler of your life nor are you helpless in the face of life."

-Shams Tabrizi

"Life was a school, but humankind didn't want to "learn" before falling into/experiencing misery one day... That is why "misery" was a "compulsory course" in the curriculum of life..."

-Deniz Erten

What is Destiny?

Have you ever wondered what the word "destiny" means?

While we do not speak using random words with those we try to guide, even with our children, undoubtedly, Allah did not choose random words in His guiding book which He descended to guide His beloved servants whom He has shown mercy to and facilitates their lives in both worlds.

Yes, every word in Quran is carefully chosen, whether or not we realize it. I will elaborate on this in the following chapters, but for now, I will try to explain it using conversational language...

The word destiny (qadar) comes from the root "QDR" and includes meanings such as, "what is deemed most suitable" and "measure, balance-scale, of which the size is appointed." Fatality is derived from the same root.

We would get a certificate of achievement or merit when we study hard at school, right?

Think of it this way... Destiny is, basically the same thing. Our worldly life is like a school where we get the diploma of our missions for which we came to this world. With every teaching we gain here, we move on to other vital stages where we will be transferred to from here. However, the painful part of it, is that our comprehension and the teachings we receive will be limited to what we have achieved here. In other words, when we taste/experience death, our ego/nafs and our spirit, when we pass to the other eternal life, cannot have insight beyond the knowledge we have gained here...

Let's delve deeper with some examples and try to comprehend two kinds of destiny narratives...

Hazrat Umar, who gave orders not to go to the place where the plague occurred, answered his friend who asked, "Umar, are you running away from the destiny of Allah?" He responded by saying, "Yes, but we are running from one destiny of Allah to another..."

Isn't that amazing?

Failure to go beyond the continuing "stereotypical" perspective regarding Islamic teachings, but if you ask me I would say "vital" concepts (because, the Islamic philosophy is basically submission, and it is the method for every person to apprehend life, yet the "Islamic" concept is sacrificed to stereotypes) have led to overlooking the "scientific signs" and turning one's own life into a nightmare with one's own hands.

Just like the story of a woman who did not lose hope in her Lord giving her a child even after Moses asked his Lord and received the answer "She will not have one," she internalized that Allah is always in a new glory and He is the Almighty and she, therefore, continued to ask for and pray to Allah for a child, and she finally had a child to

Moses' surprise.

Therefore, even if we have knowledge yet no wisdom, we forget that Allah is the Almighty and we end up confining ourselves to "cannot be" with our "limited human minds…"

While talking about destiny, which may change, with their unchanging and particular willpower, people always see themselves as "victims of destiny" because they are inclined to think negatively and to consider their egos as perfect due to their mindsets.

Yes, it is very important to consent to one's destiny, but making the same effort to avoid adversity is also a divine order given to you by Allah, and we will focus on the possibilities of destiny that can change with willpower.

Now, based on these explanations, let's distinguish between these two concepts that people mostly confuse:

"Allah's will" and "Allah's approval/consent…" Before moving on, let's explain these words; "All actions belong to Allah."

"…while it is Allah Who created you and whatever you do?" (Surah as-Saffat, Verse 96). Therefore, Allah creates the actions. However, the will to determine which path to take before the events we encounter has been given to us by Allah (as a test).

For example, when you were in high school, it was determined that you would get "physics" lessons, but it was up to you to either study or not study… Even if you intend to study and make an effort, Allah creates the actions towards that direction.

In our good and bad actions, we always think, "Allah willed it and I did it. I wouldn't have done it unless Allah willed it, right? So, that is predestined for me…"

Oh! I wish it was this easy…

While evaluating the events and deciding our actions, we can think, "However, Allah's WILL and Allah's CONSENT are completely separate concepts."

So…

Let's say I intended to do wrong, or I carried out the wrongdoing... The fact that Allah does not interfere with me and does not prevent me from committing this action in other words, the fact that Allah creates this action and allows me to choose this action with my will does not mean that Allah wants me to carry out this wrong action. It definitely does not mean that He has given CONSENT …

My voluntary choice, out of all the given possibilities, constitutes my destiny. That is, the "destiny (the most suitable)" will again originate from my willful choice, which will become the divine decree (qadâ) as of that moment due to the occurrence of that result. But this is not because Allah "predestines" by withholding our will; on the contrary, because I "chose" to carry out that action with my free will bestowed upon me by Allah. Whatever I do with my particular will is my choice. I get a certificate of approval if I study. This is given to me as a plaque at the end of the semester. I intended to study, I took steps towards that direction, hence I received this recognition. That is, what is predestined and is my free will, hence the most suitable outcome. This is called destiny….

If we were created to be puppets, we would not also be given free will... If we do not have a will, would we be held responsible and accountable for our actions?

Allah is fair without limits.

Doesn't comprehension look like this? Perceiving destiny with the understanding "You made me go astray!" as Satan told Allah after his wrongdoing in the story of Adam and Eve that I briefly mentioned above actually suggests that anyone who thinks and acts this way has a satanic understanding and it is misleading to think this way…

Let's get back to our subject. I committed an erroneous action, and my action has a "reaction/response" in the universal mechanism. Because in this quantum universe, every action constitutes a chain reaction (the domino effect) and every deed in the universal mechanism is balanced by a "counteraction" …

So, think of it this way, everything is like a simple law of physics.

Material and meaning are not separate concepts as they are sometimes viewed!

If an action has a material (physical) effect, it has a material (physical) reaction. Just as you cannot stop the ripple in the water when you throw a stone into the water, you may not avoid a response/reaction to an action in this universal mechanism built on "action, reaction, and cycle." Even if we cannot witness these responses in the realm of meaning with our five senses, this does not mean that there is no reaction in the realm of meaning.

Does our blindness mean that the Sun does not exist?

This is the set of rules that are explained as the laws of Allah under the name of "sunnatullah" in the universe. And it is actually so easy to understand, just like physics...

This is explained quite succinctly in Surah ar-Rahman, in which the rules of creation and functioning/operation are also explained.

"The COMPENSATION of a person who does good is good. The COMPENSATION of a person who does evil is evil."

The reason for the ambiguity here is that the word "COMPENSATION" is not properly understood and used correctly in our spoken language. COMPENSATION means response.

Therefore, the concept of compensation is not expressed in the Quran as it is used in our language. The concept of compensation does not have a negative connotation with its use in the Quran. Compensation concisely means "response." It is an action that occurs automatically after an action depending on that action.

It means "the response to what you do in the automatic operation of the universal mechanism."

"If you do good, you do good for yourselves; and if you do evil, you do it to yourselves." (Surah al-Isra, Verse 7)

"Whatever affliction befalls you is because of what your own hands committed. And He pardons much." (Surah ash-Shuraa, Verse 30)

These verses summarize what we want to convey.

So, this universe, which is already based on "rotation," is automatically activated, and the effect of your action will return to you with a reaction that you cannot predict.

Just like an "echo", just like a "mirror…"

You will see the reflection of your own actions unfolding before you... Why?

Because the universal mechanism was established in this way. The only salvation is Allah's forgiveness and concealment (veiling) of that action; otherwise, there is no escape from this reaction. But basically, it is inevitable to be the object of reactive energy to neutralize it just like any energy you unleash, and any situation that is against the laws of physics is against the laws of the universe to the same extent…

Of course, we will discuss the mechanisms such as repentance and charity and the veiling of these actions, the forgiveness of Allah, and of their consequences when we talk about "What should we do?" And these fall under the title, "The change in destiny is destiny," as our Prophet says…

Now...

Let's go back to Allah's WILL…

If Allah wanted, I mean willed, us all to be on the true path, our presence here would be meaningless.

It is even mentioned in a hadith: "If you were not to commit sin, Allah would sweep you out of existence and He would replace (you with) those people who would commit sin and seek forgiveness from Allah."(Hadiths on repentance by Muslim/ 9-10-11)

This is a profound topic, and we will explain later what it means in the concept of (the) LORD…

As required for us to be tested, we are beings who have been given the will to choose the wrong actions because we are given free will… Here, I will delve deeper into our subject, and from this point on, I will ask you to evaluate the statements accordingly… We have been given the will to choose an action… Allah creates what we choose… That is why Islam is based on intention… Even if we say, "I did it!" The creation of the actions belongs only to Allah… But since we think in this way in our daily language, we will explain the truth of the matter and continue in the daily language "so that it is understood." This is beyond dispute…

As it is mentioned in Ayat al-Kursi (The Throne Verse), "illa bi ithnihi," that is "Nothing will happen without Allah's permission."

So, Allah "allows" us to commit erroneous actions with our will in order for us to be tested. Otherwise, He would have interfered with our will. Then the purpose of the test would not be fulfilled, because He would interfere with everyone's actions and make them do good, then we wouldn't need to distinguish between right and wrong.

In fact, I would like to mention something here. The fact that magic is such a great sin in our religion is because it involves "interfering with the will of a person…" Even when Allah bestowed a particular will to His servant, who may dare to interfere with this?

The fact that Allah allows the occurrence of the wrong actions that we have chosen does not mean that He "has given consent for" these actions… We cannot talk about Allah's consent for the damage done both to ourselves and other servants.

"Allowing" something to happen, as required by our test in the universal system, Allah's "consent" of it, and Allah's "will" regarding something are separate things…

As long as we cannot distinguish between these concepts, it will be impossible for us to understand what is "destiny".

Let's think of it this way and let us hope there is no misunderstanding …

Your mother allows you to go out at night while you are an adolescent. Now, is the permission here to allow you to misbehave? No… But you do because your will is in that direction. When you come home, your mother learns about this, and as a means of punishment forbids you from leaving the house for a few days, for example. Why? Because within the permission given to you, you chose an action that was wrong with your will, and this is a result, a punishment, a response. Here, the sanction to stay at home is also what is "deemed appropriate" for you.

You know that your mother does not consent to the wrong action you committed. Let's say you have harmed another person. Yes, this does not prevent your mother from loving you, because you are a part of her. But she will not consent to the action you have committed. Actually, she is with you as you commit that action. She is aware of what you have done. She sees and hears. How and where will you flee to in order to avoid paying for your mistake that has a universal response?

In summary, we are the beings who are allowed to make right or wrong choices with our will, as required by our tests. Our actions will have consequences, just like when living in a society, if we steal from someone, we will account for this before the law. If there is an established order somewhere, then there is a law enacted for the proper functioning of the system. This is valid for a country as well as for the order of the universe established by Allah. While the (visible/apparent) lawmaker in a country is the servant of Allah, the lawmaker and ruler in the universe is Allah. If we see our destiny as the "reaction or punishment" issued by the universe, then it would be best for us to comprehend that we are at the center of destiny, our will, and our actions...

The fact that Allah allows an action to take place does not mean that He wills that action and consents to that action. The argument "I wouldn't have lived this unless He willed it! This wouldn't have happened!" is therefore unsound...

Allah does not consent to or wills this situation, but He allows this to happen for the sake of the system so that you can see your will and your choice in your test; that is the whole point. Because with every action you take, the whole system is restructured. The expression, "Allah is a new glory every moment," which is said for Him, refers to this with one of its insights.

Hence, it is said that even the mussels at the bottom of the sea have a right and will hold you responsible for a sin or your merit. Because each action affects the whole system. A chain reaction occurs in the whole system because of a single action. Because, fundamentally, everyone is ONE, and being separate, "unitary, partial," is just an "illusion". Just as a splinter stuck in a finger affects your whole body, each action affects this universe which is a single body that we all live in, that is, all of us are essentially like the cells of a body.

The fact that the responses to good or bad actions are seen after a certain time is because each part in that cycle is affected by this effect and triggers the next action.

When something happens to you somewhere in your body or you had an operation, you notice that it causes other occurrences in other parts of your body. This is no different in the universe which is a single body...

This situation results in you realizing that you are the perpetrator of what you think is victimizing you and that the gratifications that you get have been or will be returned to you (based on the timing of the universal cycle) because of your correct steps... Even if your name given to you in pre-eternity is a "murderer," if you choose to destroy the negativities of your ego/nafs by your will, you will be guided to the true path, but if you choose to take another life by going astray, you will fall into perversion...Forgetting that one of the 99 names of Allah is the "JUST" and trying to attribute your mistake to Allah will prevent you from understanding your mistake and repenting, and moreover, it will lead you astray even more...

It is said that Allah rewards and punishes His servant through another servant. The cyclical response for a mistake we committed from a servant of Allah who is totally different than the one whom we have wronged, is nothing more than our confrontation with our mistakes or our good deeds under the name of "Destiny..."

This is how this popular "quantum universe" works. It's a question we've heard everywhere in recent years, but when I ask what quantum means, I can't get the full answer.

The lexical meaning of quantum is "one of the possible value sets of a wave." It is used to describe the laws of physics of atomic or subatomic particles.

The Quantum Theory, on the other hand, is "a physics theory that is used to explain the energy in atomic phenomena," which the world has struggled with for years to find the answer to.

Quantum thinking theory says that our body is "a sea of energy" and contains verbal and imaginary formations designed to set a level of consciousness.

In terms of lexicon, which is the most magnificent point, it means "one of the lowest value sets of the possible values of a wave." It literally means "quantity."

In fact, we will all understand that human beings are "wavelengths," their choices are a "chain of possibilities," and that DESTINY, meaning "quantity, measure," is "one" of these possibilities which is chosen by will and its chain reactions. Like quantum, destiny literally means "measure and quantity."

Such a coincidence, right?

Shams Tabrizi

One day, a person who thinks of himself as very knowledgeable comes to Shams Tabrizi. He sees Shams building a structure that looks like a house or a small dwelling with adobe bricks. He watches the Hazrat for some time.

Shams is unaware of this person's arrival. Because he is both working with the love of worshipping and busy with the remembrance of Allah (dhikr).

The visitor notifies Shams of his arrival by coughing. The Hazrat takes a glance under his arm and has an overall opinion of the state of the visitor and says: "Sir, after coughing, praise so that you may exhibit your gratitude to the giver."

"But I do not believe," says the man.

Shams is surprised and says, "How so?"

"What of it? I mean, I do not believe!" he insists, "I came to ask you."

Shams is surprised and stops what he has been doing, "What is the question?"

"I will ask three questions to you. I would like you to answer these questions. Those who referred me to you said that you are competent in this issue. Let's see if you can answer them?"

Hazrat Shams Tabrizi is surprised, but he is also prepared because these were regular occurrences. He says, "Well then, ask."

"You insist that there is Allah. Where is He? Show Him so that we can believe in Him."

Hazrat Shams smiles lightly and says, "Ask me the other question."

"If there is the Hereafter, if everyone will suffer the punishment for what they did in the Hereafter, then let everyone in the world live as they wish. Why are you intervening?" Hazrat Shams remains silent for some time. Then he says, "Ask the other question."

The visitor pauses for a while, thinks, and asks the third question as follows; "You say that the devil was created from fire. You also say that he is infernal. Does the fire burn the fire? You see! Look how surprised you are. Now, answer them." he urges.

Hazrat Shams has noticed that the opponent is a dark, strict denier. He smiles again and takes one of the adobe bricks he has just used and throws it at the man's head. The man exclaimed, "Oh my head! What have you done? My head! Help me! No rescuer, they are killing people!" he begins to scream out loud.

A crowd immediately gathers around, and they quickly take the man before the Islamic judge (kadi) of the time. They appear before the judge; Hazrat Shams Tabrizi on one side and the man on the other…

The man complains, "Master, this man hit me with an adobe brick, he cracked my head open. I have a splitting headache.

The judge turns to the Hazrat," Why did you hit this man's head for no reason? "

He smiles and says, "I answered his questions, I didn't hit him."

"What? I do not understand. How did you answer my questions? Is this how you answer?"

The judge intervenes and asks, "Hold on! What did he ask and how did you answer?"

Hazrat responds, "Forget that he says that there is no Allah. Now he says that he has a headache."

"Yes, I have a headache," the denier interjects.

"Then, let him show me his headache and I'll show him Allah."

"His second question was, if everybody will be punished in the Hereafter, let them live as they wish." I felt like hitting his head with an adobe brick. So, I stood up and hit him in the head. Since we will be punished in the hereafter why are you questioning me now and he is complaining about me?".

The judge begins to smile, the denier is furious. Hazrat Shams asks, "In his third question he said that the devil was created from fire and asked whether the fire would burn fire. So, I answered that question: Human beings are also created from earth. Will earth damage earth? I hit him with an adobe brick. Then, why does he say that it hurt?"

This quick-wit and noble attitude of Hazrat Shams makes the judge very happy. Because the Hazrat had given the best possible answers to that vanguard. He turns to the man and says, "he answered your questions both in the practical and apparent sense and theoretically in the hidden sense. There is nothing to complain about!"

As the denier continues to say, "But I have a headache, I am injured…" the judge orders him to be thrown out.

Experience love that is "learned" not "memorized" … The "true love" born in this way, brings you together with yourself first.

11.
TIME

The rate of expansion of the universe is at such a critical rate that if this rate of expansion one second after the Big Bang had been smaller by even one part in one hundred thousand million million, the universe would have recollapsed before it ever reached its present size.

-Stephen Hawking

Have the ones that I lost defined my success
Have I failed to do anything in this life
Have the years gone by worn me out or have the mirrors
Tell me, how have I survived all this time…
My mind was a liar…
My heart was a thief…
My spirit was lonesome…
Among all this crowd…
Where would I fit in this enormous universe
Now that they do not give me a place in either world
I am untimeous…
Time… hurts…

-Deniz Erten

Concepts of Time and the Moment

We say time passes... We are actually mistaken... Time does not pass... We pass through time...

Do you know what time is?

Time is, I think, the SUPPOSED MOMENT.

You surely know Zamzam (Zemzem) water. Who knows, maybe the ancient people used the Persian word "zeman" to represent the MOMENT with "Zem" meaning "to stop". Actually, we call the MOMENTS "frozen" in the fragments of our lives "time."

In fact, when we quickly turn the pages and look at the photos of our moments that have "frozen" frame by frame, like a photo album, a concept, where the "frozen" moments pass by/flow rapidly like a movie, emerges...

While the word "time" was zeman and used with concrete meanings such as "aging, wearing off of an object, a distant period", it is currently abstracted under the name "time (zaman)" and used in exchange for "waqt – the present moment..."

The fact that the subject of time is so important and comprehending its actual meaning is essential for us to understand our lives. Otherwise, we would get lost and old because we would not be able to find where we stand among the photos flowing by.

Time is fundamental to understanding the subject of "destiny". We actually suffer losses because we have been stuck on the subject of destiny for centuries and therefore, we cannot structure our lives with a true insight in this direction...

The underlying cause of failing to fully understand matters such as "Do people have a will?" "Allah wishing, in other words, Allah willing..." "Allah consenting to something..." is the failure to fully understand the concept of TIME...

Why?

When it is said that destiny is PREDETERMINED;

The understanding suggesting that "This destiny is predetermined, it is certain that I will go to Hell anyway; then, what on earth should I strive for? I'll just sit back..." comes into play right here...

In fact, it is the deceitful devil who gives this delusion. Again, the devil misleads people with "ideas."

"It has already been determined anyway, No matter what you do. Let it go, it was his destiny to kill him. Wait and see, everything is predetermined..."

Now, let's delve deeper into this subject ...

What is TIME?

(Before starting on this topic, I would like to state that when I say time, the concept of "space-time" is meant due to the unity of time and space, but I especially did not use this expression, which remains "technical" in the current language.)

Time is actually a sort of SEQUENCE in which we perceive events. We, human beings have distinctions such as "yesterday, today and to-morrow, past and future" due to the dimension we live in; and they flow in a sequence.

Let us elaborate further ...

For us to see an object, the image coming from that object by means of light must reach our eyes... The further the object is from us, the later we see it...

More interestingly, although I will not elaborate on it right now the retina in our eyes perceives objects "upside down." I mean, the image of a person standing in front of us is actually reflected to our retina as upside down; however, our brains turn this image transmitted by our eyes into an upright position... Anyway, let's skip these for now and get back to the main point ...

Are You the Destiny?

Cosmos ... The interesting word meaning the order, law, and system in the universe; the total opposite of chaos... In short, no matter how you name it, the cosmos is the set of rules established by Allah for the order in the realm of existence, namely Sunnatullah…

Here I started to comprehend the concept of destiny while reading several books on the cosmos and the comments and determinations of Einstein and Stephen Hawking on this issue... How?

When we look at the stars, their light reaches us from millions of years away, and most of them have already disappeared even though their lights reach us. That is, we see them and presume that they exist. However, what we see may only be their lights. During this period when the images of the stars reach us thanks to the light they emit, we see a star that might have already turned into a black hole and disappeared "as if" it exists… You will be more surprised if I give an even more recent example. In fact, as our own image in the mirror reaches our eyes within a period as a result of refraction of light, that image is reflected to us with a time delay, even at a certain fraction of a second… In short, when we look in the mirror, we see the state we were in a while ago, not our current state.

In essence, when we look in the mirror, we actually see our own PAST…

In fact, it is worth considering the explanation of scientists that the universe is a momentary lag in the moment when a human, who is an observer, looks at him/herself…

One of the points I was impressed with when I started researching time to understand destiny was related to the sun's rays. The sun's rays reach the earth exactly 8 minutes late due to the distance from the earth. The moonbeams reach us after approximately 1.2 seconds. Since there is an 8-minute delay with the sun rays reaching the earth, don't even mention the fact that if the sun was to disappear, we would continue to see the sun rays from 8 minutes earlier. Yes, we would only be aware of the disappearance of the sun only after 8 minutes...

In all of these, destiny may not really be understood without understanding the "explanation of time in the sight of Allah."

In fact, the verse about time "in the sight of humankind" and "in the sight of Allah" named the MOMENT is written as follows: "They challenge you 'O Prophet' to hasten the torment. And Allah will never fail in His promise. But a day with your Lord is indeed like a thousand years by your counting" (Surah al-Hajj, Verse 47).

Everything happened in a single MOMENT in a dimension called the MOMENT beyond time in the sight of Allah. Our perception of time in our dimension through "sequencing" only binds "us." Allah already knows what we will do with our own voluntary choices because Allah is in possession of all eternity in every possibility, we would choose... All the information regarding the time period we call the "future" is already available in His presence because time is only a concept that records us, those created. However, we, who are incapable creatures and who live in a dimension subject to that sequence, do not yet know what to do when we experience something. Because, as a result of our physical limitations, we are subject to the restriction and records of our own time zones...

It may sound strange to you, but I can also give you an example...

The Universe, which broadcasts live in our presence, the servants, is sort of a "recorded broadcasting" because everything has already happened in the presence of Allah.

All wills have made their choices, the broadcast is over. We, the servants, participate in the live broadcast without knowing what we will encounter and what we will choose, and we perceive as if everything has just happened or is happening at that moment...

Our records, which have already been archived, will be re-broadcast in our memory recordings that we have taken from this world, and everything we have done will be presented to us again...

Let's give another example. Suppose that we went to another star.

When we look at the world from there, for example, we see the period of the French Revolution[4]. Who did what and how the French Revolution was written in our own period of time. We did not interfere with anyone or anything. But in our current time period, we know that specific era and its aftermath in the world. We know in advance what will transpire. We know, but those living in that time period do not know what they will experience because they cannot see it from the time period we are in. Therefore, whether they will choose right or wrong with their will is still up to their will, and in both cases, the results of their choices are already within our knowledge.

In this case, do we have a will? Of course, we have! Did these people that I saw have a choice? They had. So, what's the difference? We "knew" in advance what they would do in which situation with their own choices because we could see and know their past, present, and future due to the dimension of time we are in. The notion of TIME, namely the moment, in the sight of Allah is like this... The fact that the WHOLE of the fragmented and sequential time zone is only in His sight... Yesterday, today, tomorrow, centuries after, and before...

But Allah's unlimited knowledge, who has this information and every information, knows every state of His servants, He "is with them" anyway; yet, Allah has allowed His servants to whom He granted from His "attribute of will" to make their own choices because of that "test" that is always mentioned...

There are certain verses in the Quran that simultaneously use both present tense and past tense...

For example, "Allah sealed their hearts..." "You cannot do that, Allah did that..." In fact, although the use of future tense after a present tense, such as "Allah will do this," is correct in our dimension of time, past tense was used in this statement since all the times in the sight of Allah are folded in the time unit called the MOMENT and all of them (yesterday, today, tomorrow) have already happened and concluded...

---

4 Thanks to Hamza Yardımcıoğlu, the author of Bir Solukta Evren'in Resimli Tarihi.

As long as we do not understand the concept of "time," the understanding that people's hearts are inherently sealed brings us face to face with the question "But, what about the will?"

Here again, there are numerous explanations. One of them is as follows:

Allah knows, thanks to the "moment beyond time" in His sight, that His servant will not return to the true path even though they have been given every opportunity... And in a further description, the reason for using the past tense in such a case is explained as, "Because of the time in His sight, Allah already knows that His servants would misuse every opportunity to return to the truth unfolded before them in addition to knowing every future state of His servants." However, in this case, the use of the past tense is misinterpreted as if that person was not given the will and was subjected to injustice without thinking about it, which is truly an erroneous understanding. The contrasting explanation brought on by Ibn al-Arabi regarding this verse is breathtaking... The Hazrat states that the hearts cannot only be sealed by being a sinner but also because of the love of Allah and that some servants carry the "seal of love" and no matter how many times they err, they will eventually return to Allah because Allah sealed their hearts with His love. What a magnificent description... Remember that every verse has both Jalal (the Majesty) and Jamal (the Beauty) revelation. Allah has such an extraordinary love towards His servant that the verses which have both positive and negative meanings bear the sign that Allah will turn you towards Himself just when you think you have been blasphemous and are ruined.

Allah gives us the chance to return to Him and the true path at every opportunity. But He also knows how we will use those opportunities in all the possibilities offered to us since the dimension of the MOMENT which is beyond time and the concept of the moment is in His sight. His awareness of the MOMENT when everything happens turns the future in our sight into the past based on the "beyond time" concept in His sight… And indeed, this future issue is indicated in the past because He knows this in advance and as a sign to us…

If we do not know this, we will be at a great loss…

We believe that the Quran was descended hundreds of years ago. However, everybody's Quran is descended to them over and over again at every moment…

On top of that, every person benefits from the Quran as much as they perceive. In other words, when we say that "the entire Quran was descended…," this means that the Quran was descended to "the universe." However, whatever we understand, whether it is one verse or five verses, the portion descended to us is just that much.

Even if you recite the Quran from cover to cover many times, the meanings of the Quran that you do not understand have not yet been descended to your comprehension and, actually, to your deeds. Hence, the command "Read!" is so deep …

We will discuss this later to the full extent of our comprehension…

We have expelled ourselves from the Quran so much that we read a story lived centuries ago from a storybook that does not concern us and through the prophets and persons whom we think are unrelated to us and we continue with our lives, which, we think, are "separate" from the Quran, with a different understanding…

However, everybody has their own 'Night of Power', their own 'Ascension', everyone has the Quran as much as their own comprehension… Everyone ESTABLISHES their own MOMENTS.

Qur'an

Establish… the moment…

The one ESTABLISHING the MOMENT… (To "establish" reads as "Qur" and the "moment" reads as "An" in Turkish, an amalgamation of the two words makes up QURAN when read together).

The Quran is such a miraculous book that it is descended at every moment to everyone trying to comprehend Him... And everyone meets their own realities by ESTABLISHING their MOMENTS with the choices they make...

Our biggest limitation is to consider the words such as "to come down, to descend" as papers falling down the sky in our brains covered with patterns...

Even taking the word "Ayat (Verse)" as "lines written on the pages of Quran" before understanding the significance of "ayat (verse)" meaning a sign qualifies for a mistake in our perception of Quran not as a "living" and "the true treasure," "the method", "guideline", and even the "address book of true salvation", but a whole lot of pages telling stories...

Allah does not care about lines but hearts...

Be sure that the Quran speaks to billions of people who lived and will live and to each of you individually... He responds to your needs by directly addressing it to you...

How?

One of my dear friends called me one day... We had many conversations about Allah and the Quran. She told me these exact words:

"Deniz, sometimes people don't understand me, even those closest to me ..."

I smiled. I had been there; I had been harshly criticized. But it was a process. As with all the events that our Prophet experienced and showed us, everything was actually presented to show us what we will experience and what we should do in each situation. She said to me, "One day my boyfriend took me by surprise by telling me not to think that hard about a book written centuries ago, to be normal, and to live my life, or otherwise I would go crazy..."

Anyone who has set out to understand the Quran, Allah, and the Prophet has and will experience this. Unless one tries to be aware of the ego and the truth and frees themselves from the "slavery" of this worldly system on this path, one will not understand what is going on...

It has always been this way and will continue to be so... I smiled again..."And then?" I asked...

"Then..." she said, "I followed your advice. Like you say, if you cannot find the answer to your question, perform ablution, and ask Allah, then take the Quran, close your eyes, and open a page. There, Allah will give you the answer because you turned towards Him with your purest intention... He will talk to you through the Book and through a line on the TV or a slogan on a car as the universe is the book of Quran... Because He is everywhere...

I took the Quran. I was so deep in the dark. I said, Oh my Allah! Am I doing wrong? Show me the true path. Or am I going crazy?"

Then I closed my eyes, opened a page, and said, "Bismillahirrahmanirrahim. With my eyes still closed, I ran my finger and landed somewhere on the page..."

"Yes?" I asked excitedly. I had also experienced such occurrences. Everyone who turns to Him experiences such happenings for a certain time, especially when they first embark on this road..."Yes... then?" I asked.

"Then..." she said and started crying., her voice was trembling. "I saw my finger had landed on the verse, "they called him Majnoon", she said.

As I write this even now, I have a shiver running from my toes up to my scalp...

We both fell silent and began to weep silently. Our Prophet realized that we live in this world on the reverse side when he became aware of the knowledge of Allah... If you enter a world lived on the reverse side from one direction, people will come at you and call you Majnoon, crazy...

He is the city of knowledge but what are we? Still, the beginning of being a "seeker," a "student," or a "demandant" would encounter resistance from the circle...

Allah has told us, with the example of the Prophet, that anyone who tries to find and understand Him and who contradicts the people who are imprisoned in the world order will be called crazy claiming that they are against what is called "normal..."

In the presence of our Prophet, it is actually a narrative of what we will experience as we embark on a journey to reach Allah. Considering the Quran as a book that only talks to the prophets, to the Israelites who failed to understand what it is in many senses, to the devil, angels, and the Prophet is like wandering around the world in vain to find the treasure hidden in the backyard and eventually, finding it inside the home...

In this case, I cannot find the appropriate words to talk about how Allah approached His servant with love and gave her an answer that instantly relieved her pain... I have no words other than the greatness of His mercy and love ...

Going back to our subject of destiny ...

Allah's verbal use of time periods such as the past, the future, and the present in our dimension in the verses lies in the difference betwe-en time in the sight of a servant and the MOMENT in the sight of Allah...

The servant always looks with a fragmented-sequential unitary mind, which we call small; this is the case with everything. For examp-le, you saw a dress displayed on the right side, you cannot see the left side, but the right side is so magnificent that you want it. It must be yours...

Then you buy it, and what do you see? The left side of the dress is torn and has completely different colors and patterns all over it... What you badly wanted a while ago has now turned into a nightmare...

Here, you can see the whole dress only if you look from above...

Like everything else in life, that's how time is. We always look at the events from our side. However, the "full picture" is completely different...

Unless we try to be fully aware of every subject, our confusion will not end. Even our wishes will not end...

If one can holistically look at some things, they would find that they may not easily wish for anything...

The price of everything is like the left side of that dress unseen from the side we look at. We fall for the right side and then we are billed on the left side...

The same applies in the case of Time...

Unless we try to look at events with a view of a dimension beyond time in the sight of Allah, our suffering remains unlimited, and our understanding remains limited...

This is where surrender comes into play in Islamic philosophy, even if we cannot foresee it. You cannot see because you're only powerful enough to look from this side. Then give up that misleading little power and "surrender and abandon yourself to the look" of the One who owns the whole picture.

We tell many people that "their hearts are sealed" without having a grasp of what the situation is. Everyone thinks the other one is sealed... However, nobody except our Allah knows the situation of others. Maybe people who are labeled as such are more beloved than us in the sight of Allah. Only Allah knows who is sealed because He alone has the knowledge of the future or those whom He wanted to notify...

They asked our Prophet:

"O Messenger of Allah (PBUH), does Destiny change?"

"It changes..." he said, "but the change is also the destiny."

This explanation is actually a magnificent summary of what we have said. However, because we are ignorant and we do not strive to understand, it has become one of the situations where the deceptive demonic system uses it as an opportunity to mislead us and give us the feeling that we are "victims..."

As Allah criticizes in the Quran and scriptures, sincerely turn to Allah, not with "words" but with "hearts", without being "a talebearer" or "one of those carrying two hearts in one chest." In fact, here I am giving you a great secret and a clue to one of the most powerful means of change in your life... Even if you have never fasted or worshiped in your life, search for Ramadan given by virtue of a science as you will see in the revelations provided later in the Sign and the last 10 days of Ramadan as well as the practices of our Prophet in those days... And follow the signs... Practice them for your life... Then, write to me... I will be waiting... in astonishment...

Our Prophet, who is the master of science, has actually stated here that these are recorded in the MOMENT, which is the concept beyond time in the sight of Allah. But it is a situation where we can make changes in time in our sight with our will and that is known as the "past" by Allah, who also knows the future...

In other words, even though the changes we made with our will are expressed as the "future" based on our time period, they are all gathered in the MOMENT when all the time zones in the sight of Allah were folded...

Hence, the knowledge that a person will change their course with will is already within the knowledge of Allah, who is in a dimension beyond time. YOU are the one who does not know what will happen, whether you will go to Heaven or Hell... Maybe you will behave in such a righteous way, or you will do such a good deed that your life will change completely, and perhaps you will perform such a good deed that you will realize that you are experiencing one of Hazrat Ibn Arabi's "sealed" heart descriptions even when you think you are imprisoned for the wickedness... Just when you say, "No matter what I do, I am one of the unbelievers," you will suddenly realize with an incident that you are actually one of those "sealed with love" and be aggrieved, you will feel remorse, and apologize to Allah like a child suffering for upsetting their mother... My dear Allah... Oh, my dearest Allah... I misunderstood You... I have never known and understood You despite all Your calls and Your infinite mercy... Forgive me...

What a wonderful life .... Everything can change with our next choice…

This information is only within the knowledge of Allah because He looks at this universe and this world from "every time" period and only He knows everything…

You are a human, you are subject to time and space, you are limited... Whether you look from that star or this star, you can only have a grasp of a certain time period. However, He has a grasp of all time periods. Does that make you weak-willed? Never! On the contrary, this is the information to make you increase your effort. What do you know? Maybe you will get everything you want, but you are so conditioned that the devil who gives delusions (insecurity, ego-system) always tries to play games with negative, diverting ideas on your will for you to think "I am already ruined if it is so!" And you fall into this trap...

Unfortunately, whoever blames destiny basically blames Allah. This is the same as how the devil interpreted by saying, "You misguided me!" You have chosen the way of eternal unhappiness and the way to be expelled from the concept of Heaven…

I would like to mention this before I proceed to the difference and details of Allah's decree (Qada') and destiny…

Destiny is the constant measure and formulas applied to any one possibility chosen by the servant among infinite possibilities. Decree is whether they are realized or not. Their realization or the severity of realization is also affected by your choices…

Every choice, every prayer, every charity, and every step gives you the chance to change your destiny. If you take the opportunity correctly, Allah, who is in a new glory, in other words, who creates something new every moment, gives you selections (which are already known to Him) an opportunity when they become a decree, which is a "judgment…" Allah having all the knowledge by His side is one thing and you thinking that Allah did not give you will is another. If He wanted you to be a puppet, why would He give you the right of will, which is one of His attributes? Then what is the reason for being tested? Does this understanding match with the name al-'Adl (the Just)-Justice, one of the most important names of Allah?

Is it correct to try to understand Allah, who has limitless knowledge, with such a shallow logic?

This is actually mentioned quite clearly and Allah reminds us by saying, "Whatever affliction befalls you is because of what your own hands have committed. And He pardons much," (Surah ash-Shura, Verse 30).

Surah an-Naba Verse 29 is written as follows:

"Va kulla shay'in aahsaayneahu kiteabea(kiteaban)…"

"But all things We have enumerated in writing (in other words, we listed them) …"

How? We have written which direction you are heading to with your choices based on the possibilities. Since we know how you will act in any situation "EVEN BEFORE YOU KNOW" because we have the capacity to see your "WILLING" choice "IN ADVANCE" due to the time we are in, we wrote them all a long time ago.

For instance, in the fight between a father and son given as an example in the Destiny chapter:

1. He could leave the house early.

2. He could choose not to get angry, apologize, and leave his father.

3. His father does not obey his ego, suppresses his anger, and does not escalate the matter.

4. His father reaches for the ashtray and gives up at the last minute.

5. His father throws the ashtray outside and injures a passerby, who then comes into the house… etc.

We "listed" endless possibilities. Since we knew which of these possibilities you would willingly choose due to the time we are in, we wrote that choice as a result of the probabilities we listed…

To understand destiny, people must first understand the concepts and differences between TIME and MOMENT…

When we say time, we are talking about the time period, the sequencing in our sight…However, there is the MOMENT with Allah, and it would not be wrong if we summarize that the time period called the MOMENT is the time period beyond the time in front of Him, where all the time frames of the past and the future come together, and what will happen is already written…

I am making a movie…

There is the cast. There are various roles. And the director says, "We are going to be improvising throughout the shooting of the movie within the framework of the rules. Let everyone do anything they want to do with their own will. I will only shoot the film…"

The main actor in the film is in love with the main actress, but no matter what her father objects and they break up and marry other people.

They film another version, and there the father does not object and the two get married…

Thousands of versions like this are shot based on the choice of wills. And we watch these films...

Like in this film roll, the beginning, middle, and end of everything already exists in the same film roll…

We "choose" from the possibilities (and Allah creates the action we have chosen; this is an issue that we will later expand on under the section titled, The LORD) … Our choices are recorded by our "memory" of which one of the meanings covers the description of the "recording angels," and they accompany us in our eternal journey…

The issue of staying in the MOMENT, which we have frequently heard of in Western teachings in recent years, actually takes its essence from the Quran… We are not even aware that the MOMENT mentioned there is actually the MOMENT in the sight of Allah…

There is a magnificent example of this subject in the Quran. Each story in the Quran told as a "parable" speaks to us and tells us what to do in every situation…

The matter of time and MOMENT and how we should think to

be able to see the truth in these matters is explained in Surah al-Kahf (The Cave), which includes millions of signs from the People of the Cave (Ashab al-Kahf) and the companionship of Khidr and Moses (Musa)…

In this Surah, Moses (Musa) represents the scholar who evaluates events with his little, unitary, partial mind and lives in TIME. KHIDR, on the other hand, represents the person who is aware of the knowledge given by Allah (ilm ladunni), which is the knowledge next to Allah, and the MOMENT that Allah conducts with His holistic mind…

Like every word in the Quran, the word Khidr has been purposefully chosen… I know that we have not thought much about this symbolic identity except Khidr in the expression of Khidrallaz, where we jump over fires and write our wishes for a spouse, money, property, etc…

What does Khidr mean?

Khidr originates from the word 'khadr'… It means green. It makes our thoughts green like trees in Spring and brings liveliness and vividness wherever it goes…

The word Khidr means khadr, which in Turkish reads as "hazir" meaning "ready" …

It is a nickname given to a person in the Quran, so it is an expression of a rank and understanding that can be valid for each of us.

Khidr is THE ONE WHO IS READY IN EVERY AGE.

Furthermore, the word 'Hazrat' also has the same meaning. The one who is ready at all times, the one who is always alive…

What about the word 'religion'? Do we know what it means?

Do you know that I couldn't get the correct answer from anyone whom I asked this question? I could not get a direct answer to this question, not even from a single person out of the hundreds of people who heartily claim to be Muslim, atheist, or deist believing in the Creator but not the religion… Interesting, isn't it?

Doesn't one know the definition of what they claim to believe or what they claim to not believe?

We do not even try to understand the truth of the things whose existence or non-existence we defend beyond the "patterns" that we are forced to memorize! However, if you ask, we all know everything…

There is a saying, "I once used to know everything. I was very unenlightened back then."

Now, all I know is that I don't know anything… I asked my friends who claim to not believe in religion… 'What is religion?'

No answer…

''When you say religion[5], you mean the PATH. And when you say you don't believe in religion, you're actually saying you don't believe in the path. Do you know that?

"Oh," said most of them. And they just looked at me. If you say, "I do or don't believe in the Creator, 'I have my own way'," then I tell you "Your path is yours, my path is mine…" After all, this is the MAIN PATH. The beginning and end are definite; only the path to follow is up to you. Are you going to choose the path with shortcuts and with no detours (which is the "sirat al-mustaqim, the straight path, whose meaning we don't know) or the rather sorrowful and painful side paths?

Whichever way you choose if your departure and arrival points are the same, why are you driving yourself into the ground rediscovering America? I did the same thing myself on those paths, I suffered from my own "self-inflicted" pains, which I now deem "futile" with my current understanding … Finally, I cast myself adrift, I surrendered because I realized that it was my own shadow that I was trying to fight against. It is very painful to realize that the one you are fighting with is yourself. The moment that people find themselves is the exact moment when the true "civilized" part of their lives, in other words, their "Medina" begins. I will address the topic of Medina and its true meaning when

5 "The word "deen" (religion), which is closely related to the word "deyn" (debt) in its origin, also means "method, path, and system."

we come to the subject of Hijrah (the migration).

Now, let's go back to our topic. Religion means 'the path followed, the path to go'. If we do not break our conceptual patterns, we will be trapped in time while everything happens in the MOMENT...

''Religion means the path shown by Allah, the Almighty in order to lead people to eternal bliss. '' (Hazrat Ali)

Now, let's get back to the main reason we have given the definitions of the words, 'religion' and 'Khidr'.

To the subject of Time and Moment ...

In Surah Ali 'Imran Verse 19, the Quran says, "Inneddine indallahil Islam ..."

In other words, it says: " Indeed, the religion in the sight of Allah is Islam. " We will explain the Islamic dimension of this issue in the chapters to follow. Right now, I will first offer an explanation regarding our subject related to Time and the Moment.

In this line, He says: "Surely the religion before Allah (in the sight of Allah) is Islam (to surrender)."

That is to say, there is also the understanding of the religious path that is not with Allah ... And unfortunately, most of us "are stuck in the religious path before the servant, which we have determined and interpreted with our own partial limited intelligence." The story of Khidr and Moses (Musa) below also tells the truth about us being led to our own unhappiness by losing the "holistic intellect" representing Khidr because we are the Moses, and we think that we know everything...

Here, the difference is between the path with partial perspective and the path with universal perspective... Unfortunately, as long as we evaluate the PATH from our own perspectives, we will not be able to understand the path "explained by Allah from His perspective."

In order to understand the path that Allah explains from His perspective, one must first "reach Allah". How will you witness that scene before you reach Allah, that is, before meeting Him?

Do not react as if I have just said some unusual things here.

How does 'Wuslat', meaning "the reunion" of the friends of Allah, happen? How did and how does the ascension happen? Why are the awliya who reach certain ranks on their spiritual journeys considered mature? What rank did they reach?

Of course, to Allah... to the Truth...

Being a wali of Allah, a man of Allah on the journey starting from the ranks of ego and extending from the Lordship to Divinity, fana fillah, baqa billah, and many more... From the journey to the Truth to the journey in the Truth; these are the issues only to be told by the friends of Allah...

All these issues, such as reunion with Allah, annihilation in Allah, and subsistence in Allah, belong to an incredible journey that has long and profound meanings, stages, and ranks in terms of Sufism...

Cemal Nur Sargut magnificently enlightened us regarding this matter in her explanation of "Ana al-Haqq (I am the Truth) ..." She tells us that the name "Allah," which is "al-Ism al-Jami" meaning the sum of all words, the attributes of Allah which He refers to as "I wished to be known..." manifests in the locus of meaning, in other words, the name "Allah" does not come to the Earth, and it is located in the locus of meaning... Even in worldly usage, while people are named after the names of Allah such as as-Samad, al-Jamal, and al-Jalal, this usage is not possible for the name, -Lord forbid- Allah...

What we need to remember is that the name Allah appears with the name The Truth (Haqq) when it manifests on Earth... And Sargut expresses it as follows: '' When the name of ALLAH manifests on Earth, it appears with the name The Truth (Haqq) and the name the Truth (Haqq) is the appearance of all names and attributes on Earth; it is the truth of the Prophet, it means Hazrat Muhammad (PBUH). Therefore, the Truth in the Prophet manifests itself as a Truth in all of us, in the people, and I have one or more of those names, and so do you. If I reveal these names in my own existence and give up my egocentric desires, I will have the right to say ANA AL-HAQQ since there will be nothing but the Truth (Haqq) of Allah in me; yet, I cannot say that out of modesty, but that's beside the point."[6]

After a certain point, the friends of Allah who made this journey no longer have "selves" (personalities). They have returned to the state in which they were when they arrived here... They are like the hollowed-out reed flute, they only reflect the voice of the blower... They are called HAZRAT, meaning the one who is always READY IN THE PRESENCE OF Allah...Now that they subsist with Allah, they are free from time and space... Their spirits have overruled their bodily records and broken the chain of the "impossible" because they reunited with Allah while living...

They neither know time nor place; they are ready and stand beside you when their names are called...

So, since Khidr is "always in the presence," he was allowed to benefit from the "holistic" knowledge of Allah, and therefore had knowledge about the future that Moses could not see with his partial perspective...

The only "path" that we understand without reaching the religion next to Allah or turning to the friends of Allah who have reached that religion is the path we find with our own limited perspective. And this is the only PATH where everybody looks from different angles, and which is basically the sum of all angles when viewed from above...

That is why we are very stuck in the concepts of TIME and MOMENT...

Although we claim that we have knowledge, unless we try to look from the perspective of Allah, who has holistic knowledge, we are stuck in the dimension of time and evaluate events from that dimension...

We have to surrender to Allah, the Prophet (PBUH), and the perfect people ... For this reason, the friendship between Khidr and Moses (Musa) could not last for a longer period ...

Moses questioned Khidr's actions with his perspective confined to the "partial knowledge and intellect" within the dimension of "time."

6 Serpil Çavuşoğlu, Cemal Nur Sargut, "Herşeyin Allah Olduğunu Görmek", "http://www.indigo.com/"

However, the future would show Moses the real face of Khidr's actions, but Moses could not be patient, continue, or surrender to this, and his behavior resulted in him losing Khidr...

Being a scholar with apparent knowledge is not enough... It is necessary to be a scholar equipped with the "knowledge of Allah..."Ilm ladunni (the divine knowledge) is required...

The Quran likens some scholars who do not act with their knowledge and who do not adopt their knowledge to be "donkeys laden with books." As a matter of fact, in our prayers, "we take refuge in Allah from useless knowledge..." Because knowledge only makes sense when we experience it... Even the stance of such a person that we call a "state" is like a whole "lesson" for people...The science of truth is holistic. External sciences, on the other hand, are fragmentary and partial and can alter with changing data.

'MOMENT' is the place where yesterday, today, tomorrow, eternity, past-eternity, and all information are folded and meet... And the MOMENT is only next to ALLAH... The subject of the MOMENT is not properly understood as it has been covered in the superficiality of the statement 'to linger in the MOMENT' which has been mentioned in Western teachings for years. Does "enjoying the moment" refer to this or does it suggest for you to linger in the MOMENT in the presence of Allah so that you do not imprison yourself and your eternity in a past that you cannot solve, a future that you cannot see, and an understanding of now that you cannot grasp...

Stay with the only owner of knowledge at every moment ... Whoever is ready in His presence finds peace...

It could either be Khidr or Hazrat...

As long as you reach Allah not because of causes beyond your control like death, but by willfully dying before death... Experience your spirit predominating over your corpse, discover it...

Return the Amanah (trust/guardianship) you have been carrying to its owner while in this world...

I am leaving it here right now so that we understand the concept of destiny that is the basis of the subject.

And I say that this is what the Quran is for... That is, to ESTABLISH our MOMENT, our present, and our eternity correctly... Now, it is the time to ESTABLISH your MOMENT with the permission of Allah...

The Good and the Evil, The Last Supper

From Paulo Coelho, the author of the Alchemist by whom I was impressed: Leonardo da Vinci faced great difficulty when he thought of painting The Last Supper... He had to depict the Good in the form of Jesus and the Evil in the form of Judas who decided to betray Jesus in the story of the last supper... He left the painting unfinished and started looking for people he could use as models for these two people. One day, during a choir concert, he noticed that one of the choir members was a perfect fit for depicting Jesus. He invited him to his studio to pose and drew numerous sketches.

Three years passed, and The Last Supper was almost complete, but Leonardo da Vinci had not yet found the model to use for Judas ... The cardinal of the church where Leonardo was working began to pressurize the painter to finish the mural painting as soon as possible. After searching for days, Leonardo found a young man who had aged ahead of his time. Leonardo told his assistants to move this tattered man dressed in rags to the church even if the task might prove difficult due to the man's inability to move on his own because he had no time to sketch.

When he arrived at the church, the assistants raised the man to his feet. The poor man did not understand what was happening to him.

Leonardo was portraying the non-belief, sin, and selfishness seen on the man's face...

When he was finished, the hobo, who had just been liberated from drunkenness, opened his eyes, and saw this wonderful mural.

With a voice full of surprise and sadness, he said, "I've seen this picture before..."

"When?"Leonardo da Vinci asked equally surprised.

"Three years ago," said the man. "Before I lost all my assets. At that time, I was singing in a choir, I had many dreams, an artist invited me to model for Jesus' face..."

So, the faces of Good and Evil are the same...
It all depends on when they get in one's way...
                -From The Devil and the Young Woman, Paulo Coelho.

The Treasure We Are Looking For Is In Our Backyard

Everything is possible next to Allah... In the anecdotes about the folding of space and time by the friends of Allah, you can see the truth of the famous "time machine" concept that is the subject of many films... Will Allah, who carries the lights of the stars from millions of years to you and to the present moment, not allow His friends to experience travel in time?

People who carry the spirit breathed by Allah cannot see or notice how the devil strives to prevent them from realizing the extent of the power they are equipped with...

However, if the spirit, your only asset, which provides your life belongs to Allah, nothing is impossible... The whole point is to discover the treasure given to you... This is the reason why you came here... To be able to BE the one that you were sent with the capacity to BE... Being able to only BE with that power and knowledge that is available in the seed of spirit sown in the soil of the body and with the one within you, and to emerge by piercing that soil is such a great story of existence that anyone who discovers their own truth in this journey also discovers the universe...

How magnificent... The more people, the more treasure... The greatest time machine is the human being... its spirit... Everything we call technology may actually be our dependence, becoming primitive and growing apart from Allah and what He bestows upon us ...

When we look at the remains of some ancient societies that we think of as primitive, seeing that they did what we failed to achieve with this technology may also suggest that the technology is not a means of liberation but a means of enslavement by taking us away from our own nature and capacity that are the greatest treasure and secrets, and prevents us from discovering our spiritual powers and secrets...

Just like our memories with terrific capacities losing their functions and becoming blunt while the machines that cannot even be a single fraction of our brain are recording phone numbers... For example, we need to check whether so many people had memory problems in the past, or whether our functions that we no longer use because we rely on machines have been dulled under the name of "technology" ...

I do not know if you have ever paid attention, but to the science of Allah, human beings are taught about how much they can be glorified while in the virtual worldly system we live in, people are always taught and indoctrinated to believe what they "cannot be or cannot do", and in short, "their power is insufficient and limited"...So that they are under the illusion that they are trapped in their bodies until the grave.

A few days ago, a friend of mine told me that he turned to Allah pure-heartedly and that Allah suddenly showed him a vision of the place of what he lost... "It was impossible for me to see this; how could it be? Especially the part where I saw something that was impossible to have been there just by closing my eyes was unbelievable."

The body equipment we have is extraordinary, but its use requires a guide as it is with every new item... Just like our newly bought television... Discovering yourself and understanding what this magnificent power that is given to you is capable of, will be your own "Laylat al-Qadr" (the Night of Power) where your life has changed... When you try to get closer to Allah, you will realize that you are surrounded by His armies besides the gifts bestowed upon you, and thus, you will have a spirit freed from all kinds of fear and loss, and you will feel "safe"...

Even though there are many references to time from the throne of Balqis brought next to Hazrat Suleiman in the blink of an eye, to the explanations of dreams, and to Miraj (the Ascension). Humankind is a kind of "box" hiding a power beyond the reputed leading-edge technology of creation and design. We need to think carefully about the purpose of "concealing" these features by creating deceptive patterns ...

Remember, kafir (unbeliever) means "the one concealing the truth". A person experiences helplessness on their own, and they experience what can be described as a "miracle" with Allah... It is the devil and his system that conceals the truth and makes you feel helpless though "Allah is with you"...

The devil is in exile in the world... Our Muslim scholar Mehmet Ali Bulut says: "Devil is the name given to the Satan sent down to the world..."

The main purpose of the devil is to make us forget our powers and what we are capable of and to lead us to transgressions that serve the realization of the apocalypse and to immediately return to the place he came from by defeating Adam, whom he regarded as his rival....

Allah communicating with us through signs and symbols makes the devil try to deceive us through symbolism...

Discovering the power and spirit of Allah in you means that the devil is defeated by Adam... That is why, with his system, he tries to make people turn outwards rather than inwards to prevent this from happening...

While human beings have the perfect equipment by nature that can never be matched by any matter or technology, the devil keeps whispering the delusions from all corners (whether through the media, the worldly system, or through friends and family) that they must "consume" wildly and they need to feel dependent on matter and they may only be "valued" when they have what others possess to prevent them from being aware of his abilities...

This system that is kept alive reminds us of the narrative in the Torah... When the devil tells Adam and Eve, "If you eat the fruits of this tree, you become gods and eternal...," he instills the consciousness that what makes human beings valuable is an external object...You start to move away from your truth, in other words from Allah, with your bodily and material concerns... You believe that consuming and possessing various belongings will make you valuable and you throw earth on the treasure buried in your heart... The interesting thing is that you feel this situation from within, and you cannot be "happy, peaceful, and powerful" with what you have. Look around, you can see dozens of examples...

If everyone went after what was in themselves and not in someone else as Islam recommends, they would understand that there is not only one treasure, but infinite treasures attached to this one treasure... But this is the feeling of greed, one of the devil's favorite sins...You may be blind to and deprived of your own treasure if you are deceived by greed...

This is the life story of the traveler who traveled the world in search of the famous treasure everyone was after and found that great treasure in his backyard...

Now turn to yourself...

"We are closer to him than his jugular vein ..."

(Surah al-Kahf, Verse 16).

"Then put your trust in Allah alone ..."

(Surah An-Naml, Verse 79).

III.
THE JUDGMENT DAY

The most magnificent system can only continue to function with the
management of a very powerful and very intelligent being.

-Isaac Newton

And 'remember' when your Lord brought forth from the loins of the
children of Adam their descendants and had them testify regarding them-
selves. 'Allah asked,' "Am I not your Lord?" They replied, "Yes, You are! We
testify." 'He cautioned,' "Now you have no right to say on Judgment Day,
'We were not aware of this.'

-Surah al-Araf, Verse 172

It is said that...

In the pre-eternal world where we were created by Allah, Allah addressed us...

''Alastu bi Rabbikum?''

Meaning: "Am I not your Lord?"

And it is said that people were so awestruck by the magnificent beauty of Allah's voice that they constantly searched for Him, always missed Him, and always wanted to hear Him. And this is why they tend to hear beautiful voices upon their arrival on the Earth...

The longing for the unique beautiful voice of Allah...

And "whirling" adopted by the travelers of love is actually the spiritual and bodily response to that divine voice ...

Allah's voice encompasses and reverberates everywhere. The universe is "a sea of vibration and frequency…" Just like our inner world.

As I approach the matter of "the Judgment Day," I wanted to start with this because the subject of "Sound" is the key to it.

"They ask you 'O Prophet' regarding the Hour, "When will it be?" Say, "That knowledge is only with my Lord. He alone will reveal it when the time comes. It is too tremendous for the heavens and the earth and will only take you by surprise." They ask you as if you had full knowledge of it. Say, "That knowledge is only with Allah, but most people do not know." (Surah al-Araf, Verse 187)

My perspective on the concept of the Judgment Day, which has puzzled people for hundreds of thousands of years, first started to develop upon encountering the following narrative...

They asked the Prophet: "O Prophet of Allah (PBUH), when will the Resurrection Day come?"

He replied as follows: "There are three types of Resurrections: The first is the small Resurrection that is for you on the day you die. Whoever dies it means their Resurrection Day has arrived.

The second is the medium Resurrection which begins when you are put in the grave. This is also called the torment of the grave (adhab al-qabr).

And the third is the great resurrection. It is the Resurrection Day when all living things will die and resurrect. This is the general Resurrection Day."7

7 When the Resurrection Day begins, it is said that it is appropriate to think of it as a period of time since there will no longer be a world day... It is stated that the Earth, the Sun, the Moon and the stars will fall apart and be torn into pieces one by one... "It is forty between two blows..."
Thereupon, Abu Hurayra was asked:
"Is it forty days?"
"I don't know." "Is it forty years?" "I don't know". "Is it forty months?"
"I don't know. Afterwards, every part of a person will rot and crumble, but the bone in the coccyx (the bone like a tiny marble) will not rot. People will resurrect and rise from that bone."(Musnad, II, 322; Bukhari / tafsir: 3/39, 1/78, Muslim / fiten: 141)
It is said that at the moment of Resurrection, the spirits of the believers will be taken

After reading these words of our Prophet, I saw that my stereotypes on the subject began to crumble.

As Quran delicately opened itself to me as I continued to turn towards each page, surah, and verse, the first thing I understood was that I was about to experience something that reaches deep within my spirit.

"And on the day of the great Resurrection, every person will be resurrected in the state in which they died. A person who performs good deeds while dying will be resurrected in a good way, and those who perform bad deeds and do not repent will be resurrected in that way..." In one of his hadiths referring to all these matters, our Prophet said:

"In whatever state you spend your life, you will die in that state. In whatever state you die, you will be resurrected in that state."

With an expression that I later understood, "my journey of dying before I die begins" and my world which I built, and which consisted of dreams and far from the truth was getting ready to fall apart...

The deep sleep which I was living as a result of confining the concepts to certain patterns and considering dreams and tales "true" and the truths as dreams and fairy tales was about to end.

---

earlier and therefore they will not feel the Resurrection; the Resurrection Day will be for those called "infidels/unbelievers.".

FIRST, MATTER

While the smallest unit of matter was thought to be an atom, the discovery that this was an illusion and that the smallest part of matter is subatomic particles, a kind of energy, completely changed the world's view of matter.

Actually, all matter was energy compressed into a slower vibration. It was a much more intense and concentrated state than other energies (according to Einstein it could turn into incomparably more energy than a small mass volume).

With his "theory of relativity," Einstein showed that matter and energy are equivalent. By approaching energy mathematically, he revealed that besides time and space, which we also call place, matter and energy exist, and that matter and energy are basically the same (equivalent). Matter was just a special kind of energy... Yes, all the forces we can see in the universe, each one, were nothing more than "electromagnetic waves with different wavelengths and frequencies, that is, vibrations..."

Let's start with the expression of "resonance," which is important and fundamental to the subject...

We have now understood that the basis of matter is the energy fields that form the magnetic energy that gives the "appearance" of that matter... Yes, resonance (magnetic resonance) is the name given to the vibrational sound or melody of these magnetic fields. All space-time is a sea of energy in the quantum sense. And everything in this sea of energy, whether a table or the stars are subatomic energies with the same building blocks and different vibrations and resonances...

This reminds me of the following words by Rumi:

"We came from the sea; we go to the sea..."

Scientists now describe the universe as "a sea of energy," and with the change in the perception of "matter" and the realization that "everything is fundamentally energy," they say that we are "peculiar floating frequencies in this sea of limitless frequency…"

This led me to the definition of the friends of Allah (e.g., Rumi) written centuries ago of human beings and the universe. Here, we were like a glass of water taken from the ocean. We were neither the same nor separate from the ocean…

While I was thinking all this information took my breath away, I was reading Surah al-Jumu'ah on a Friday and the first verse caught my eye in a different way.

This is the beauty of the Quran. Each time you read it; you discover something different. And here lies its miracle. What is perceived based on comprehension expands and develops as the comprehension increases and coincides with a timely expression. The same verse opens a different door in every reading in your comprehension, in your awareness…

Each of the words in it holds thousands of meanings, but we all get our share. Just like Rumi said:

"No matter what you say, what you say is as meaningful as much as others understand…"

It was the exact nature of the Quran; it held innumerable meanings as many as the stars that were invisible and ignored due to the sun during the day, but we limited the sky of our comprehension to the extent we saw.

I started reading Surah al-Jumu'ah. The first verse had so far appeared before me many times with different statements, but it had a beginning that was similar in content…

"Whatever is in the heavens and whatever is on the earth 'constantly' glorifies Allah; He is the Owner of the Dominion, He is the Most Pure, He is the All-Mighty, He is the All-Wise…"

After reading a few more surahs, I came to Surah al-Hashr. Its first verse was familiar to me:

"Whatever is in the heavens and whatever is on the earth glorifies Allah. For He is the All-Mighty, the All-Wise."

So, what is the first thing that comes to mind when we say "tasbeeh" prayer beads? An accessory that has recently become a traditional habit. Or the tasbeehs comprising ninety-nine beads (101) used after prayers. Initially, it comes to mind as an item.

But what did "tasbeeh" actually mean? For example, we say Subhanallah 33 times after prayer, the word 'Subhan' comes from the same origin as the word 'tasbeeh'.

I picked up the dictionaries. I started to search for the words tasbeeh and subhan...

Tasbih: An expression of praise stating that Allah is above any imperfection, exonerating Him, and expressing His absolute transcendence...

Subhan: To praise, to exonerate.

Here, I came across that wonderful word above all these beauties. The magnificent meaning of the word that connects all the pieces together...

"The word Subhan from the Arabic root SBH. The root meaning is to SWIM (without sinking), rolling forward, moving away quickly, being fast."

Yes, SUBHAN meant to SWIM.

I started to understand, albeit from the edge, what kind of SCIENCE was hidden in the Quran statements called "AYAH" (verse) meaning SIGNS, in the hadiths of the Prophet, and the words and couplets of the friends of Allah that we deem poetic...

Particularly some scientists now argue that the basic structure of matter consists of electromagnetic fields, not matter particles. Everything was united under a single energy field, and this made it inclined to remove many things from the title of "impossible" (teleportation, time travel) ...

These recently discovered scientific data gave us clues that we are all energies floating in the sea of limitless energy of Allah's names and attributes (meanings).

The "verses" that we think are the lines written in the pages of the Quran meant "the signs of Allah". A leaf was a verse and a human being...

Everything around us, including us, was nothing but the "signs" of Allah. Everything between the earth and the sky was the signs of Allah and they surrounded us. I glanced over; I was surrounded by verses. Even the gentle breeze that I felt at the back of my hand was actually water vapor. And it was as if I am swimming in this endless sea in both that water vapor and everything else around me.

"O day, rise! The particles are dancing. Spirits are dancing headless and footless in ecstasy. Those in this universe are all dancing for Him." (Rumi)

If a glass of water was taken from the sea, would it be separate from the sea? No. Would that glass of water be the sea itself? No. We were "the floating frequencies" in this limitless sea of energy that was formed by the revelation of the meanings of Allah's names and attributes…

We were exonerating Allah; we were glorifying Him. And we were trying to find our way in His limitless sea of energy...

"O, Muslims! I do not know myself; I do not know myself. I am neither a Christian nor a Jew nor a Muslim! I am neither Oriental nor Western ... Neither divine nor servile... I am neither of nature's pillars, nor of spinning flanks! I am neither from India, nor China ... I am not from Iraq, nor the lands of Khorasan... My distinction is being indistinct, my place is "placelessness!" (Rumi)

"We are neither from here nor there. We came from above, we go up! We came from the sea, we go to the sea, we came from an out of place, we go to an out of place!" (Rumi)

I think we need to be equipped with additional information before we delve deeper into the Resurrection topic...

WHAT IS THE ATMOSPHERE?

The atmosphere is a big computer...

Every person has an atmosphere. And every human being is a small world... And each of us will have our own Resurrection Day for our material and spiritual awakenings...

Have you ever reflected on what is the atmosphere which we don't feel the need to learn about except for the obligatory classes in our primary and secondary schooling, yet on which the creation of life depends?

The information we were taught in our childhood and adolescence flew away into the atmosphere a very long time ago. After this stage in your life, you must be thinking that you do not have the time to search for such topics in all the turmoil from love-sickness to lovers, from university to business, from marriage and kids to the struggle of making a living. Then you see that an entire lifetime has passed, and all that remains is the regret of those things we have not done ...

We think we invest in our own material future, but in that moment we lose our "essence," which is our most precious treasure that will carry us to eternity and happiness in both realms. And the material is temporary, it actually does not exist, and our essence is eternal and unique ...

Anyway, now that we've found a few hours in all this hustle and bustle, at least come, let's understand together, what is the atmosphere ...

Atmosphere: "It is the layer consisting of gas and vapor that surrounds the earth, retained by gravity. It is a mixture of gases, mainly oxygen, nitrogen, and water vapor, that is called air. As the earth rotates around its own axis, it is a thinner cover at the poles and a thicker cover at the equator."

The atmosphere, designed as a cover to envelop our world, protect it, and make it a living space, is actually like a big computer on top of all this.[8]

The atmosphere absorbs the solar radiation, called ultraviolet, and balances the temperature difference between the day and the night, resulting in the earth being a habitable place.

The plural version of the word "Sama'", the Arabic word for "Sky", is "Samawat" and it is mentioned repeatedly in the verses of the Quran. Just like the use of the word sky in our language, the word "sama'" is used in the Quran to refer to both the nearest sky and all atmospheric layers that cover the earth. When we say, "clouds in the sky" we mean the nearest sky but when we say "stars in the sky" we use sky to refer to the entire universe. The same is true for the word "sama'" in Arabic.[9]

In addition to this, based on the description of "sama'" and "ard" related to the world and the explanation identified with the world in the "hidden/covered" sense and originating from each of us being a "realm," "ard," that is the earth, represents the human body and "sama'" represents the human consciousness …

Every person is a sample of the universe and the earth. Dimensionally reduced and folded. However, in terms of content, it is even bigger… In short, if we think about it, picture the world like this: Think of billions of "small worlds" on the big earth (planet earth).

Here, each one of us is the "small worlds". We have our own bodies and consciousnesses as well as our energy fields, that is, our atmospheres … (The energy field described as the aura is a kind of atmosphere belonging to human beings. It is a kind of cover that protects the person from damages based on the individual field strength by filtering various electromagnetic fields like the evil eye) …

In the attribute of the "Lord of the Worlds" lies the meaning of both our world and the realms of many beings as well as the meaning of the Lord of each person, each of which is a different realm, that is,

8 Our teacher Mehmet Ali Bulut states that the blue color of the sky originates from the refraction of the sunlight as well as another important factor which is the electromagnetic radiation somehow released from the brains of people…

9 The explanation of the seven layers of the sky in the Quran may also refer to its layers, dimensions, and gravitational fields.

the world.

Now, let's go back to our topic of sama' and sky ...

Here, in this narrative, let's take a look at another meaning that SAMA' is referring to in various verses of the Quran in the narration of ard and sama'.

In the Quran or even in our conversations[10] when we say "sama'", we limit our comprehension to the "sky". One meaning of SAMA' is the sky, the heavens, and fate. Yes, but besides this, SAMA' also means "to hear" ...

Doesn't the word SAMA', originating from Allah's name as-SAMI, which means "the All-Hearing", explain the nature of the sama' better to us? ...

SAMA' means "the one who hears" and is like a memory and a computer that records us.

On the other hand, the power of the word "prayer" is made clear in the hadith "The weapon of the believer is prayer" means "to call, to invite."

In short, I am trying to say this: We make a call to the "All-Hearing" with each of our prayers and invite what we want ...

Basically, even if we do not do it with the consciousness of "prayer", we are constantly in positive and negative calls and communication with the universe because "our every word" is perceived by the sama' ...

Every verbal input to the atmosphere, which is the universal computer, will activate the energies associated with that subject.

Don't let this narrative seem strange to you ...

With technology, even smart houses that are voice commanded, from the hologram, have emerged. Moreover, when you want to search for something on the internet using the new versions on the computers, for example, when you make a verbal command and say "Einstein," the computer that receives the voice command, offers you a response like: '' 150,000 results were found for this search. '' You choose one by

---

10 SAMA'- SAM'A

clicking on what is known as a LINK and the information is given to you. Of course, the results you get vary depending on how you use this.

In the narration of Necdet Ardıç (Terzi Baba), a friend of Allah, I heard this: "Do not think Noah's Ark was made of wood. Noah's Ark had such advanced technology that it had VOICE command ..."

Later, when I began studying the people of Noah, I read the following in Surah Noah, verse 15:

"Do you not see how Allah created the seven heavens one above the other?"

Scientific investigations and research reveal that the sky surrounding the earth consists of 7 layers.[11]

The expression here, "Do you not see?" is striking. It turns out that the technology is so advanced that it could mean that the layers of the sky are clearly visible, or it could mean that you already have this knowledge ...

I mean, in this world where the hints of the advancement of technology were given beforehand, it did not seem impossible to have VOICE-commanded computers and mechanisms that run with them...

As people progress in technology, they tend to forget that Allah's technology is beyond any technology.

In fact, when my friends use the term HI-TECH, I tell them "I use the technology of the al-HAYY and the ONLY (TECH, a pun for the word TEK, which means "Only" in my first language, Turkish)."

When we were children, we were told a fairy tale called Ali Baba and the Forty Thieves ...

Ali Baba finds the treasure in a cave and learns that the cave is opened by voice command. Speaking the right words will open the cave allowing him to acquire the treasure ...

"Open sesame!"

Why would not a similar cave that opens layer by layer with the right words exist in the universe and offer us the treasures it contains?

11 troposphere, stratosphere, mesosphere, thermosphere, exosphere, ionosphere, and magnetosphere

"Open life, open!"

Of course, it should not be forgotten that after finding the treasure, Ali Baba becomes the target of thieves. Therefore, here you have to decide well what you want or the distress of the fulfillment of what you want may be more than the pleasure and comfort it will bring.

For this reason, is it not best to approach the sky that hears us with the prayers of the Prophet, that is, the calls of the Prophet, which are the advice of Allah?

When we call someone we say, "I CALLED you. I texted you".

Our brains are like radios; magnificent devices designed to be both a receiver and a transmitter ...

What we say is so important that it is said that our words find "spirit" in the science of Sufism... The Prophet advised us to have a "good opinion (husn e zan)" in every comment. Even though we cannot see the energies of our words "for now" with our physical eyes and this dimensional perception, this does not mean that these energies do not exist ... This concept of "good opinion-positive (good) thinking," which has existed in us for centuries, is presented to us as anew discovery under fancy names such as "the power of thought" and "positive thinking" by Westerners in recent years.

-Allah is the All-Hearing. Yes, He hears and sees us everywhere, anytime. He records everything with the magnificent system He has established from His own names and attributes and embraces us.

What we share with the universe, that is, our words, in fact, "the nature of the energy they produce" is so important, because as we have already stated, matter is essentially energy... For example, is it possible that Hazrat Muhammed [PBUH] who advised us among other recommendations not to tell anyone about a bad dream and recommended that we blow or spit three times towards the left and take refuge in Allah from the evil of the devil and read Ayat al-Kursi would advise you to tell your dream which may carry a negative CALL to the "sama' hearing you," that is the celestial computer surrounding you all over?

The science of dream interpretation warns and teaches you that you should not tell your dream to those who would interpret it unfavorably, or even if you tell, say, "Rabbi Yassir wala tu-'assir. Rabbi tammim bil khair" meaning "O my Lord, make things easier for me, do not make things difficult for me. O My Lord, let my affairs end with goodness."

Whether or not we know it, even when we are vocalizing something we are thinking about, we activate a mechanism related to the energy of that thing. Because our intention or thought becomes a CALL and "the sound is the energy that carries knowledge, that carries information," and as per our designs bearing the meanings of Allah's names and attributes that manifest in us, we are like devices provided with the mechanism to realize energy...

The sama', which is the ALL-HEARING main computer that we can also call the headquarters, will start to wander and seek the response to the energy it creates, like any energy that does not disappear. Like a word you enter on a Google search, the sama' will list and download the expressions of the energy you produce.

Whether it is an action or a word, basically everything carries information and energy. When you wish for something, you must act in the direction of what you want, not only verbally, but also with your actions. Likewise, apricots are not only grown by sowing the seeds. That apricot seed will turn into a tree once it is fertilized and watered, and the necessary precautions against natural disasters are taken. Otherwise, it will rot away...

That is why, like every word, the action to reach every call is a call. This is because the actions you take to realize your wish, also known as "actual prayer," will also release energy, just like words in the very nature of a prayer or a call...

For example, there is the following advice: "If you have sinned, do good deeds immediately. Here, the issue is as above. When we commit an action - which the universe perceives as a call - it is also a targeted call, or when we make a verbal call/invitation (like I wish I had a car) we are unaware that we have actually prayed to the universe...

Trying to NEUTRALIZE an erroneous action with a good deed is nothing more than an effort to balance the negative energy parcel we have revealed with another positive energy that can correspond to it. However, for some sins such as "rights of individuals" it is impossible to produce a positive energy in that direction without taking the positive energy of that person yourself (without making an effort for it). For example, asking for forgiveness from that person or fulfilling the requirements of being forgiven by that person.

For instance, it is said that sins and good deeds will be weighed on a scale called "Mizan" on the Day of Judgment.

"So, whoever does an atom's weight of good will see it. And whoever does an atom's weight of evil will see it," (Surah Zilzal, Verses 7, 8). There are verses regarding the weighing of good deeds and sins on the Mizan, which is called the Scale of the Day of Judgment.

It is said that everything in the world that is produced from words to thoughts will "take shape" and goodness will be bright, and evil will be dark.

If there will be a different method of recognizing or reading energy in the dimension we will be transitioning to, then it is likely that we will see what we see as matter in other forms and what we see as meaning in other forms...

The universe is made up of sound and light... The definition of information and energy is limited to the perception of the computer reading it. Think of it like this, if a media reader is not installed in the computer, the computer cannot read a YouTube video uploaded, right?

However, after that program is installed, the link that is the "connection" of the information which is the "invisible" data becomes visible to you ...

For the purpose of being tested, we came to this universe and the world with certain limitations, and for this reason, perhaps we cannot see that a good deed, such as feeding the poor triggers the formation of a "heavenly room" in a dimension that we cannot see at the same time that we perform this action.

Ignoring what our brains and perceptions cannot read or see would be to belittle the universe. There are so many things that we cannot see and hear in this universe, which has been created by the word "BE" from the science of Allah and which is an infinite genius, that our Prophet said, "The sky is so crowded that it creaks."

Islam, which explains that the main purpose is to be cleansed and to pursue SCIENCE, recommends making an effort to know our Allah, who says, "I am as my servant thinks I am," with the closest comprehension by forcing the limits of our perception as much as possible.

"I am as my servant thinks I am." In other words, I treat my servants based on their comprehension of Me.

Then, the more we know about Him, the more our comprehension will change and increase.

"The righteousness and acceptance of a deed depends on the righteousness of the heart. The righteousness of the heart depends on the righteousness of the intention." (Mutarrif bin Abdullah)

Some malevolent people who saw our Prophet reciting "Astaghfirullah (Forgive me Allah)" 70 times a day would ask, "If prophets were sinless, then why does he ask for forgiveness?"

Here, we perceive repentance only as cleansing from "sins." We have categorized everything. Sins and good deeds, religious and irreligious, this and that.

However, even expressions such as sin and good deeds in religion are about ensuring that human beings, who are actually an information package, an energy, attain the right energy and be in the right communication with the universe.

Our Prophet recommends the concept of repentance to us by doing it himself, and there are many reasons for this. But one of the most important reasons that beautiful sinless person was doing this was to be cleansed from the COMPREHENSION of the previous day.

Our Prophet saying, "If you are the same as yesterday, you are in a loss ..." expresses that we need to add new knowledge and comprehension to ourselves daily. Islam is the religion of science. Even the attribute of our Prophet "UMMI" is not fully understood. For our Prophet, we say, "He was ummi," as if we were telling a story. "Ummi" means illiterate in its apparent meaning, which is certainly how Allah deemed it appropriate due to various wisdoms. Allah predestined our Prophet to be illiterate because He didn't want our Prophet to be accused of reading the Bible and the Torah preceding the Quran and quoting information from them.

However, there is another meaning of "ummi" that is unnoticed and overlooked as the comprehension improves....

Do you know what IMAM means? Imam comes from the root ''um" and um" means mother. Although some may say, "Allah will punish you," "He will put you in the fire," or "You are an unbeliever" from time to time, in the religion of Allah, "imam" means "the person who calls the lost children of Islam to the right path with the compassion of a mother."

With the compassion of a mother ...

Portraying the religion of compassion and mercy as the religion of punishment and torment is such a great crime that scholars warn people to convey the religion correctly otherwise there may be a great punishment.

As we see, "um" means "mother." This expression, in which the mother of knowledge, the conscious one is hidden, actually refers to the profound knowledge of Muhammad (PBUH) ...

In other words, our Prophet was UMMI, but he was not like the stereotyped scholars who are literate, and who are likened to "a donkey carrying a book" in the Quran. He was the one who "acted" based on his knowledge. He was not limited by being a porter of information who only carries and transfers information, he was the one who converted information into wisdom by turning it into a STATE.

Our UMMI Prophet, whom we know to be illiterate, was also the MOTHER OF KNOWLEDGE.

Likewise, when he was ordered to "Read!", he said, "I don't know how to read and write, I cannot read ..." And Jibril (Gabriel) (Gabriel means the mightiness, power, force of Allah) said to him: "Read in the name of your Lord ..." (Surah al-Alaq, Verse 1)

The Prophet who read in the name of his Lord became the mother of knowledge. We bypass this miracle by giving formal meanings to his illiteracy. Each state of the Prophet was the very nature of the miracle if we only knew it. We must walk after our Prophet, not Abu Jahil, who is, the father of ignorance.

That is why we must READ, in the name of our Lord. Because, if He, who knows everything informs His servant of His might and makes them the mother of knowledge. In the blink of an eye...

The life of Terzi Baba, loosely translated to the Father of Tailoring, one of the great saints raised in Anatolia, contains a profound message on this subject...

Terzi Baba began to learn tailoring to have a trade, at the request of his parents, after he had studied basic religious knowledge. Hence, he is famous as "Terzi Baba." He had no interest in the world. He was too inclined to the hereafter. While he was busy with his trade, he did not abandon worship and made maximum effort to disobey the desires and wishes of his nafs (ego). He met with Sheikh Abdullah Mekki Effendi, one of the caliphs of Mawlana Halid-i Baghdadi, and became his student. Thereafter, Terzi Baba's spiritual rank progressed day by day. He reached very advanced ranks in struggling with and disciplining his nafs, as such Abdullah Mekki Effendi authorized him to practice as an Islamic/Sufi teacher. In Ottoman Turkish, this was described by the word, "icazet" whereby the student is authorized to guide, train, and teach others on Allah's path.

His meeting with Abdullah Mekki Effendi was as follows: Terzi Baba both sewed and chanted Allah's name with both his tongue and heart. While sewing in his shop, he used to push the needle through the fabric, saying Allah's name with his tongue and heart. He was a gentle and humble person. He did not want anyone to know about his state. He loved the poor very much and his affection for them was evident.

One day, one of the poor travelers came to Erzincan. The coat he was wearing was too dirty to handle, as was very old. This person visited the tailors in the city one by one to have his coat mended. But all the tailors he visited, did not sew his coat, they were even hesitant to touch it. Tailors cynically told him, "There is Terzi Baba over there. Take it to him, he will sew it". The poor traveler found Terzi Baba and told him what he wanted. Instead of rejection from Terzi Baba, he was welcomed. Terzi Baba said to him, "Leave your coat, I will have it ready by tomorrow inshaAllah." He then, washed it well, dried it, and sewed it. The next day he handed over the coat to its owner. He did not charge for all this. That poor traveler was very pleased to see his coat clean and mended. He looked at Terzi Baba and made a wish from his heart that may Allah Almighty let him reach the discourse of his loved ones.

In those days, Hazrat Mewlana Halid-i Baghdadi sent Abdullah Mekki Effendi, one of his caliphs, to Anatolia. Abdullah Mekki Effendi stopped by Erzurum, then he turned towards Erzincan. When he approached Erzincan, he said to his friends, "The town our teacher described to us is this, Allah knows. There is someone here and we have to give him an item that was entrusted to us." When Abdullah Mekki Effendi honored Erzincan with his visit, people flocked to see him. Terzi Baba was among those who came. Abdullah Mekki Effendi stood up when Terzi Baba, whom he was seeing for the first time, entered the room. He invited him in and sat him by his side. He paid Terzi Baba a compliment that he had never paid anyone before. "We have an item entrusted to us from Hazrat Mewlana Halid-i Baghdadi. I deemed you deserving of that item. It provides you with many benefits. If you accept it, I will deliver it to you," he said. Terzi Baba responded,

"You know, sir if it is a material benefit then I will not utter the name "Allah" for anything related to this world". When Abdullah Mekki Effendi received this answer, he said, "My son, you have found what you would have discovered eventually. The entrusted item that I will deliver was nothing but saving you from the love of the world." He looked at him with himma (spiritual aspiration) and delivered the item. This led him to be disciplined and reach maturity on the path of Shahih al Naqshband al Bahaeddin Bukhari. He gave caliphate to Terzi Baba and assigned him to teach the religion of Allah Almighty to the servants of Allah and allow them to reach the marifatullah (the knowledge in Allah). Thereupon, Terzi Baba's state immediately changed, and he dived into a sea of spiritual blessings.

After these events, Terzi Baba's high rank was known far and wide and word of it spread among the public. Everyone came to him to benefit from his spiritual blessings. Over time, the number of Terzi Baba's students increased day by day. Those who were envious of this state started to gossip about him. They said, "So many people gathered around such an ignorant ummi." Even those who had a bit of knowledge started saying such words. Thereupon, the mufti of the town invited Terzi Baba for a test. His purpose was to ensure that when Terzi Baba was unable to answer the questions, he would understand his ignorance and give up the role of guiding people. Terzi Baba accepted the mufti's invitation. He saw that a large scientific council had gathered. When Terzi Baba asked the mufti why he invited him, the mufti responded, "We invited you for a test. There are many rumors about you. We need to put an end to this. We will now ask some questions. You will answer." Then he asked about the number of affirmative (subhuti) attributes and many other things.

In order to reveal a great truth, Terzi Baba answered, "Allah Almighty has seven affirmative attributes according to the inhabitants of this town and eight affirmative attributes according to those in other towns. According to this town, the affirmative attributes of Allah Almighty are Ilm (Knowledge), Sam'a (Hearing), Basar (Seeing), Irada (Will), Hayah (Life), Kalam (Speech), and Takwin (Bringing to Being). According to this town, Allah Almighty does not have Qudra (Power) as an attribute. Because the people of this town deny Allah's attribute of Qudra (Power). If the people of this city believed in the attribute of Qudra (Power), they would say that Allah has the power to create the ability to allow an ummi servant to guide other people to the true path..." Immediately after his answer, those present were convinced that Terzi Baba was a spiritually mature man with the knowledge given by Allah (ilm ladunni). They asked for forgiveness. Thereafter they were hospitable and respectful.[12]

"Ilm (Knowledge)" is the most important thing in our religion. Years after our Prophet started receiving revelations, the system that regulates prayer times was given ... In our country, when someone converts to Islam or wants to practice the obligatory worships, we say, "Perform salah!" without explaining some of the basic information.

Of course, one should perform salah, there is no other gathering like salah. But in doing so, you also need to understand what you are doing, what you are saying, and what a magnificent road you have actually taken. Only then will you embrace salah more and become seriously attached to it. Thus, you will also understand that the true salah is not limited to five times a day, but the "Permanent Salah," which is also indicated in the Quran.

Friends of Allah are in a state of permanent salah with their hearts. Even if they stood on their prayer mats at least 5 times a day, their foreheads remained in prostration at every moment. They comprehended that they were always in the presence of Allah, whether they were sitting or standing, or when they were all alone.

In one of the discourses when Jibril (Gabriel) came to teach Islam, he asked the Messenger of Allah, "What is Ihsan?" Prophet Mohammed (PBUH) replied, "It's worshipping Allah as if you see Him ....

---

12 Encyclopedia of Saints

Even if you do not see Allah, Allah sees you." So Ihsan (doing what is beautiful) is to worship and behave with this comprehension…

With the comprehension of being with Him at every moment …

If we could all be like this, would the world be in its current state?

Isn't that the reason why the surah beginning with ''Kul hu" is called Surah Ihlas? Have we never contemplated the reason why a prayer that does not contain the word "Ihlas" is called Ihlas?

We perceive prostration as simply putting our foreheads on the ground. Whereas, in addition to its meaning "to prostrate, to worship by falling on the ground," prostration means "to submit, to obey and, to comply with." It is turning towards Him not only with your body but also with your spirit and comprehension. For this reason, Allah says, "There is no veil between me and my servant in prostration, it is the moment when he is closest to me."

Believing, obeying, and submitting actually exist in the creation of the human "essence," that is, in its nature, even if the spirit desires for it to be forgotten. Even the word 'nature' is a sign of this…

Nature is "the inherent characteristics of a being that come from its creation …" You know, to "submit" to someone is to follow that person, to be subject to, and be dependent on them. So, human nature involves submitting to Allah…

Even the word "tab," which is also the first syllable of "tabiat (nature)," means "to stamp; seal, character…"

The universe is the seal of Allah… Seeing that seal, stamp on yourself, knowing that you carry it, and glorifying it, and the sense of belonging is the way one's nature is satiated, it is the way of finding peace…

What lies in the word "prostration" is the expression of this obedience. Prostration is an expression of obedience to the Creator. Prostration to Adam means submission resulting from obedience to Allah. The words obedience (itaat) and nature (tabiat) are interrelated.

Everything that exists in the Universe is obedient to the Creator.

So, obedience is an inherent and intrinsic aspect of humanity ... The search never ends before one experiences this ... That person cannot find peace nor feel a sense of belonging ...

There is such a beautiful narrative that Allah is actually hidden in everything that exists in the universe ... This becomes apparent to a highly perceptive person, but those who fail to comprehend this think that they are in love with other things or that they tend to be inclined towards other things ... In fact, Allah kind of spared us with His sole existence and manifestation everywhere and prevented us from falling into this sin, the sin of drifting away from Him.

It is not about seeing what does not exist, but not seeing what exists ... It is only about comprehension ...

Truth is always with us, in our nature. We either agree to see this or not ...

As long as we do not, we will live as expelled from being ourselves and go through the pain of resisting our nature and betraying our existence with a spiritual dwarfism caused by the uncracked seed that failed to become a giant tree...

Love is neither in your lover nor in your head.
Love is only in you...

-Deniz Erten

Yes, when it comes to ilm (knowledge), I felt that I should briefly address the matter of the Sahaba (the Companions of the Prophet).

Have you ever thought about what is the meaning of Sahaba?

Sahaba means "master of suhba (discourse)" and "the possessor." But what did they possess?

The knowledge imparted by the mother of knowledge in his discourses. A while later after they started to possess the knowledge, the calendars for salah were determined (in the Ascension). There were so many things they perceived and prostrated in their consciousness that they reached the peak by prostrating physically ...

They said, '' Subhana Rabbi Al Ala" in prostration; when they said, "My Almighty Lord, I exonerate you," they exonerated Allah even from their own comprehension because they comprehended that Allah is a great power and Being that is beyond comprehension.

I hope that anyone who devoted themselves to the knowledge and discourse of the Prophet would be on the way to becoming a Companion spiritually inshaAllah. Because the Messenger of Allah (PBUH) says, "A person is with their beloved one."

What more can he say?

In Fusus al-Hikam, Hazrat İbn Arabi discusses this issue as follows:

"When a person acts as an imam to his inner realm and the angels performing salah with him (as stated in a sound hadith, since the angels stand behind the person who performs salah, everyone who performs salah is an imam) for this person, he attains the rank of prophethood, and this rank is to be a representative of Allah.

When he says, "Sami Allahu Liman Hamidah (Allah hears whoever praises Him)," he informs his ego and the angels behind him that Allah has heard, and those who are there with him reply by saying "Rabbana Lakal Hamd (Our Lord, praise be to You) ..."

For there is no doubt that Allah Almighty says,Sami Allahu Liman Hamidah" through the mouth of His servant. So, take a look at the magnitude of the rank of salah and where it leads the one performing salah. However, a person who fails to reach the level of observation during salah cannot attain the purpose of salah. Because such people fail to see the Truth to Whom they invoke and thus, they do not have that light in their eyes. If they do not hear the response of the Truth during salah, it means that they are not of those who heed (the Truth). And anyone who is not present in the presence of their Lord because they do not hear and see is not actually performing salah. Such people are not from the class of observers and listeners ...

We will meet again on this subject in the book. Now, if we have quite understood the importance of ilm (knowledge) in Islam, let's continue with a few authentic hadiths.

Knowledge is so important:

"And these examples We present to the people, but none will understand them except those of knowledge." (Surah al-Ankabut, verse 43) Below are some noble hadiths:

"The ink of those of knowledge is weighed by the blood of the martyr and the ink of those of knowledge is heavier than the blood of the martyr."(Khateeb, I. Najjar, I, Raafai)

"Those of knowledge are the candles of the earth, the caliphs of the prophets, mine, and the other prophet's heirs." (Abu Nuaym, Ibn Adiyy) "The first of those who will intercede on the Day of Judgment are prophets, then scholars, then martyrs."(Daylami, Abu Sheikh Khateeb)

"Those of knowledge are the caliphs of the prophets in the world, and they are martyrs in the hereafter."(Khateeb)

It is explained over and over in the verses that our religion is not meant to be brute force or brutality, but to actually "fight with the ego" and to reach the knowledge of truth, which is the only reality.

"...Are those who know equal to those who do not know?..."(Surah az-Zumar, Verse 9)

All we understand from the Eid al-Adha is only physically fasting and then sacrificing a ram. We do not examine why the day before eid is called "AREFE (EVE)." Is this word that comes from the root of the word "arafa" meaning, "knowing, wisdom, informing about the future" chosen for nothing? The word sacrifice comes from the same root as the word "affinity" meaning "to approach." Here, the real Eid al-Adha is the day when we sacrifice our egos and approach our Allah. A person who has become acquainted with the knowledge and worship of Allah, that is a person who "knows" or "has reached awareness" as defined in Western terminology, will certainly celebrate Eid al-Adha as one who has received the good news of getting closer to Allah. Could there be a better reason?

Mount Arafat is the mountain of love where people end the ignorance they had until then and where they were thus forgiven just a moment before they become those of knowledge, that is, those who are "aware" and those who "know" on Arafat, on the last hill between the perception of the world and the perception of truth coming along with the knowledge of Allah.

We do not live anything by knowing, yet we still bewail the veils in our prostration.

I will come to this topic under another heading. Now let's return to science and energy...

It is interesting that for example there is a concept called "zakat" in Islam. Zakat means "to be cleansed, to be purified, to be cleared of crime." Zakat of not only property but also knowledge, even beauty, and health should be given in different ways...

Repentance means "to return and to give up sins".[13]

This word means "returning" from the mistake with negative energy in the Aramaic / Syriac language from which it originates. Interestingly, the Arabic equivalent of the word "thawab (reward)," which is the reward of goodness in Islamic law, is "to return."

It is interesting, isn't it? Is there a message to be given to us?

Or are we told, "Whether you do good deeds or commit sins, it will come back to you!"?

It's because the system is based on "turning" and each energy must return to its source where it is produced with equivalent energy...

As even water is poured, the light energy of equivalent intensity, as opposed to its energy, climbs up from where it is poured.

In this world, the negative energies loaded on our information package, which we call "the spiritual or energy body," must be cleared. If we do not clean them up, we pay for it with diseases, distress, etc. and with the punishment of the grave after death, with blessings granted

13 Since the word "devil" means being away from Allah, repentance, in another sense, means returning to Allah after drifting apart from Him.

to us (through charity, zakat), or, if still short, with sufferings on the Day of Judgment, or we pay for it by staying in hell if intercession does not remove them. Adam means "nothingness." However, this nothingness points to existence with the subsistence of Allah in the absence of "one's own relative existence," which is described as "the seas of the nothingness that could not possibly exist" and a journey from humanity to Adam. Therefore, it becomes necessary to lose oneself in Allah in order to exist in Allah... With the eternity in their spirit and with the representation deemed to exist in this realm, humanity is actually nothingness... The story of every human being is the story of the journey from humanity to Adam, who overcame the sufferings in the war between the finite and the infinite, who passed through their barzakh and disappeared from their own end and reached their eternity ... For this, you must first understand that you are a human being ... That is, you are nothing... You must first empty your CUP of existence ...

When dust falls into a glass of water, the water added to it is nothing but the growth of dirty water. Therefore, the first step is that the CUP should be emptied, and refilled with clean water and that clean water should be increased with knowledge ... In the Zen doctrine, which is very popular in the West, it is recommended to be an empty cup. The orientation to Zen philosophy is that it means "the path; the path to our essence." It is called a path that is independent of religions. However, it must not have been understood that the word religion means "the path" and that it is the path to Allah, to our essence...

In order to exist with the right energy, you must first disappear, and in order to exist with Allah, you must first lose yourself in Allah...

Whether on Judgment Day, in the grave, or in the world, people suffer due to the deficiencies and mistakes in their comprehension of knowledge. This is the knowledge of truth. Therefore, the responsibility of those of knowledge is enormous, and the magnitude of the punishment of those who lead people to the wrong path and lead them to drift apart from Allah is repeatedly stated in various verses in the

Quran.

Expressions such as "Do not make it difficult, make it easier, there is no compulsion in religion" involve many meanings.

People fall into the distinction between good and evil because of their ignorance. As such, the Messenger of Allah, knowing that our way of understanding is always through "matter" and "form," converted everything taught to him by Allah into matter, physical appearance, shapes, and symbols.

"And We have truly set forth every 'kind of' lesson for humanity in this Quran, yet most people persist in disbelief." (Surah al-Isra, Verse 89)

While Abu Jahil is also a name given to a pattern and a person, it is actually a criticism brought to the system of survival where religion, the "path," is only bodily rituals and understanding.

Regarding this person, whose real name was Amr Bin Hisham and who was the enemy of the Prophet and Islam, everyone gave an opinion on what nickname should be given to him based on the popular Arabic practice, and our Prophet deemed it more suitable to call him ABU JAHIL. Why is that?

Why did he deem it appropriate? What does ABU JAHIL mean?

Abu = father, jahil = ignorance. Here, again, a concept is taken out of the pattern of a "person" and turned into a "system" ...

By pointing to Abu Jahil, who lived centuries ago, is it possible that our Prophet meant that regardless of who they are, whether they live now or centuries later, Islam has only one enemy, and it is an "ignorant" person? This ignorance is Islam's worst enemy.

We continue to hold a grudge against him in our own way by considering him as an individual and to be defeated by our "Knowledge was a single point, but the ignorant have multiplied it ..."(Hazrat Ali)

Rights of Individuals

It is ordained, "There is no person without sin."If we are penalized for every sin, it is truly an unthinkable punishment. However, the mercy of our Allah is so great that He says He will count our thawabs as ten-fold and our sins as they are. O Settar (The Veiler of Sins) covers sins with the name At-Tawwab (the Accepter of Repentance). For if we suffer for our every sin, there will be incredible pain and anguish. When a thawab is committed, an angel comes to you; the sins of the previous day are not written until every afternoon salah, so as can be understood from the teachings such as ask for forgiveness, the benefit of thawab is to eliminate sins. It is an attempt to prevent our SPIRI-TUAL BODIES from losing power by balancing the negative energies we load on ourselves with positive energies. However, as stated as an example, the rights of individuals are very important and we cannot pay them with "nafl (supererogatory)" prayers. This will be paid by fard (obligatory) prayers or by adding the great sins of that person to the spiritual body. Every unit of energy that will be transferred from our spiritual bodies, that is, from our energy bodies to the opposite party will reduce our energy power in our painless transition to another dimension ...

Not one sin or thawab will be wasted because the energy released from these actions survives like every existing energy. They are weighed on a scale called mizan which maybe weighs energy. Knowledge and information are also energy, and while Allah's friends warn that thawabs can be quickly melted away by our sins on the mizan, they mention the fact that the knowledge of truth is not like that.

One is treated based on whether sins or thawabs weigh heavier.

One day I was reading a book by Ibn Arabi, I think it was Fu-tuhatal-Makkiya. In it, Iread something very interesting: the Sufis (the word Sufi has many meanings; pure, clean, purified from dirt, possessing the knowledge of the truth, and it is said to come from the word 'woolen clothing') from the friends of Allah, transmitted a kind of energy among themselves as if they were holding something from the abdomen. They already had it in their comprehension as they had a grasp of these kinds of narratives about the energy body as well as the knowledge of truth that they possessed for centuries that is above every knowledge.

I don't know if you have ever thought about this, but there is a mention of Allah's gaze. So much so that the pilgrimage time is defined as the time when divine mercy and wisdom are the most intense and it is said that Allah looks at His servants ...

There is a concept called "nadhar (consideration; to gaze, to look)" in the science of Sufism. The murshid transfers energy to the murid by looking into the eye. Since energy is also a transference of knowledge, it leads to different discoveries in that person's comprehension.

Another version of this is REVELATION. Revelation is one-to-one unlimited energy and power. It is the transference of knowledge and energy from Allah, the Almighty, and the All-Knowing, to a being. In this way, there will be great revelations in the person who suddenly receives it. However, this energy transfer is such that it jolts the person who is loaded with it. In fact, if we consider the chronicles about how our Prophet trembled and what he experienced on the day he received the first revelation, we can perhaps comprehend how the energy of a person with lower knowledge, that is energy, will rise with this new charge.

It is also stated that even those who receive inspiration experience a state of difficulty and trembling as if 100 watts were loaded into a 50-watt light bulb...

We can think of it as follows, aren't we surrounded by electromagnetic fields?

Although we cannot see, there are electromagnetic fields surrounding us like the internet, mobile phone base stations, wireless net, television receivers, satellites, etc.Can we see them? No, we can only see the related devices, but our eyes cannot READ, I mean, see and perceive these currents.

There is an "unlimited flow of information" around us. Here, the brain of a person is a receiver and a transmitter like a radio or a cell phone. What do those whose Internet data runs out do? They reload the energy package so that it can be connected to the flow of information, albeit "limited".

While there is an unlimited flow of information, we are limited to our own package, and each package contains information. Every package uploaded to us increases our communication and connection. So, the universe and our brains are just like the relationship between a computer and the internet.

Our television or radio will be exposed to the flow of information of the frequency of the channel it is switched to, and it will be deprived of perceiving all other frequencies. Couldn't the situation be like this? There are already all dimensions and entities around us. While all dimensions are intertwined, just like the electromagnetic fields surrounding us, we are only in connection with the channel that we have the password or the channel we set our radio to, and therefore, we do not know what is in the other channels because our settings are not directed to those channels.

When information comes from the upper consciousness like inspiration, that energy containing KNOWLEDGE originating from the unlimited power and knowledge will increase the voltage of that person. Even the concept of burning may possibly be originating from this. As our energy, in other words, our knowledge increases, our electrical field, in other words, electromagnetic field, also increases, so we actually burn.

Interestingly enough, the friends of Allah also talk about burning ...
"I was raw ...I ripened ...I burned ..."
Mawlana who says, "There is a difference in burning... Wood becomes ash when it burns. Human beings become servants when they burn

..." might have actually offered us knowledge under a poetic narrative?

Aside from everything, a being whose lungs are fed with oxygen, who burns the food eaten and turns it into energy is already burning.

This burning and this "fire" are a different kind of fire ...

By the way, the word "halal (permissible)," for which we opened a parathesis above while writing about forgiveness under sins-thawabs, means to UNTIE, PERMIT. We are actually tying ourselves and our perception and our transition to the energy body with negative information burdens called sin, such as the rights of an individual. Those bonds must be untied by forgiving ...

It is even stated that our energy body will "shine" with the thawabs of our spiritual body. Shining means LIGHT. Lightening ...

Even the expression ENLIGHTENING, which comes with the Western teachings, is also based on Allah's knowledge of truth. How?

Allah orders us to be enlightened. He invites us to the truth.

People who have encountered death speak of a light. Remember ... Let's look at verses 35 and 36 of Surah an-Nur:

"Allah is the Light of the heavens and the earth. His light1 is like a niche in which there is a lamp, the lamp is in a crystal, the crystal is like a shining star, lit from 'the oil of' a blessed olive tree, 'located' neither to the east nor the west,2 whose oil would almost glow, even without being touched by fire. Light upon light! Allah guides whomever He wills to His light. And Allah sets forth parables for humanity. For Allah has 'perfect' knowledge of all things."

"'That light shines' through houses 'of worship' which Allah has ordered to be raised, and where His Name is mentioned. He is glorified there morning and evening."

Here, nur means "light, radiance" in Arabic. And the believers are invited to the nur, that is to say, "light", "enlightenment" inside and outside ...

Cleansing of the spiritual body, the brain, and reaching the light. The brain, which is an electrical system, always radiates rays. Some people will describe a person and say that his/her face is radiant. Why? The concentrated knowledge inside, the loaded energy is reflected on the outside, that is, on the body ...

There are saints with radiant faces. Didn't we ever think why a person had a radiant face?

The Light of Muhammed is said to have covered the universe. The Quran mentions those who torment their nafs (egos). We will talk more in detail about the ego in the next chapter, but do you know what "cruelty" is? What does the word cruelty mean, and to whom do we refer as "cruel"? To whom does the Quran refer as "cruel"?

The description of this verbis "the one who domineers, a wrongdoer" it has the same origins as the word "gloom, darkness..."

So every time we torment our nafs (egos), that is, every time we fall into error, our hearts and the energy surrounding us darkens and we become cruel, that is, we will be the ones "in the dark ..."

Islam is a path that invites to the divine light and enlightenment. The heart enlightens by possessing the knowledge of truth. Its darkness dissipates, and the light inside reflects on the face, after a while it is reflected on the outside and the light intensifies. That is perhaps the reason our Prophet did not have a shadow. Yes, it is said that Prophet Muhammad (PBUH) who prayed to Allah, "Turn me into divine light," did not have a shadow ...

How can pure divine light have a shadow?[14]

Accounts are not just kept on the Day of Judgment. Allah swiftly settles the accounts with His name "Sari-al Hisab" (Swift at Reckoning).Our actions will positively or negatively return to us in accordance with the universal mechanism.

14 The Messenger of Allah did not have a shadow. When he stood in the sun, his brightness would overwhelm the sun's light. When there was an oil lamp next to him, his light would repress the oil lamp's light."(Ibnul-Cevzi Ibn Abbas)
Zekwan: "The shadow of the Messenger of Allah was not seen in the sun or in the moonlight." This is narrated by al-Hakim al-Tirmidhi and regarding the wisdom in this, he explained that this was to avoid stepping on his shadow to insult him...
Ibn Seb: "His shadow was divine light. When he walked in the sun or in the moonlight, his shadow was invisible."(Prophet's Collection)

The troubles that we encounter in this world are generally the penalty of the sins in the sense of "erroneous action ..."

The word sin is described using different words in the Quran (sin, guilt)...

To understand the concept of committing a sin, we need to understand well what Allah advises us. Allah does not want anything from us for Himself, He wants from us what is good for "us". Even if we resist this belief, Allah wants us to fulfill our worship again for us. If the All-Mighty wanted anything for Himself, He wouldn't say, "There is no compulsion in religion!" Allah does not need our worship.

We are the needy. The qualification of our erroneous deeds as "sins" is because we harm ourselves or others.

Like the understanding of worship, the understanding of sin is considered as something done for Allah. However, Allah, who also calls Himself "as-Samad" and does not need anything or anyone, has completely recommended a kind of individual and public structuring so that we can live in a righteous, happy, and peaceful life and that people do not harm each other.

I usually give the following explanation to the people who say they don't worship Allah because they don't understand why they should worship.

Think of your parents. They try to make you study well and be a successful person, right? Sometimes they punish you when you don't study, but in all likelihood they love you. In all probability, whatever you do, they'll embrace you. What do they expect after all?

I have never seen a parent who does not love their child and does not forgive them in any case. Even if a parent does not forgive initially, but they always feel a certain pain for their children.

After all, what do they want from you? Is it something for them? No...

"They strive for your own peace, strength, success, and happiness in your future life." It may happen that they do not do what you want because they want to protect you. You think they don't understand you. However, they do not expect anything from you, and although they are people in need, they think of you first ... From time to time they want to protect you from yourself...

"As long as my daughter is happy and successful. She may live abroad when she grows up. I hope she will be happy even if I don't see her..." I know many parents who say this "...

Every time I hear that I think about how Allah loves us, and I think of how He likens Himself to a mother to express His mercy.

Is it possible to think that Allah, who says, "If your mother's mercy is a drop, mine is the sea without limits," who has limitless power and needs nothing awaits us to commit sins to burn us in hell?Of course, not, as Allah expresses Himself in His own words, His mercy exceeds His wrath...

Allah, who loves us so much and says "My mercy exceeds my wrath ..." loves every servant individually...

He wants every servant to save themselves. From time to time He wants to protect us from ourselves and He does so. While we think we ended up in a dungeon like Yusuf or in the belly of a fish like Yunus, He is actually protecting us from ourselves...

One day, an arranger friend of mine asked me the following question:

"Deniz, I pray so much, and I pray for the things that I want, but Allah does not give them to me. Why? Why am I praying then? It is as if He does not hear me."

This was my response to him:

"Murat, you have a three-year-old son. If he turned to you now and asked you to buy him a motorcycle, would you buy it?"

"Don't be silly, no way!" he responded.I asked, "But why?"

"What kind of a question is this, Deniz? Why could that be? It would hurt him, of course, I would never do such a thing!"

I smiled.At that moment, he looked at me and tears welled up in his eyes. At that moment my heart quivered, and my eyes teared up.

"You see..." I said. "Just like a parent who predicts where and how his son will hurt himself, Allah does not give His servant what he thinks he wants in his ego, with the knowledge He is aware of and with His unlimited knowledge... Actually, while His servants cry asking why does He not give what they want or whether He loves them or hears them, He withholds from them so that they do not come to harm, He says that He will give them one that is better and more beautiful. But we cannot hear it, more precisely, because our egos are deaf to voices other than their own.

Wouldn't the world be an unbearable and chaotic place if every person received everything they wanted? That thing that you persistently asked for is given to you one day because you prayed so much. But the price that you failed to foresee hits you in such a way that, after some time, you may say "O MY ALLAH, I WISH I DIDN'T ASK FOR THIS!" "You may complain that your prayer is not accepted, but one day you may be thankful that your prayer is not accepted," (Shams Tabrizi)

It happened to me a lot ...

Afterlife shows you this once or multiple times, you try hand over after making some effort towards what you want, learn to trust in Allah, and live by adopting this state...

Because you know that good and evil change based on perspective and time... Because you know that Allah may deprive His servant of any position, possession, property, job, or spouse in order to protect him from his ego and from the tendency to deviate from the right path that even one cannot confront or accept ...

Because you know that Allah protects you from yourself ... Don't ask "What does it mean to protect you from yourself?" Everything is inside human beings, both friend and foe... The echo is the voice inside...

You buy a car and you think it is good for you. Three months later, a tax is imposed and you say, "O my Lord!" Here is how the place of good and evil changes over time ...

Or you are dismissed from your job, someone else gets that job; this is good for which one of you and bad for which one of you?

Somebody better explain it to me...

"But if they turn away, then say, 'O Prophet,' "Allah is sufficient for me. There is no god 'worthy of worship' except Him. In Him, I put my trust. And He is the Lord of the Mighty Throne." (Surah at-Tawba, Verse 129).

In total, there is no distinction between good and evil ...

That is why when reciting "Amantu (I believed)" which comprises the fundamentals of belief, the friends of Allah say " Khayri-hi" and "Khayri-hi"[15], not Khayri-hi and Sharri-hi. Because everything that comes from Allah is good ...

Partial/unitary minds and egoic understandings are subjects of the distinction between good and evil. However, just as in Einstein's theory of relativity where all beings and physical incidents of beings are relative, the concepts of good and evil in the realm of meaning are relative and change depending on each person!

Yet, everything that happens is good for the "universal whole" and for everyone. Because Allah protects and loves each of His servants. Does a mother distinguish among her children? Why would Allah distinguish among His servants unless they go astray?

"No matter what they do, do not think your sins are greater than my mercy!" In fact, He says, "you come, I forgive", does He not say that my compassion is so abundant to my servants?

So, He established the system to allow us to come through the procedure with minimum pain while changing dimensions[16], to protect people from themselves, and to give the same liberty to each servant. And not to heat up the boilers for us in the place called hell.

This arrogance in people, this self-love, and setting too much value

---

15 "hi" refers to "His" in Arabic.
16 "Akhirat," the word for afterlife in Arabic also means metamorphosis.

on worships and even sins is something that is really inconceivable.

Among all the names of Allah regarding mercy and love, starting with the idea that Allah is always tormenting us leads to worships performed for the sake of interest and out of fear...

Every word spoken to the universe is "an enlivened energy" and will certainly be a reciprocal energy creation within the universal mechanism ...

For example, you reproach your husband for being very angry at you and exhausting you. This is a call for the sky that hears this! And, unfortunately, these words and thoughts trigger a mechanism in this direction whether or not you notice ...

Even if you are not aware of it, something may happen to your husband and you will be affected by this situation ...

Therefore, Allah says in Quran that bad words have a response to the one who utters them and good words are like a beautiful tree with strong roots ...

This is one of the reasons why malediction is forbidden ... If you are really a victim, the mechanism you call into action may be created on the side of the said person with the coordinates determined by you and with consequences that may cover you as well, but you will be affected by this...

Let me explain it differently to make it clearer; SAMA', which has unlimited knowledge, is like Google with a large and unlimited database. All the information in the universe is recorded in the sama' and we can call all the information we are looking for with SOUND which is basically vibration...

Think of it like the communication systems ... By pressing certain keys on a telephonic device, we reach different people over the "same wire" or since we are using "cellular phones" through the same "base stations" by simply dialing different numbers..., It is a serious matter!

If you reflect upon it, this is really quite weird!

Just like reaching a store, a person, or a workplace you want by dialing numbers in the sea of numbers ... So the relationship between SOUND, thoughts, and sama' is making a call towards your pursuit just like dialing the same telephone number ...

Moreover, Ibn Arabi, who is one of the greatest friends of Allah and who, based on his knowledge, became famous for his foresight on many subjects including "letters," says the following about words consisting of letters:

"Once these verbal letters floating in the air come to existence, they won't die; written letters are not like this, because the form of a written letter or word may change and disappear for they are present in a place that accepts change and perishment. As for verbal shapes, they are present in a place that does not accept change or perishment. That is why there is subsistence, permanence, and eternity for verbal letters. Therefore, the air and the sky are filled with the words of the world. The ones with kashf (unveiling) see them as permanent representations."

With the verbal letters floating in the air, he refers to "the words we speak, the words that meet with our breath," and he states that they may not disappear, in other words, die for they are an energy release. He highlights that this does not apply to written letters and words. He says that there is "subsistence" in verbal letters, which means there is permanence and eternity. He even adds that those with kashf can see them as permanent representations...

Don't think this is strange. Can we say that a word is different than a representation, that is, matter, since our understanding of matter in the universe changed into energy after the discovery of subatomic particles, and energy is expressed in units with individual "vibrations and information"?

In fact, I say it for the sake of contemplation, there is a verse of which a point in its content really shook me when I "FIRST" realized ... In three places in the Quran, it is stated that Hazrat Isa (Jesus) is "a word from Allah."

"So the angels called out to him (Zachariah) while he stood praying in the sanctuary, "Allah gives you good news of 'the birth of' John who will confirm the Word of Allah and will be a great leader, chaste, and a prophet among the righteous." (Surah Ali 'Imran, Verse 39)

"'Remember' when the angels proclaimed, "O Mary! Allah gives you good news of a Word from Him, his name will be the Messiah, Isa (Jesus), son of Marium (Mary); honored in this world and the Here-after, and he will be one of those nearest 'to Allah'." (Surah Ali 'Imran, Verse 45)

"O People of the Book! Do not go to extremes regarding your fa-ith; say nothing about Allah except the truth. The Messiah, Isa, son of Marium, was no more than a messenger of Allah and the fulfillment of His Word through Marium and a spirit 'created by a command' from Him. So believe in Allah and His messengers and do not say, "Trinity." Stop!—for your own good. Allah is only One God. Glory be to Him! He is far above having a son! To Him belongs whatever is in the heavens and whatever is on the earth. And Allah is sufficient as a Trustee of Affairs." (Surah an-Nisa, Verse 171)

Elmalılı Muhammed Hamdi stated that certain beings indicating a particular or a universal meaning by causing an effect in the mind through the sense of sight when the universe is observed along with the pronounced meaningful sounds and transcripts may also be called words and that Messiah Isa (Jesus) being a word should be interpreted accordingly.

Allah has the attribute of Kalam (Speech). All beings, except for the revelations from His attribute of Kalam, and the book of the universe consisting of them is a materialized book consisting of material words. All the sentences and words of this book are creatures; they are created afterward. The wisdom of Messiah Isa (Jesus) being referred to as "the word of Allah" is because he was born without a father. It is even stated that his condition is like that of Adam, who was also created from no-thing and was through the word of Allah. I mean, Messiah Isa (Jesus) was created by a verbal command; he is the product of "kun fa-yakūnu (be, and it is)." Allah said, "Be!" and he "was." Since the order was a verbal command, Messiah Isa (Jesus), who is a product of that order, was given the title of "The word of Allah."

It is fitting for me to mention the following matter here. In fact, we are all words. How?

When you say "Deniz" (which means "sea"), that word, which is actually a meaning, brings me before your eyes with all my characteristics, right?

Whether it is my physical characteristics or spiritual characteristics, a word, that is, a meaning brings the object into view by just saying, Deniz.

For example, when we say table, a table, which is actually a meaning, materializes and integrates with the object of table before our eyes...

So, words carry meaning and meanings are not separate from matter. The greatest illusion of human beings is to separate matter from meaning and the world from the afterlife.

Then, what is SOUND?

Sound is "periodic pressure changes in the atmosphere that can be perceived by the hearing organs of living things." In short, it is a type of energy formed as a result of the "vibration" of molecules in that matter in air, in liquid, or solid environment...

It spreads in waves. Sound is spread by vibrating the particles of the matter from which it emanates. It cannot propagate in space; therefore the sound of starbursts cannot be heard in space. The speed of propagation is highest in solids, then in liquid, and then in gas. Sound propagates in particles; the denser the particles, the faster the sound propagates. Depending on the external factors such as temperature differences of the air, it propagates at different speeds. Its general measure is 340 meters per second ...

Let's explain it as follows. First of all, sound occurs as a result of the "vibration" of objects. What we hear is the reaction of those air molecules...

What is frequency?

Frequency is the number of vibrations of any sound source per unit of time.

The unit of measurement of sound "hertz" is "the unit used to describe and measure the propagation frequency of sound waves in 1 second"... How?

In addition to the sama', which means "hearing", prayer means "to call, to invite"...

Discovered in the 19th century, the ionosphere is "the third layer of the atmosphere on the earth" and its most important feature is to ensure that "the electrical energy and radio sound, and electromagnetic waves are wirelessly transported from a very distant point to another.[17]

Now, let's contemplate together on the narration of the Day of Judgment.

The Day of Judgment is an incident that has been the subject of numerous movies and books. Whether people believe or claim that they do not believe in its existence, they all have a hesitation about the Day of Judgment and in fact, they feel a certain fear...

Since we are guided to live with a single understanding of the world and live in both worlds (the world and the hereafter) with formal and material concepts (mansions, houris, fruits, etc. in the heaven), we are all secretly curious about the Day of Judgment for we perceive that day as the "perishment of the one world for eternity" without noticing that each one of us are individual worlds walking on this world.

The biggest mistake about the concept of the Day of Judgment is the understanding that there is and there will only be one Day of Judgment and then everything will perish...

---

17 Allah, who is aware of everything, has given people abilities such as speaking, hearing and understanding so that they can communicate with each other. In addition to the ionosphere layer that reflects the skywaves, it has also organized the ground waves for a near viewing angle and beyond-the-horizon communication by crawling on the earth.

I don't know if this is because of our arrogance but we cling too much to the idea that we are the only ones and each of us is a superior exemplary being in the universe...

For example, in Surah al-Isra Verse 70, it is ordained "and privileged them far above many of Our creatures."

In a universe that is approximately 13.7 billion years old, it is not very reasonable to think that we are the only human beings who have been living for only a few thousand years in a world that is said to be 4.5 billion years old...

There is a narration about tens of thousands of human beings that passed through this world... I saw it in Ibn Arabi's narration for the first time.

Adam is our father, that is true, and he is from the earth like us, and there are also narrations that each earth consists of the formation of the world with new elements after a Day of Judgment. Therefore, it is stated that the structures of Adam are different from each other ...

That dear friend of Allah Ibn Arabi, that beautiful person, talks about seeing a man, among tens of thousands of people circumambulating Kaaba, who is incredibly tall and strangely does not have a shadow during one of his visits to Kaaba in his 2-year stay in Mecca:

When the tall man notices that he was noticed, he says, "We are circumambulating this house just like you..."

Ibn al-Arabi approaches him. He asks who he is.

The answer he receives is surprising:

"I am one of your great ancestors."

When asked in which century he lived, he replied, "I passed away forty thousand years ago."

Ibn al-Arabi cannot hide his surprise, "How can it be? In our opinion, even the emergence of Adam dates back 6-7 thousand years ago ..." The stranger replies:

"Which Adam are you talking about? Are you talking about the Adam close to you or us? Be aware that one hundred thousand Adams have passed away before Adam, who was the first ancestor of man."

Perhaps this explanation has something to do with what is mentioned in Surah al-Baqarah Verse 30:

"'Remember' when your Lord said to the angels, "I am going to place a successive 'human' authority on earth." They asked 'Allah', "Will You place in it someone who will spread corruption there and shed blood while we glorify Your praises and proclaim Your holiness?" Allah responded, "I know what you do not know."

We can say that this verse sheds light on how the angels knew in advance that Adam to be created will shed blood ... Again, the secrets hidden in this verse, which we read without thinking, are actually a statement that takes us to a place of enlightenment if it is read with a little more thought. In addition to the answer by Said-i Nursi to the question which should be asked by everyone reading this verse, "How did the angles know that Adam would shed blood?" That it is possible that this was notified to the angels by Allah, they might have seen and read the feelings of wrath and lust of humans at a lower rank than them, or they might have read it in the Preserved Plate (al-Lawh al-Mahfooz) (the genetic code of people, that is, DNA, is the small Preserved Plate; all this information recorded in the genes of people is like a downsized sample of the Preserved Slate), it may also be possible that there are Adams, who were re-created many times, with the same bloodiness, malice, and self-interest in the unknown history of the universe.

There is plenty of "veiled" information kept from us by those who run the world order. While we are of the understanding of referring to those who are not born as Muslims as "kafirs (non-believers)", the real kafirs, meaning "those veiling the truth," may be those claiming to be Muslims and busy manipulating us.

The concept of justice has actually been destroyed by people in this world order. However, Allah, who embroiders the Quran, which we think is incomprehensible, is the only power acting "openly and fairly" with His words to anyone who thinks a little while we devoted all our time to the temporary expectations that appear to be "value" in the life of the world. The whole point is to think and investigate. To slow down life, to focus on the truth. To pursue the "self" inside, not the shadow play that appears outside ...

If we actually chose to reject the verses that we could not understand without diving into their essence because of our own laziness and misuse of our egos, it means we deserve to be slaves ...

Allah is the only power that will free man from his slavery... We are continuing our own slavery because it is difficult for us to prostrate to Allah five times a day and try to find the meaning of this although we prostrate to so many people and positions and interests.

Anyway, let's not deviate from our subject and continue ...

In different verses, the Quran uses expressions such as "We created Adam for heaven. We created Adam from water. We created Adam from clay," perhaps to indicate different Adams.

If we limit our view, we cannot grow ... Everything is possible to Allah.

The fact in the Quran that the world has a very old past, is obvious to a thinking person.

"Have you not 'already' received the news of those who were before you: the people of Noah, 'Âd, Thamûd, and those after them? Only Allah knows how many they were. Their messengers came to them with clear proofs, but they put their hands over their mouths and said, "We totally reject what you have been sent with, and we are certainly in alarming doubt about what you are inviting us to." (Surah Ibrahim, Verse 9)

Wouldn't it be covering the truth to limit the Quran, which is open to unlimited interpretations, with a single line of translation? We cannot know those who preceded us; only Allah knows, and of course, He makes known if He wishes ...

In the Quran, there are many verses mentioning the civilizations that lived and were destroyed in the past ...

"Have they not seen how many generations We destroyed before them which We had established upon the earth as We have not established you? And We sent [rain from] the sky upon them in showers and made rivers flow beneath them; then We destroyed them for their sins and brought forth after them a generation of others." (Surah al-An'am, Verse 6)

In light of the above statement, when we read this verse, I think we all think almost the same things. And even, the statement "We have given them the blessings of the sky as we have not given to you," may refer to both the higher civilization levels of other civilizations, the level of technology, and the possible connections with celestial beings or beings in the extraterrestrial world. Everything is possible to Allah. If Allah exists, and He does, then there is no impossibility. The impossible is something that is only in our perception. As you get to know Allah, there is no room for either dreaming or believing that there is anything impossible. If Allah allowed me to imagine something, it means that He also allowed me to do it. It is up to my effort. And nothing is impossible to Allah, therefore it is not impossible for His servant who has surrendered to Him with everything. Because the servant, who has surrendered with everything, has surrendered their existence to Allah. Before death...

Our Galaxy (The Milky Way) came into existence 13.8 billion years ago. And our source of life, the Sun, came into existence 4.6 billion years ago and 4.5 billion years ago, the Earth was not habitable for approximately 700 million years ...

However, our atoms are not from this world and did not form in this solar system. Because the structure of atoms changes at nuclear temperatures, most of the heavy elements were formed in the nuclei of supernovae in stars hotter than the Sun. Even the vital iron atoms found in our blood came to the world from outside the solar system.

The Sun has a core temperature of 15.6 million degrees Celsius and a surface temperature of 5500 degrees Celsius. Iron can only be formed at temperatures of up to a few hundred million degrees Celsius. In other words, it was formed only in the stars that are many times larger than the Sun, which are called nova or supernova. That is to say, the iron in the world comes from outside of the solar system; the iron dispersed from an exploding supernova descended to the world ...

In Surah an-Najm verse 1, the "star", which is described as "By the stars when they fade away!" represents our existence in our egos along with many other meanings...

The iron in our blood, such an important element that keeps us alive, comes from the stars. Maybe that's why every ego wants to behave like a star. Everyone likes themselves the most. And popular celebrities are called "stars" ... Because we carry stardust.

"The nitrogen in our DNA, the calcium in our teeth, the iron in our blood, the carbon in our apple pie were made inside the collapsing stars. We are made of the material of the stars ... '' (Astronomer, astrobiologist Carl Sagan)

Surah al-Hadid (The Iron) Verse 25: "Indeed, We sent Our messengers with clear proofs, and with them, We sent down the Scripture and the balance 'of justice' so that people may administer justice. And We sent down iron with its great might, benefits for humanity, and means for Allah to prove who 'is willing to' stand up for Him and His messengers without seeing Him. Surely Allah is All-Powerful, Almighty."

The descension of iron which was mentioned in the Quran centuries ago has always attracted the attention of those who are interested in the Quran as well as scientists. Yes, iron was sent to the world from the stars...

In the Quran and hadiths, in the narrations of the DAY OF JUDGMENT, the phenomenon of blowing into the SUR (the Trumpet) is mentioned ...

When Allah wills to end this world and the angel named Israfil (Raphael) blows into a horn-shaped horn called SUR (the Trumpet) that is wide between the earth and the sky, the Day of Judgment arrives.

"The Trumpet will be blown and all those in the heavens and all those on the earth will fall dead, except those Allah wills 'to spare'. Then it will be blown again and they will rise up at once, looking on 'in anticipation'." (Surah az-Zumar, Verse 68)

All living things and beings, except the servants whom Allah wills, will die instantly ...

"And when the trumpet is blown, that will 'truly' be a difficult Day - far from easy for the disbelievers." (Surah al-Muddaththir, Verses 8-10)

"The Trumpet will be blown 'a second time', then—behold!—they will rush from the graves to their Lord." (Surah Ya-Sin, Verse 51)

"And 'beware of' the Day the Trumpet will be blown, and all those in the heavens and all those on the earth will be horrified 'to the point of death', except those Allah wills 'to spare'. And all will come before Him, fully humbled." (Surah an-Naml, Verse 87)

"No! When the earth has been leveled - pounded and crushed And your Lord has come and the angels, rank upon rank, and Hell is brought forth on that Day—this is when every 'disbelieving' person will remember 'their own sins'. But what is the use of remembering then?" (Surah al-Fajr, Verses 21-23)

I will continue on this subject, but the issue that needs to be addressed here is this: Why the blowing of the Sur? Again, the act of blowing ... What is the SUR?

Who is ISRAFIL and what does it represent?

Israf-El: Allah's breath, ... IL that means EL refers to ALLAH. In short, Israfil means the breath of Allah.

Israfil represents properties that express the power of life and vitalization.[18]

In other words, it is narrated in the Quran that the living things that have just been destroyed will resurrect and rise ...

18Israfil enforces the orders and wills of Allah regarding "vitalization" with the name "al-Muhyi (The Maintainer of Life)." Especially in the ressurection during spring, Israfil is in charge of the manifestation of the name "al-Muhyi." Another of Israfil's tasks is to notify the angels about their tasks by looking at the Preserved Slate before him. Moreover, the angels commissioned in the Preserved Plate are under his command...

"On that Day We will roll up the heavens like a scroll of writings. Just as We produced the first creation, 'so' shall We reproduce it. That is a promise binding on Us. We truly uphold 'Our promises'!" (Surah al-Anbya, Verse 104)

"The Trumpet will be blown and all those in the heavens and all those on the earth will fall dead, except those Allah wills 'to spare'. Then it will be blown again and they will rise up at once, looking on 'in anticipation'." (Surah az-Zumar, Verse 68)

(The subject of white holes: The white holes actually represent re-birth like the Big Bang. The verse states that the world will be restored to its original state after being rolled up. "The day comes and We fold the sheet of sky just like a scribe rolling up the sheets written. Just as We started to create in the first place, it is Us to resurrect. This is a promise binding on Us. It is again to make this happen.") [Al-Anbya, Verse 104]

Let's get back to our topic for now ...

Why Sur?

The life that started with the Nafas ar-Rahmani (the Breath of the All-Merciful), who caused the existence of the universe, will also end with a breath blown into a horn interpreted as a pipe and then return to life ...

Now let's contemplate on the subject...

I am a musician. This is merely a tewafuq (a pleasant coherence).

One day I was working with a high-pitched soloist. He turned to me and said, "You know, if I raise my highs even higher, I can crack a glass or window."

Ever since I began to contemplate about the statements on the Day of Judgment, this event has literally shed some light to me ...

Once you reach the resonance, not only can you crack a glass, but many other things...

What did a sound that could shatter glass into pieces do to me and my cells made up of molecules and atoms at that moment?

Yes, it was about SOUND.

The great program in the universe was based on SOUND. I even began to understand that the universe was a cave that opened with a sound like in the tale of Ali Baba and the Forty Thieves ...

Everything was sound, vibration ... In a sense, the sound was like light molecules hitting the air.

Everything was light, that is sound, and everything was vibration ...

At that moment I realized that Google hearing me was just like a smart and voice-operated computer...

And just like in Ali Baba and the Forty Thieves, "Open sesame open!" I decided to say. "Open life open!"

Sensation

Our perception of "hearing", which is among what we perceive with our 5 senses, is actually not as simple as we think...

We measure the universe with what we hear and perceive. However, what we hear is restricted by Allah due to our body machine and many other reasons for the purpose of being tested. I will mention the subject of being tested elsewhere because it is unfortunately perceived in a shallow manner and is one of the subjects of which the meaning is not fully understood. Returning to our topic, what we understand is; we limitedly perceive a limitless universe and try to measure, understand, and grasp it with limited minds formed by the senses...

As Hazrat Ibn Arabi explains: "No matter how much our comprehension increases, we open our doors to the flow of the knowledge of truth on the day we accept that it won't be possible to fully comprehend the infinite might and mind of Allah."

For this reason, it is said that the biggest obstacle between us and Allah is our bodies, which are limited machines, and our "partial-unitary-personal minds" formed by the senses and ideas of bodies equipped with these restricted machines, are the greatest obstacle between us and Allah...

Even after they start to deal with the knowledge of truth, people often hear others say, "You will go crazy!" or "look, don't go too deep, you will go crazy!"

However, the answer here comes from Hazrat Mawlana:"One is not called a dervish before being called crazy..."

SOUND

Sound occurs as a result of the "vibration" of objects and is generated by pressure waves. Sound and vibration studies are interrelated. For example, sound pressure waves vibrate our vocal cords, and these pressure waves are detected by making our eardrums vibrate ... (The interesting thing when I first learned about this subject was that the "stones" in the organs that provide balance in the inner ear are called crystals, and the ear and the inner ear resemble a horn...).

For sound to be transmitted, a "medium" such as solid matter, air, or water is required, and it is also described as "transmitting changes in very small pressure waves in the air."

The speed at which sound is transmitted depends on many factors, from what kind of material it is transmitted to, up to the air temperature...

As for what vibration is, vibration is the mechanical oscillation around an equilibrium point. "Oscillatory motion occurs as a result of the periodic change of physical properties of an object. This physical property can be displacement, velocity, pressure, temperature, etc. These oscillations can be periodic or irregular."[19]

The most important example of vibration can be an "earthquake", which is our nightmare. Beyond that examples range from the jolts of your washing machine to pendulum-type movements.

If you want to reduce the noise somewhere, you need to provide

---

19 "Sound and Vibration in the Quran Verses," Sami Polatöz, http//www.sizinti.com

the effect that will reduce the vibration of the material that causes that noise.

The Wave

Both sound, light, and even the particles that came into our lives with quantum mechanics propagate in waves.

Sound waves propagate in the air at a rate of 340 m/second...

The difference in the propagation of SOUND and LIGHT is that SOUND requires a medium to propagate, and thus, the sound is qualified as a mechanical wave.

Light does not need this; light, which is therefore qualified as an "electromagnetic wave," consists of the periodic vibrations of electrical and magnetic fields by charged particles without requiring a medium, and it moves in the space as such...

Sound, which requires matter to propagate, cannot travel in space, and thus, we cannot hear the sound of great starbursts. On the other hand, light, an electromagnetic wave that does not require a medium to propagate, can propagate and travel in space. Because of the differences arising from the variations in wavelengths, they are named radio waves, microwaves, infrared, ultraviolet, etc...

So, in principle, "sound and light" are waves that carry "information and energy."

I will explain how this relates to us later on in the book...

What is Frequency?

Frequency is the number of "vibrations" made by any sound source per unit of time. The stronger the wave, the higher the frequency...

HERTZ, which is the unit of sound measurement, is used to describe and measure the propagation frequency of sound waves within 1 second...

Now let's get to people...

Which sounds does a person hear?

We can hear sounds of 20 to 20,000 hertz through our body machine ears. Even this is theoretically so; we best hear the speech frequency region of 250 to 3000 hertz. Animals can even perceive sound frequencies that humans cannot perceive. For example, elephants and dogs, etc.

It has been proven that Chinese frogs living in waterfalls and rivers in China do not have communication problems between their own species thanks to the "ultrasound" supersonic waves they produce to communicate in their intense and high-water sound environment. The human ear cannot perceive these sounds...

The Quran has numerous verses on sound and vibration and I aim to contemplate on these by identifying them with the Day of Judgement.

Sounds at 20 hertz and below are called infrasound, that is, low-frequency sound... Ultrasound (supersonic), which is a term we are familiar with, is the sound above 20,000 hertz that we cannot hear. You or your relatives have definitely been screened by ultrasound in hospitals. The ultrasound device produces sound waves above 20 thousand hertz into the tissue, and as a result of the reflection of those sound waves, an electric current is given...

As we can see, sound waves are divided into three...

There is a quartz crystal called the piezoelectric in a device called a probe that is placed on the body. When the electric current is applied, the crystal rapidly changes shape, and this change of shape causes vibrations and consequently sound waves. When the sound waves or pressure that comes as a reflection reaches the crystals, they start to transmit an electrical current and this electrical current transmits the result to us in "images" by "reading the tissue ..."

An example of the conversion of sound to electricity and its conversion to the information carried by the sound is the image of a baby growing in the womb. The information captured by sound energy turns into electricity, and that turns into an image.

As you can see, the information that actually comes as sound is converted into electric currents, and an image is obtained from the vibrations. In other words, the reflected sound wave was converted into an electric current and read as an image.[20]

"Whether you speak secretly or openly – He surely knows the best what is 'hidden' in the heart. How could He not know His Own creation? For He 'alone' is the Most Subtle, All-Aware." (Surah Al-Mulk, Verses 13-14).

Isn't it possible that the expression "essence of the chests" refers to the finest details of both the spiritual nature of human beings, including the inner voice which people think is only heard by their brains and all biological characteristics?

This can mean many things, let alone reading the energy of thought, which is said to achieve 80 percent success by scientists all over the world ... The image of an object is generated by collecting and reading ultrasound, that is, the transonic waves reflected. With these images, important information about our internal structure is obtained.

A very important concept about vibration is resonance; when one of the sound sources with the same frequencies vibrates, the other sound source vibrates with the effect, and this is called resonance.

Every system has a frequency that it generates while oscillating without interference, and the amount of displacement during this oscillation is called amplitude (the difference between the rise and fall of a wave from its normal state). If the frequency of the force applied by an external force is equal to the natural frequency of the system, "resonance" occurs.

An example is a building under the effect of oscillations caused by earthquake waves.

If the sudden and variable breeze of the wind under a bridge under

20 The quartz crystal both produces and perceives sound, and this is another indication of the importance of crystals in the science of truth.

the influence of another intermittent and variable wind is an example, the Tacoma Narrows suspension bridge, built-in 1940 in the USA, was destroyed by a resonance shortly after it was put into service.

Now let's come to the point where this connects the matter with us...

"When Our command came, We saved Shu'aib and those who believed with him by a mercy from Us. And the 'mighty' blast overtook the wrongdoers, so they fell lifeless in their homes," (Surah Hud, Verse 94).

Imagine such a sound that has the quality of a sound wave that can destroy the cells of a human body's internal organs.

Human beings are in the same type of oscillation as electromagnetic radiation, in other words, radio waves.

Could the main purpose of religion, that is, the path be to ensure this electromagnetic radiation emitted by people is in harmony with the universal radiation?

Could the use of sounds, which involve endless meanings of the Quran and which have a kind of "magnificent" sound quality such as 'Allah' or 'inna', that we call DHIKR with intense and quivering vibrations and thus, increasing our frequencies be a coincidence?

Leave Islam aside, I am sure you have all heard the yogis using magnificent sounds with high vibrations such as "Ommm!" during meditation.

I wonder whether the cry that is referred to as a loud sound will not apply to those whose vibrations are changed because they wish to reach Allah and are people of dhikr and whether it will apply to those who do not wish to do so?

If resonance is being exposed to the same frequency, will those with different frequencies not be affected and harmed by this sound?

While even the layers of the earth are destroyed at the matched frequency of sound, is it not possible for the human body, which is already named EARTH, to turn upside down like it does after an earthquake? Could it be for the same reason that it is said in verses 28 and 29 of Surah Ya-Sin, "We did not send any soldiers from the heavens against his people after his death, nor did We need to. All it took was one 'mighty' blast, and they were extinguished at once."?

While it has currently been discussed globally that it is possible to spread sound waves by propagating equal frequencies with a certain region and generate an earthquake in various regions obtaining resonance, does the idea that a person created from the earth could be destroyed by sound seem impossible?

Similarly, in verse 41 of Surah al-Mu'minun, it is ordained, "Then the 'mighty' blast overtook them with justice, and We reduced them to rubble. So away with the wrongdoing people!" People whose organs and cells are destroyed by the resonance generated by the sound wave to a point where they are likened to rubble ...

In verse 40 of Surah al-Ankabut, it is ordained, "So We seized each 'people' for their sin: against some of them We sent a storm of stones, some were overtaken by a 'mighty' blast, some We caused the earth to swallow, and some We drowned. Allah would not have wronged them, but it was they who wronged themselves."

Because of the use of expressions such as "tremors", "earthquakes," and "jolts" in many other verses of the Quran and because the disaster that occurred was actually a sound-borne noise, it might have destroyed the bodies with resonance ...

In earthquakes that destroy the earth, the sounds of earthquakes are investigated by using hydrophones.

The destruction of the people of Thamud is also expressed in verse 78 of Surah al-A'raf as follows: "Then an 'overwhelming' noise struck them, and they fell lifeless in their homes." Although the word "rajfa-tu" mentioned in verses 91 and 155 of Surah al-A'raf is interpreted as earthquake, do you think that what is meant by this word is actually a resonance caused by the sound? The destruction that sound waves can cause is also expressed in verse 31 of Surah al-Qamar as follows:

"Indeed, We sent against them 'only' one 'mighty' blast, leaving them like the twigs of fence-builders."

"Had We sent down this Quran upon a mountain, you would have certainly seen it humbled and torn apart in awe of Allah. We set forth such comparisons for people, 'so' perhaps they may reflect." (Surah al-Hashr, Verse 21).

This verse has dozens of meanings that we perceive and have not yet perceived. Apart from the most frequent narrations, I would like to examine this verse in reference to our topic of SOUND.

"If we had brought this Quran down to the mountain." The Quran comes with revelation, isn't it?

And that "higher information" carries an enormous ENERGY like every other information …

The "information, that is, energy" in the form of "sound" energy has such a vibration that it is strong enough to shatter a mountain from which it is descended …

There are many mountains, which seem impassable and uncrossable, that can be broken into pieces with sound and resonance. So, how sublime is the source of that sound that with a revelation, mountains that seem indestructible can be shattered …

Think about what can be done with SOUND, vibration, and resonance …

Well, just as there is a sound that can destroy, is there a SOUND that can build a barrier?

The depiction of the Day of Judgment talks about the disintegration of those who do not believe, that is, those who could not enter the frequency of the believers, with the first blow of the Trumpet and their re-integration with the same SOUND.

In Surah an-Naba (The Tidings), which is named after the information it provides about the Day of Judgment, it is stated that the animals will be raised again after being disintegrated and becoming dust, and the people who will be raised in the image of "animals" will emulate the animals leaving without being questioned and say, "I wish I were dust!"

It is said that if you recite Surah Ya-Sin Verse 9 when you want to go unnoticed by those who make you feel uncomfortable they will not be able to see you. Of course, it does not mean that everyone reciting the verse will experience this; this requires a great deal of concentration, and even beyond that, for the correct transmission of that sound vibration, there are conditions such as the righteous intention of the receiver and the transmitter and being in a pure energy state. These conditions are prerequisites because of their influence on the energy, to be able to enter that frequency with these words ...

Let's go back to the verse.

It is interpreted as follows: "and have placed a barrier before them and a barrier behind them and covered them 'all' up, so they fail to see 'the truth'."(A translation from the Turkish Religious Foundation).

An explanation on when and how this verse was descended to the consciousness is as follows; those who did not want the Prophet to leave Mecca alive and therefore came to kill him were waiting in front of his house.

He was asked to say this verse with the "higher information," that is, "revelation" that came to him."

"And have placed a barrier before them and a barrier behind them and covered them 'all' up, so they fail to see."

As he recited this verse, a barrier that could not be seen with these eyes was placed before and behind the polytheists (those who associate Allah with partners), and the Messenger of Allah (PBUH), by reciting this verse, walked among them unseen and left.

If we see this in a science fiction film, we might think it is possible, but for some reason, when it is described in the Quran, we displeasingly exclaim, "How?"

In a universe that is a software made up of words, letters, and numbers that we cannot possibly receive with our limited perceptions and in a universe that existed at Allah's command, "Kun! (Be!), "do you think it is impossible for such things to happen with the generosity of Allah offering us to use His attribute of Kalam?

When you send beautiful words, that is, beautiful sounds and vibrations, to water, the shape it takes changes; then why can't the dozens of "objects-and-beings" that we do not see around us take different shapes? Especially when every living creature was created from water ...

Especially, when it is ordained, "... And We created from water every living thing. Will they not then believe?" (Surah al-Anbya, Verse 30).

Do you know what the science called alchemy is? Where does it originate from? This word, originating from Aramaic, means "symbol, sign"...

So, what did the verse mean? Symbol, sign...

Is it too difficult for Allah, the owner of words, to destroy the mountains and raise them again, to split the Moon and merge it again? None of these are difficult for Allah, and He is the One who allowed Isa (Jesus), whom He made the intermediary of His might, to bring the dead to life and to open the eyes of the blind by enabling him to say, "Bi'ithnillah (with the will of Allah).

That might belongs to Allah, and He furnishes His servant with that might to the extent of His servant's strength. He says, "And We charge no soul except [with that within] its capacity." He "offers" to His servant from His own attributes and names.

In the name Quran al Kareem (besides the many meanings we know), "QURAN" refers to the Self and "Kareem" means generous and noble... In short, the Quran is the GENEROSITY of that Almighty SELF to His servants...

It is such a treat that, if truly understood, it would make His servants His caliphs. It is a method that He offers to His servant to facilitate their existence and to mature the capacity they have reached. It is a treat to allow His servants to live in both worlds, their eternal life in their most mature state...

I only take into account the people who talk about Allah, religion, and our Prophet when I see what they know, how much they research, and how unbiased they are. Because the more one learns and knows, the more one is drawn and the more they want. They want to be "the one who knows". They want to be "the one who finds." And finally, they want to be "the one who becomes." They want to understand and live the religion and to evoke the same feeling in others, happiness.

This is the reason our Prophet and the friends of Allah are said to "lead to salvation." Salvation is to know, find, and become.

It is to become everything in nothingness.

And Allah wants the servant whom He loves and has compassion for to return to their "essence", that is, "to Him", and to exist in the eternal power with his absence as before for the sake of His servant's good, happiness and maturing...

QIYAM-AT

There is enough light for those who want to see,
and enough darkness for those who do not.

-Blaise Pascal

One day, while my mother and I were having a conversation, she said, "Wait, I'll perform my salah and come back..."I said, "OK" ...

Since my mother was widowed at a very young age, she is a person who has dedicated herself to the path of Allah. She prays for hours. During the years I didn't fast, she fasted without a break despite her age, worshiped for hours, and on top of all that, she would read scientific narratives about the Quran. May Allah bless her, she still reads.

She came to me after performing her salah.

"Deniz!" she said. "When I was at qiyam, something came to my mind, my concentration was disrupted. Fortunately, I managed to gather myself.""When, when?"I asked. She looked at me and responded, "At qiyam ..."

O, Allah! Something stroked me on the head ... ... "While at qiyam." I leaped from excitement that for a moment she failed to understand what was happening.

"Mom, I don't believe it! You said qiyam?" I asked.

She looked at me puzzled and asked, "What is going on?" I said, "Mom! Don't you understand? Qiyam ... Wait a minute."

I immediately turned on my computer to start a Google search. I opened an Arabic dictionary and entered the word "qiyam."

Here was the meaning right in front of me. Qiyam: 1. To stand up. 2. To wake up ...

Qiyam, that is, when we are standing while performing salah, also meant "to wake up" as well as "to stand up."

Then "Qiyam-at[21]" meant "stand up and wake up."

At that moment there was a "jolt" in me ... A deep jolt ... The connection between "qiyam," which was a concept that I know from salah, and "qiyamat" was clearly evident before my eyes.

The earth I was standing on began to slip and my world fictionalized by my brain began to crack ...

Qiyamat was "standing up and waking up from a dream into the truth..." This was why this word was attentively selected ...

This information, which they have attempted to convey to us through imported information under the name "awakening" for years, originated from the Quran, the One ESTABLISHING THE MOMENT ...

How did I fail to notice such an exposed treasure before me?

Allah was saying "Stand up. Stand up and wake up, my servant! Wake up ..." I had to immediately find the surahs related to the Qiyamat. I conducted a Google search... I wrote " Surahs related to Qiyamat" on Google and began reading the translations ...

The first ones that came before me were surah az-Zalzalah and Surah al-Qiyamat ...

It felt like I was going crazy. As I was wondering what was happening to me, I saw the translation of the verse of Surah az-Zalzalah that was right before my eyes ... "When the earth is shaken 'in' its ultimate quaking, and when the earth throws out 'all' its contents, and humanity cries, "What is wrong with it?" ..." (Surah az-Zalzalah, Verses 1, 2, 3).

---

21 "Qiyamat" is spelled "Kıyamet" in Turkish, and while Kıyam" refers to "Qiyam," "-et" is the third-person singular for the Turkish verb "etmek" meaning "to do, to practice, to make."

O Allah!

What was happening? The place I stood on, that is, my "beliefs" was shaking under my feet. What was happening to my beliefs and my fictional world? What about me, what was happening to me?

In fact, this incredibly amazing feeling was also accompanied by some remorse ...

Because I have "slept" with virtual realities in this world for years, and because I fictionalized my beliefs and pained myself supposing that my world was the true one.

Suddenly I felt an ache in my belly ... Something had happened to me ... I felt like I had been a fool all this time. I felt like the alchemist who had searched for his treasure outside for years, but found it in his backyard after traveling all over the world ... I was deeply saddened ...

Tears began to flow from my eyes ... My mother was right next to me, but since I was in a state that she could not understand, she must have felt nothing but panic ...

"My girl!"she said ... "Deniz ... Astaghfirullah... What's going on, my girl?" "Mom ..." I just said. "Mom ..."

Sometimes words are not enough, you can't describe what you really feel. Some states are only experienced but cannot be explained. They cannot be described without being experienced...

"I'm fine, there's nothing wrong. Don't worry ..." I said, my voice trembling ... "My girl, you've lost your color ... O Allah, I became frightened and just asked what's going on?..."

She stood up and headed towards the kitchen.

This time, I reached out to the Quran and began reading the verses from Surah al-Qiyamat ...

I felt deep painful remorse for not hearing Allah calling me for so many years ...

Then I returned to the Surah al-Qiyamat ...

"I swear by the Day of Judgment! And I do swear by the self-reproaching soul!"

This was me! This earthquake that I felt right then, this regret, this pang of remorse I felt could not be explained better than this, my Lord ...

I was crying. Tears began flowing down my face.

When I was little, I used to cry at night so that my mother could tell me a story. Sometimes she didn't want to tell one because she was tired. I would cry throwing myself on the floor. "Please!" I would beg.

Then she would spare me and allow me next to her saying, "Okay, okay. Come on, let me tell one ..." and she would start telling my pre-ordered tale about a witch ...

Then, I would begin crying again from remorse for upsetting her and for making her even more tired when she already had a tiring day.

Then, because I felt fatigue and remorse, I would start crying again anyway ...

My feelings at that moment were so similar to those I felt then. Let there be no misunderstanding. I kept asking for something from my Allah. I cried when my wishes were not granted. Either secretly or outwardly. However, I had a Lord with unlimited compassion who was thinking of me and trying to reach me, and He was always there for me ... And He was always with me. But I was deceiving myself, by attributing my ignorance of Him to His indifference, and although I was in the palm of His hand, I was suffering as if I was away from my home ...

Although I was sobbing, I continued to read Surah al-Qiyamat through my tears. I was having trouble reading and I was trying my hardest to suppress the hiccups induced by my sobbing ...

"O, my Allah ... I always expect You to understand me, but if I tried to understand You, everything would have been resolved..." I said to Him.

Verses 14 and 15 responded to me: "In fact, people will testify against their own egos, despite the excuses they come up with."

16: "Do not rush your tongue trying to memorize 'a revelation of' the Quran.

17: "It is certainly upon Us to 'make you' memorize and recite it."

It means that it was He who placed it in my heart and compelled me to read. He was also telling me along with His Prophet.

It was the first moment that I understood that when Allah spoke to our Prophet in the Quran, He actually spoke to each of us.

Shame on me. Oh, shame on me. My tears were flowing and I continued to be astonished and surprised. He was talking to me like He was addressing the inner me.

Was He within me? Ah!

"There is an I within me deeper than I!" That was my Allah ... O, Yunus ... Ah ...

Surah Qiyamat Verses 34, 35, and 36:

"Woe to you, and more woe.

Woe to you and even more woe!

Do people think that they will be left neglected?"

"Is Allah, who did and created these, unable to bring the dead back to life? Of course, He is ..." Of course, He is able ...

In the Western accounts I have come across, the fact that Allah brings the dead back to life corresponds with the question of reincarnation ... However, the fact was finer and deeper than that ... I was dead. I was as dead as my fantasy world that I had been blindly living in until then. But at that moment, I was being awakened ...

To be resurrected into the truth ...

And a hadith I learned years later summed up all these that I am trying to relay in the best and yet summarized way ...

The Quran was sent by Allah to "be lived and understood". How did I fail to understand a sequence of words that I considered to be just words to recite after the dead? ...

Surah Ya-Sin, Verse 69: " We have not taught him (Prophet Muhammed [PBUH]) poetry, nor is it fitting for him. This 'Book' is only a Reminder and a clear Quran."

Surah Ya-Sin, Verse 70: " to warn whoever is 'truly' alive and fulfill the decree 'of torment' against the disbelievers."

"Reminder ..."

I once heard a saying. The Quran is read to the living dead. To resurrect dead hearts ... This was what I was living ...

My failure to see the concept of death outside those patterns significantly delayed my confrontation with the realities.

Ya-Sin! So, what did this surah called "The Heart of the Quran" mean? I typed in the name "Ya-Sin" prompting my online dictionary to find the meaning. The answer was before my eyes ...

"Ya – O" "Sin - Human ...""Ya-Sin." "O Human ..."

I took my mother's Quran ... I opened page 441, Surah Ya-Sin ...

A'udhu billahi min ash shaytanir rajim ... "Ya Sin ..."

"O, Human ..."

"It is a clear reminder ..."

I felt exactly the same way as you do when you read it by knowing that someone outside is calling you, "O, human."

What was human? What is it about this word that we must remember? ... What did I forget and what was I reminded of?

Human

I am sharing the dictionary meaning and explanation of the word "human" with you ...

Two words are mentioned as the root of the word "human." The first of these is the word "Uns". Uns means "friendship, affinity". It refers to living as a society and being "close" to people while, on the other hand, it expresses the affinity to Allah above all creatures ...

It is said that the word human comes from the verb "nasiya". Nasiya means to forget. In this case, human means "the one who forgets ..."

In the Quran, in Surah Taha Verse 115, it is ordained:

"And We had already taken a promise from Adam before, but he forgot; and We found not in him determination."

It felt like I was losing my sanity ...

I don't know about you, but I was "the one who forgot," and I was being "reminded."

The Quran, which I could not even open the door of its true meaning because of my arrogance until then, shook me to my core and reminded me of how "small" I was ...

The word "dhikr" in verse 69 of Surah Ya-Sin stood out right in front of me as another concept whose content we do not know.

It was a completely different understanding to say, "I try to remember what I have forgotten ..." Rather than saying "I recite Allah ... I recite the Beautiful Names of Allah ... I am doing dhikr ..."

The Quran has a special structure, which opened itself and emitted its scent the more you studied it layer by layer like a rose. Therefore, a shallow form of studying it, reading in my mother tongue Turkish, was not recommended.

Of course, it was not a coincidence that such a rich language was endowed with words carefully selected by Allah...

When Allah spoke with His servant, He carefully chose these words and concepts. The fact that even the language chosen in the Quran belonged to a special tribe, the Quraysh, was actually a clue to the depth of the issue ...

Like most of us, I was stuck in the shallowness of Arabic in the Quran in the Arabic countries we know. In fact, the Quraysh dialect was specifically chosen.

They say, "The older the time, the younger the Quran ..."

There are people who say that the Quran came to a tribe called the Quraysh years ago and try to perceive it as an ancient storybook ...

I have heard many times that if the Quran is understood, it actually covers all ages, but sometimes it is necessary to live in order to understand something.

The Word "Quraysh"

1. The tribe, which lived scattered before, was given this name because they gathered together and subsequently began to live together.

2. The tribe, consisting of people who collect goods, deal with, and earn through trade, was given this name, which means "to earn, to gather" due to these characteristics of its people.

3. This name was given because they search for the needy among the pilgrims and meet their needs.

4. There is a monster (shark) in the seas called "qirsh."

It is said that this animal is very powerful, it eats others, nobody can eat it; it overpowers other animals, but none can overpower it, and the following couplet is narrated:

"Quraysh is the one that lives in the sea, here is the Quraysh in its name. "When I first started my legal career, my American boss told me, "I'm throwing you among the sharks … So that you can learn to deal with them as soon as possible … "

Now I ask you; are we a society that lives on matter, on earning? Our values are ruined. Our understanding of virtue is lost. Everything has become fame, reputation, and money.

Has everything now been traded? Is there any justice left?

Are the strong right in all probability?

Well, has that made us monstrous?

As long as the human ego is undisciplined, it is condemned to become monstrous and materialistic. It is a good sign for the one who understands that the name of the guardian of Hell is designated as MALIK. Is it not the person who wants to have everything, who wants to possess everything, who forgets that Allah is the only owner of everything and internalizes matter to this extent, turns their world into hell, and guards it?

History repeats itself … Many countries and nations lived, yet failed to survive. Many large corporations collapsed when they thought themselves the most divine. Did you know that this effect was even given a name in economics? "The God complex".

Since the way of life is one, its rules are also one. Those who consider themselves untouchable, indestructible, eternal, that is, divine have entered the destruction period; no matter what they do …

In this system, no tree can reach the sky. This is not permitted. This situation is no different from the law of nature.

Actually, this tribe, which we storified as the Quraysh and we consider ourselves apart from it, still lives … This tribe is us. Regardless of nationality, the people living in the world at the moment are monstrous tribes with the same understanding (sharks).

We are still burying our girls. Look at the news and tell me that the brutality of the girls' burial was at the time when the Quran was revealed! If we consider burying only as putting in the ground, this is true; but if we understand burying to cover the concept of "killing while living," we realize how women and girls are "buried …"

What if Allah whom we always question spoke to us in our mother tongues? Our questions like "Can't we perform salah in our native tongues?" would become meaningless.

There was an ego within me that was becoming monstrous with an inclination towards matter, and Allah called me in its dialect …

It was then that I realized that the book I was reading was not plain Arabic.

It was A-RABB-ic, that is, the language of Allah.

In the continuation of this chapter, I will explain to you, in my own comprehension, why it is for our own good to try to learn this language, which is Arabic, that is actually A-RABB-ic, namely, the language of ALLAH, with its meaning …

I would understand later that every word and even every letter of this language, of which each word is originating from the "MOMENT," and thus, covering all the times, has hundreds of meanings …
It was a door that I should try to open to reach Allah …

And now I was firmly determined to open this door slightly and try to figure out what was behind it ...

"Who really understands the Quran knows that even the untied shoelace is written somewhere in the Quran."

Scare Them!

The Quran was not a book that could be understood with the carelessness of translations into mother tongues, harsh words, and translated expressions ...

You know the narrations of the Day of Judgment. Believers and unbelievers know more or less about this concept which has been the subject of many movies over and over. The world will be in shambles, The Trumpet will be blown. Every living thing will be shattered, and neither the world nor a thing will survive.

Then the Trumpet will be blown again, and everyone will be resurrected.

Such a scary narrative, isn't it? I do not believe that there is any person, be it a believer or an unbeliever, who is not afraid of the Day of Judgment and its signs, even if they do not show it.

The fact that Allah and religion have been imposed on us since childhood with elements such as fear, punishment, and burning fire has turned into some kind of relationship based on self-interest mixed with fear rather than loving Allah and only fearing Him without knowing Him, and this is such a bitter situation and such a great loss ...

In fact, every human being is a realm. And the Lord of the realms is in direct contact with them. Every person is a different world. They have orbits, the sun, and the stars, rains, winds, seas, and treasures... Every person has a sama', that is, "consciousness." The human was created from the material of the earth's soil. The Human is earth, and this is their "land" in the words of the Quran.

Without realizing it, we create our own "realm", our world within this. Our own truths, beliefs, patterns, loved ones, and dislikes…

As we continue our lives in a way without being "properly" aware of Allah, something unexpected suddenly happens in our lives. Either we lose someone we love, or we experience a betrayal we never expected from someone we trust, or we lose what we believe in, our health or our property …

At that moment, we see that our beliefs, our values that we built in our own world, and everything that we wasted our youth and lives on is suddenly upside down …

Life is a road. Although everybody thinks that they are going through different things and that nobody can understand them, I have news for you. Caring for ourselves is something we all need, I know. This ego cannot even tolerate the idea that we are alike. At the very least, it cannot tolerate this being exposed. Because each of us is particularly magnificent, particularly beautiful, particularly different, particularly weak, and particularly strong …

The generosity of people towards themselves and their stinginess towards others is also among the virtual deceptions brought to us by the undisciplined ego.

Rumi said: "Are you looking for a defect? Look in the mirror …"

How wonderful are these words? We claim that we are only exposed to concepts such as defects, guilt, and ugliness. It is usually the fault of others. We have always been deceived; we are victims.

"Everyone thinks of changing the world, but no one thinks of changing himself …" (Tolstoy).

"As strange as it is to say this, for me being Muhammadan stands incomparably higher than worshipping the cross (Christianity). If human beings had the right to choose, every sane person, without doubt, and hesitation would have accepted the one Allah and His prophet … "(Tolstoy).

Merkez Efendi of the friends of Allah

Merkez Efendi is one of the spiritual sultans of beautiful Istanbul. His real name is Musa, he is the son of Muslihuddin.

Musa bin Muslihuddin came to Istanbul, where he settled after completing his education in numerous Muslim schools (madrasahs) and joining the class of scholars of Islam and Islamic law (ulema). He gained an exceptional position in a short time. But the course of his life would change thereafter.

It is Sümbül Efendi, the beloved of Allah and his teacher, who taught Musa the truths in the Quran and the knowledge of Allah. In fact, he was one of those who had revoked Sümbül Efendi at first. But Allah, the Almighty informed him through a dream that he was in error.

In his dream, Sümbül Efendi was resting on the door of his house. Despite all the things they had piled up behind the door, Sümbül Efendi had knocked down the door and entered in one move. Musa bin Muslihuddin, who woke up from his dream with the sound of that door smashing, became lost in thought. The more he thought, the wider his horizon became and he knew that this dream had a great meaning:

"What a great heedlessness we were in!"

Musa Efendi impatiently waited until the morning. It was not the time to stop. He left his house upon hearing the loud sound of the call to salah (azan). The wind went like the leaves before him, and in a snap, he had completed the winding paths and finally reached Sümbül Efendi's lodge. Without being seen by anyone, he crept in slowly, took a post as a shield and sat behind it, bowed his head to his chest, and waited.

After a while, Sümbül Efendi started his speech that poured pearls into the hearts. He spoke in an enchanting sweet, warm, and soft language. Every word penetrated the hearts of all those in attendance like a bullet. Many pearls of wisdom of here, there, and the beyond were spoken.

A window had already been opened to Musa Efendi's heart. He thought he was swimming in a completely different realm, and a warm light filled and illuminated him. Everything was more beautiful, at that moment Sümbül Efendi gazed at the dervishes with his eyes full of light:

"No, you don't understand! But the one behind the post! He completely understands because I am saying all my words for him today!" The one behind the post was miserable. How did the beautiful Sümbül Efendi know he was here? All his education, all the madrasahs he attended were useless. The waves of the sea of unity were cascading in this place.

From that moment on, Musa bin Muslihuddin held tightly onto Sümbül Efendi and dived into the sea of Sufism with the knowledge of Allah he received from Sümbül Efendi, and received his share of many spiritual blessings from Allah. A grain of divine love had fallen into the heart of the young man from madrasah. That grain of love is far better than large quantities of gems. Now the heart of the young man from the madrasah was beating with a strange melody.

One day, Sümbül Efendi subjected his dervishes to a tough test. He said to them:

"O souls made up of a handful of earth! If you had created the world, how would you have created it?"

How could this question be answered? Each dervish offered answers in their own way. However, none of them were capable of giving the answer Sümbül Efendi wanted. It was Musa Efendi's turn, and Sümbül Efendi, with his face shining like diamonds, said with a sweet smile, "Well, tell me, Musa Efendi, what kind of world would you want? If you created the world, how would you create it?"

Musa Efendi answered without looking up:

"This is not possible! But if it were possible, I would leave everything in the center! The world is in such a sweet order that it is unimaginable to add or reduce something!"

This was what Sümbül Efendi wanted. An unprecedented light resembling the moon appeared on Sümbül Efendi's face and he said, "Well done dervish Musa! So, you would leave everything in the center? So may your name be Merkez (Central) Musliheddin from now on!"

After that, Musa bin Musliheddin's name became Merkez Musliheddin and from then on, he would be cherished in people's hearts with the name Merkez Efendi.

Again, one day when the dervishes were around Sümbül Efendi like moths to a flame, Sümbül Efendi again wished to give them a test.

"O, dervishes!" he called. "The manifestation of the mercy of Allah; flowers of all kinds and colors gush out from the bosom of the earth. Each of you will bring me a bunch of flowers. Our hearts and eyes will be enlightened with those flowers scattering musk."

Nothing could stop the dervishes. For the first time, Sümbül Efendi wanted something from them. All the dervishes rushed out. They ran towards the fields and gardens and gathered bunches of flowers, and the lodge turned into a flower garden with the flowers they brought.

All the dervishes were laughing, their laughter was like a reflection of the flowers on their faces. Only Merkez Efendi was thoughtful. He had one withered and dry, daisy in his hand. What value would a dry daisy be among these colorful flowers? He came before Sümbül Efendi and lowered his head:

"Oh, the light of pure souls! Whatever flower I touched, I found it trembling with the dhikr (remembrance) of Allah. I could not pick those beauties crying out Allah, Allah. So, I came to your high presence with this dry daisy! May you forgive me!"

This was what Sümbül Efendi was waiting for. He looked deeply at Merkez Efendi:

"Praise be to Allah, who touched your inner eyes with divine wisdom!"

After receiving this good news from his murshid, Merkez Efendi became Sümbül Efendi's son-in-law. He married his daughter Rahime and moved to his own lodge. Merkez Efendi had drank the syrup of divine love with his heart's lips.

It was now a link in the chain of Allah's guidance.[22]

---

22 Source: Osmanlı Kültürünü Yaşatma Derneği

IV.
HUMAN

"What is this existence for if my end would be nonexistence?"
-Necip Fazıl Kısakürek

"A little philosophy inclineth man's mind to atheism, but depth in philosophy bringeth men's minds about to religion."
-Francis Bacon

"A good question is half of the knowledge..."
-Hz. Muhammad (PBUH)

"O believers! Have faith in…"
- Surah an-Nisa, Verse 136

"Fortunately, people do not know that they are immortal …"
-Deniz Erten

INTELLECT

Even though there have been attempts to portray Islam as a "formal" religion, it is an intellectually-based understanding.

In every few verses, the Quran invites those who read it and try to practice what it offers to "reason and contemplate ..."

And it emphasizes contemplation (tafakkur: a word used for expressing an opinion originating from the root "fakara") and thinking so much that it says that a person who contemplates for a moment gains a much greater reward than supererogatory worships, which are said to be useful.

The use of expressions "thawab (reward)" and "ghunah (sin)" is actually a way of encouraging people who are fed on "relationship of interest, matter and reward" to continue with such behaviors. Because human beings live in a three-dimensional universe that they perceive to be extremely limited ... They cannot see what they form as energy in response to their actions or thoughts ... To avoid them becoming harmful by getting the idea that their actions do not have a response, these behaviors that will have a response in the hereafter are restrained with the concepts of sin and reward as if to say, "Don't worry even if you don't get a response now!"

If one digs a little deeper to know basically what the reason is, one begins to realize that in fact, nothing is willed by divine grace for no reason ...

The fact that the orders and prohibitions of Islam are for people who are mentally stable and that mentally unstable people are not "held responsible" for Islam shows how "rational" this religion is.

In every few verses, Allah encourages people to ask questions and use their minds with questions such as, "Are you not thinking at all? Are you not using your mind at all? Are you not contemplating at all?"

Besides being a "religion of logic", it is a religion of "faith" by asking to "believe" in Allah and His Messenger (PBUH). Faith means "to believe". It means to trust.

The place of faith is in the heart, the intellect of a person is limited but the heart is unlimited.

It is so limitless that Allah says, "My earth and My heavens cannot encompass Me, but the heart of My believing servant encompasses Me."

And in a sense, what is actually required of us is to use the "mind of the heart." Do not ask, how that is possible.

In some verses of the Quran, the word "heart" is used instead of "intellect." "They have hearts, but they do not understand with it (with those hearts) ..." "Do they not wander around the earth so that they have hearts to think?" "Or are their hearts locked?"

Islam means "to surrender" and besides being a religion of logic, it expects people to surrender in matters that they cannot understand with the partial/unitary intellect ...

I mean, on the condition that there are "correct translations and interpretations," there are of course matters that we cannot "perceive" in some verses. This is not because the matter is "rational/logical," but because our comprehension is not yet capable of perceiving it.

When you explain a 4th-grade subject to a first-year physics student, perhaps it may sound "absurd" because the information will cause a gap. But when that student comes to the 4th grade, he/she will defend what they previously found "absurd" as a person who has studied and understood the subject and filled the gaps with their knowledge.

Whereas, we usually say, "What is this? Look! This is what it says here. Why should I implement something that happened many centuries ago? It is very unreasonable!" Unfortunately, we can make comments such as this and more.

What we should realize is that the verse written there is not unreasonable, but that our mind is not yet able to comprehend that verse.

I know, this artificial, hypothetical veil called EGO wants people to think that others are inadequate instead of accepting their own inadequacy.

This leads us to a place even more wrong than where we started. The brain is like a computer. If you have made a "judgment" on a matter, it closes the file and locks it. As you know, when a file is closed in the legal system, you cannot file a lawsuit on the same matter with a definite judgment again ...

However, our way of thinking here is related to the most basic meaning of the word Islam, TO SURRENDER.

If you say, "I cannot comprehend it now, BUT Allah may make me comprehend it in the future InshaAllah," and leave that file "open," your thoughts will become energy seeking its response in the universal computer, so sooner or later the logical information about that file will be transferred to you.

Faith is believing. You believe even if you cannot see it, you believe even if you cannot comprehend the reason at that moment.

I want to give an example from my own experience.

As you know, the topic of "veiling" is a popular topic of discussion for all of us. It has even been used to the extent of creating discrimination among people.

However, Allah tells us that "considering humans separate from Allah," which is the basis of discrimination between the servants, is the greatest sin of the devil and He explains this in Surah al-Baqarah verse 34 as follows:

"And 'remember' when We said to the angels, "Prostrate before Adam," so they all did—but not Iblîs, who refused and acted arrogantly, becoming unfaithful."

I have to give some explanations in order to convey the message that is being told here ...

The devil is a symbol of a way of thinking and confuses us by giving an idea. We make "demonized" discriminations amongst each other, and we are thus expelled from heaven, which also has a hidden (deep, veiled) meaning of "peace and happiness" in addition to referring to a place.

I thought a lot about the verses about "veiling." I read the comments of Allah's friends in various interpretations.

Since each verse of the Quran contains limitless meanings, I came across a vast amount of information.

I realized that some scholars have comments on the hidden meanings of veiling indicating that veiling adornments also refer to veiling your values such as intelligence, knowledge, happiness, and beauty that may lead to positive or negative reactions from those who understand, those who have good intentions, those who don't, or those who are ignorant so that you don't come to harm.

But the outward "veiling" was still valid in the statements made by the scholars. Why?

While my ego, which desires me to become devilish was making suggestions to me claiming that this was nonsense and this was intended to suppress women, etc. I continued to work on this with full faith in the fact that Allah, by implication, will not put anything into the Quran for no reason and that this definitely has certain benefits for humankind.

I saw that in many past civilizations, it was not only women who were veiled, but many friends of Allah were also in veils regardless of their religious affiliations.

Then one day, while reading the fashion pages in the newspaper, I saw the following article:

"This year hats and sunglasses have become larger in size. Women who do not want to suffer from aging and wrinkles caused by the rays of the sun will be able to wear these branded hats and sunglasses comfortably this year ..."

A lightning bolt flashed in my head. Perhaps another communication link was established between my brain neurons ...

The thing underlying the determination of salah times, the recognition of salah at night, and the request for veiling could have an interesting connection with the brain, body, and the sun ...

We will address the relationship of sun rays with salah and the brain under the salah and brain section InshaAllah and we will also discuss what kind of connections there might be between the brain and brain functions and the protection by the DNA.

In this context, it is very interesting that you cannot just say that I cover my head, because there is a magnificent connection and logic that shows the relationship between Islam and science in the brain's perception of the sun rays and its activities affected by it ...

I am really not interested in the political aspect of the matter because I know that the Islamic path is a universal arrangement beyond politics, and moreover, I am not yet covered in the literal "form." What I'm trying to say is that along with all the other statements on veiling, this topic can also have something to do with the matter of "energy." May Allah forgive me for not yet drawing myself into my highest energy. In fact, why should Allah forgive me, I am harming myself, we think that Allah is affected by our mistakes, and we become arrogant by thinking that we are veiled, performing salah, and fasting for Allah! We are harming ourselves!

This undisciplined ego is such a thing that we think that we even make the distinction between sin and reward for Allah. What does Allah have to do with it? Does Allah become greater with my worships? Never! Does He need my worship that there are expressions that "frighten" us in the Quran?

In fact, Allah is trying to protect us from ourselves. Otherwise, whether we worship or not, it does not affect Him. He is after all an ETERNAL MIGHT. It is not even possible for us to express Him in words. With what comprehension can you praise or question the Owner of such power and knowledge?

He is trying to encourage us through the mercy of a mother for our next life and existence, which is our eternal journey. No wrath? There is, of course, because He looks after every servant and does not want us to harm each other. But this is what He says, "My mercy prevails over My wrath. No one should consider their own sin greater than My mercy. Come until the last breath. Come one step towards me, and I will come ten steps ..."

We ignorantly refer to others as kafirs (non-believers). However, Hazrat Ali told us that we should not call anyone 'kafir'. But if I ask you what 'kafir' means, your response will be, "the one who does not believe in Allah," and you will stop there.

No. Have you thought about what the word "kafir" means? Does a kafir mean a person who does not believe in Allah?

Well then, who is the one committing shirk? Does it also mean the one who does not believe in Allah? No!

As we have stated before, 'kafir' and 'kufr' come from the same root and mean the ONE VEILING THE TRUTH. So, it is not a non-believer, they actually know the truth! But depending on their interests, VEILING the truth suits their cause and they do so! In fact, they have a full grasp of the truth!

Then, what does shirk or mushrik mean? Don't say the one who does not believe in Allah ...

Shirk means associating partners with Allah. Anyone who commits shirk knows the existence of Allah, but they also adopt other deities. And the most painful thing is that many people who do not understand Islam in a "scientific" sense and consider themselves to be believers are in secret shirk. We will explain this later.

Now let's go back to the subject of veiling. If I deny my contemplation of veiling or covering the truth, I will be accused of being a "kafir ..."

One of the facts underlying the necessity of veiling that I became aware of by researching is for the protection of the energetic field of the servant; a piece of advice for the servant... And Allah tells us these things to protect us, not to force us ... As described in Surah al-Kafirun, everybody's servitude binds them ...

When you look at the practitioners of either religious or ancient teachings, you see various veils and caps with geometric shapes. These are based on a "science" ... Once we explain that the human body and soul are actually an "electromagnetic" field in the upcoming chapters, we will start to think that the head on the body is a kind of "dish antenna" and that the turbans, cone-shaped caps and all the other head coverings of various shapes may also serve to draw electromagnetic fields to the body and prevent the energy received by the mountain, that is, the body, from being scattered, especially through the hair which is considered as an antenna ...

No sunnah (practices and traditions of the Prophet), or advice is purposeless ... A great religion and a great prophet ...

In the world right now, whether it is a dental filling or a tattoo, the materials contain elements such as mercury, and these "disrupt" the electromagnetic field and frequency of human beings and it is accepted that certain diseases such as "panic attacks" occur following such procedures ... Moreover, I would like to ask you to investigate whether the generations of certain families who are in the center of power in the world, such as those who are nobility, royalty, or aristocrats have tattoos ... There are, for example, some statements indicating that this is not "tolerated" by God in the Bible ...

Tattoos were also a symbol of the social class differences constructed in the age of ignorance before our Prophet ... Being tattooed was a sign of social status difference ... This is one of the reasons why it is discouraged ... When we look at the current world order, which I will refer to as demonic, there is an attempt to cause discrimination by giving us a sense of class difference and superiority through deceit, and actually, we are made worthless in this way ... For Allah's sake, is it this system that imposes that we can become superior through only our blood, lineage, or the possessions we have accumulated?

Does being developed individuals refer to the hypocrisy where we claim to "protect nature and natural resources" after spoiling nature, erecting concrete buildings everywhere, and then bragging about our residences to our friends?

However, when you see the importance given to herbs, flowers, animals, trees, the sun, and the moon, even in the remains of the eras that we call "primitive," you can see who is primitive and who has stepped into a new era.

Assess how "meaningful" is one of the most common statements about Islam claiming, "that what was required in the previous ages, no longer applies in this current age. ...

The only change is the numerical description of time, but the repetition of history will not change unless we try to improve the human ego ...

Unfortunately, we cannot see the fact that we react to formal "Islamic" views with formal "anti-views" unless we understand that the dos and don'ts prescribed by Islam are for our good health and wellbeing ...

To give an example, I read in a source that the Prophet had a suggestion to keep our hair long ... Later I came across numerous accounts about keeping hair long, from Indian to many other ancient civilizations. There had been some researchers claiming that thoughts result from perceiving the surrounding frequencies and certain regions of the head can perceive certain feelings and this is achieved by the hair in that region perceiving the frequency or vibration of that feeling, that is, by being a certain kind of antenna, and that thoughts are formed by "downloading" from high-level creatures through an antenna, just like with computers ... When you look at ancient civilizations, we see that hair had a distinct importance and there are chronicles about the relation of supernatural powers, the transference of spiritual information and spirit with head and hair; it is customary to keep the hair long; customs and beliefs such as the relationship between certain veins and nerves on the head with hair, and the protection of the head by covering ... There is even some scientific research suggesting that vitamin D from the sun can be absorbed more by keeping children's hair long ...

And even more, some people conducting long-term research on the matter brought up that hair and body hair could be a communication tool between various regions of the world and even between other planets, they bear the records of previous generations of human beings, and they attract the sun heat and photon waves in the atmosphere ... When we look at Rumi's writings, there is an interesting connection between these narrations and the "attraction and receiving" strength of hair like an antenna:

"There is a head adorned with a golden cone; there is another head of which the beauty of its curls (hair) is veiled with a golden cone and a crown embellished with gems. Because the curls and the love of the beautiful are very attractive and they are the throne of the hearts...[23]"

I do not know in which form it would be, but it does not look like an improbable possibility for a kind of veiling to become necessary to protect ourselves from the sun (which is known to be constantly approaching us) and for us to do this voluntarily ... Because we know that the sun has a deformative effect on DNA when it exceeds a certain extent ... It has been long claimed that our hair acts as an antenna and our brain, that is our head acts as a "radio" ...

It is not a distant idea that all these may be related to the "closure" of the receiving and transmitting properties of the "hair" and "head" to external influences due to the ever-increasing technology and electromagnetic fields, perceptions, photons emitted from the photon belt, and new expansions in the universal mechanism ...

It is not absurd that it may be necessary to protect consciousness, to "avoid being manipulated by frequency and derivative uses", to prevent the " interference" of frequencies and waves that we take from and spread to the universe, or to prevent our thoughts from being "spread

23 Antropolik ve Sosyolojik Açıdan Saçlar ve İnançlar (Hair and Beliefs From an Anthropological and Sociological Perspective)," a book by Nermin Öztürk, S. U. Faculty of Theology, Professor of History of Religions

or read …"

Otherwise, it is really strange to be ignorant enough to think that the All-Mighty Allah will have an interest in our relationship with two pieces of cloth … Arrogance, oh arrogance …

I Interrupted the subject here and opened a parenthesis about veiling because my relative self was in charge when I first read the relevant verse and it was trying to "distract" me with my perception at that moment saying, "No, no, I don't think so!" And I was actually at the test of trust at that time. If my response was, "Come on, no way!" and I let it go, this "explanation of reasons" that had become interlinked in a short period of time would not have been brought before me. In fact, this is what Allah wants the most from His servant, and when this happens, He shows grace again. Faith must actually originate from TRUST in ALLAH. This is one of the greatest tests. Although we are actually being tested, unfortunately, I don't want to say this but, we are kind of testing Him with our ignorance and small-mindedness! However, whoever trusts in Him wins everything. Allah's love for His generous servant and His love towards His servant who does not respond to cruelty with cruelty is because of the fact that this is all an indication of the servant's trust in Him. Allah wants us to trust Him, and faith not based on trust is only "formal."

Despite my ego saying, "It is not possible!" regarding that verse, I said, "If my Allah says so, there should be wisdom in it, and even if I cannot see it, He will show me the insight," and that silenced my ego.

Thank Allah. He is the One who quickly shows His grace to His servant who trusts in Him. He is the One who pleases His servant for trusting in Him... Of course, you don't do this to be pleased, but because you feel that way out of your love and faith. He is so generous and Glorious that He immediately responds to you. Try this out and see. Your affection and admiration for Him will increase. Be sure …

In such cases, when your intellect is not enough, if you adopt the idea of faith, that is to surrender even if you don't understand and to trust, different doors will open to you. Because Allah does not break His promise. He has so much mercy that He says, "I will come ten steps when my servant takes one step towards me ..."

Teachings such as "asking for something without any doubt and as if it will come true" which have been recently popularized are the same as the teaching recommended in Islam, "Ask from Allah without any doubt; while you are praying, your prayer will be accepted InshaAllah ..."

Now, let's get back to our topic on faith...

The Arabic word for faith, iman, means "to trust and to sincerely believe," and it originates from the root "amn;" it was lexicalized from the words "believe and belief." The word "amanah (trust/guardianship)" which means "to trust" and "emin" meaning "trustworthy/confident" and "amin" which is the expression we use at the end of our prayers by sincerely believing that they will be accepted are also derived from the same root word. The word to end off prayer, "Amin" means "it is so" and signifies trust and confidence.

Of course, it is not a coincidence that the name of the Prophet's father is Abdullah (the servant of Allah) and his mother's name is Amine (Emunah - confident in heart, no fear in her heart). Our Prophet is referred to as "Muhammad al-Emin" because everyone in his tribe acknowledged his trustworthiness and he was given this nickname.

(This is basically because he trusts in Allah. Those who trust in Allah also become confident in themselves. For example, Allah loves the generous because He is generous Himself. The more we become generous, the more He becomes generous to us. Allah wants His servant to adopt His mannerisms. They asked Isa (Jesus), "What must we do to avoid the wrath of Allah?" He said, "Protect yourself from your wrath." Because we become whatever we do, and Allah will increase that side of ours. If we act with wrath, He continues to treat us with wrath. Because that servant is oriented towards that name of Allah, and this gives rise to that name. Hence, it is recommended to be forgiving among many other reasons. People basically do everything to themselves because everything that comes across is basically their own reflection in different mirrors ...)

Well now, what is intellect, pure reason besides faith meaning to believe?

We are children of artificial "intellect" molded by "conditioning".

(The word intellect (aql), which is also related to the word "people (halq)" can also mean "created afterwards").

INTELLECT comes from the root UQL in Arabic and means "to bind, to restrain, to bend." It even means "to pledge, to seize" in Hebrew.

We perceive intellect as drawing conclusions by establishing a connection between objects, events, or people. Yet, the intellect, which is the outcome of our analysis based on what we perceive with our ego, nature, and five senses and what we were taught and conditioned for, actually "takes us as hostages and binds us" even if we do not notice. So much so that we cannot go beyond the mold that our own intellects put us in. And since we do not admit being "bound" and fail to get out of our molds because of our lack of comprehension due to our egos, we, as a direct defense, find "the subject before us" insufficient, meaningless, and even absurd.

People that we refer to as very intelligent and having eyes like a hawk are basically those who establish "logical connections" between objects, information, matters, and concepts and extrapolate from them. Although these inferences are valid for unitary and partial truths, they may not apply to wholistic truths ...

We think that these people are good observers and analysts.

This is exactly where the difference between personal development through religion lies. Personal development advises people about what they can acquire with their intelligence. Yet, religion explains that "that intellect should be the wholistic intellect and not only the personality but also the spirit needs to improve ..." Personal development generally guides one's mental disposition on controllable traits, but life is not a small, fragmented thing. The picture we see is only a point compared to the whole picture. Every individual is a cell of a universal body ...Therefore, there is an inevitable state of interaction among us ... Even if we cannot see the whole picture, people can be at peace and achieve continuous success only by surrendering to the one who sees and developing their spirits and personalities through a holistic intellect. Otherwise, the house of cards that people have built may come down with a light wind as a result of a stumble in their lives or the lives of their loved ones.

The technique of quantum thinking is actually developed for this, and in fact, it consists of a different way of conveying the advice of religion, that is the PATH.

So, people whom we regard as "rational" should bear in mind that intellect is a double-edged sword such that people can get injured by their own intellect. This situation is transferred to us with the decree "we do not wrong you, but you wrong yourselves."Because our intellect, in fact, is loaded with data, that is, information that was caught in our brain-computer and that is subsequently written upon the conditioning and orientation of our families, our social circles, our education, and the conditions of the world.

We can read life and scenery with this partial, subjective, that is, unitary intellect based on the data and information entered in our upper database.

The same word can mean different things for two different people.

When you call someone a "donkey", that person would see it as a compliment if they were raised with the belief that a donkey is cute.

When someone else is called a "donkey," it is likely to be perceived as meaning "stupid" or an insult because that person understood it from the perspective of how they were brought up.

While living with our perceptions, as proven facts, even our perceptions are not the essence of reality, which is why this situation is a slippery slope for "pure rationalists."

The personal intellect of each of us is the BEST for us, and this tragicomic situation is widely expressed with the saying: "The intellect was put on the market, yet everyone still purchased their own mind..."

Now you will say, "Well, the Quran repeatedly recommends that we use our intellect."

It is asked, "Don't you ever use your intellect? Don't you ever contemplate?" So what intellect is this?

With this advice, the Quran points out to us that it is the Universal Intellect (which is the intellect of the heart) that we need to reach with our partial intellect, and faith and by surrendering ...

Here is the distinction between the partial and universal intellect which is frequently mentioned in Sufism.

The word AQL (intellect) means "to bind" and the intellect works by analogy. Have you ever thought about what the word QALB (Heart) means? I was very surprised when I wondered and researched it one day.

The word QALB means "heart, changing, conversion, reversal."

Reversal!

I always say that "We live in reverse, brothers, and sisters!" When I read this meaning, it was impossible for me not to see the wonderful intelligence and humor of my Allah here.

My Allah! We really live in reverse. We are trying to get to the heart with intellects that are "bound by the conditions". However, if we try to reach the intellect of the heart, it already connects us with the holistic mind.

In fact, the word "qalb" comes from the same root as the word "revolution (inqilab)".

We were actually asked to change, develop, move forward, and break the molds that imprison us. Even the meanings of those two words (aql and qalb) were actually enough to convey the message to a "heart open to understanding". What kind of intelligence do you have, my dear Allah?

In fact, when I learned that the word "inqilab (revolution)," meaning "being turned upside down" has the same meanings as the heart, I thought, "Hazrat Shams once again did his part as the sun."

What was Hazrat Shams, Allah's beautiful friend, saying? May Allah be pleased with him:

"Instead of resisting the changes that Allah brought before you, surrender. Let life flow with you, not despite you. Do not worry that your order will be disrupted, or your life will be ruined. How do you know that the downside of your life will not be better than the upside?"

"It is a matter of the heart to proceed in the path of the Truth, not of the intellect. Let your guide always be your heart, not your head on your shoulders. Be one of those who know their ego, not those who erase it!"

Do you know that our Prophet's migration from Mecca to Medina is basically related to this subject? Do not ask, "how, what is the relevance?"

If our Prophet, that beloved servant of Allah, made a wish, would all the troubles and the Hijrah be necessary? No, they would never be necessary. But here, our Allah created this event and makes it communicated through the verses to explain a message with examples, to show us the attitude of His most beloved servant, and to show us what to do in similar situations.

First of all, we need to understand well what Mecca is. (It is called "Mecca" coming from the root word "mecca" meaning a place where people rush into because it is a holy city that absorbs the dead, cleanses the sins, and is the center of the earth).Before Islam, Arabs circumambulated Kaaba by blowing whistles. For this reason, another view states that the name Mecca comes from the word "muka," meaning to blow a whistle.

Some say that "Mecca" is also called "Becca" that comes from the root "BCC" with meanings such as "to split, to belittle, to separate, to make crowded, and to break off," because it overpowers and belittles the arrogant and it is a crowded place since it attracts people from all over the world.

On the other hand, the difference between these two concepts is explained by saying that the Haram region is called Mecca and the masjid area is called Becca.

When you go to Mecca, you will notice that people try to tolerate each other and avoid unfavorable reactions in every condition because the aim there is to adopt Allah's manners, which is actually what is desired for every part of the world. For this reason, it is also called Umm Rahm (Mother of Mercy), Umm al-Qura (Mother of Cities), or Umm Zahm (Mother of Hardship) because of the hustle in the crowd. We should remember that wherever there is "hardship and mercy" there is "Ahmet". In pre-Islamic poems, SALAH, meaning salvation, "Basse," for disciplining the deviant, or "Nasse," because of the removal of the disbelievers, were used (Prof. Dr. Ali Akpınar).

When we went to Mecca, we were told the people of Mecca were short-tempered and stern, but people were different in Medina, and they were gentle and compassionate. Mecca, which was named "the Honored (al-Mukarama) by our Prophet after Hazrat Ali broke the idols in Kaaba on his shoulders ...

It is as if the narrations about Mecca represent our current life. People are fond of trade and material goods, and they are aggressive and stern, but they carry the Kaaba, "the house of Allah," in their very center and their hearts. This place which is the center of the world is actually us, isn't it?

A person who has become aggressive and materialistic in life, but who has Allah in the heart and forgot about Him ... The heart is full of idols that they do not realize they are idolizing ... Spoiled ...

When people orient towards the path of Allah and tend to believe with their intellect, then other people close them out and even humiliate them. As they begin to behave in ways that are contrary to their old habits, they attempt to distract them from this path by calling them names such as "insane" or questions such as, "what are you dealing with at this young age?"

They are subjected to humiliation and are accused of lying. They are called insane or "majnun (crazy)" just like our Prophet was called. Because those people begin to turn their backs on everything based on materialism that is brought about by the mentality of the worldly people. They break down accustomed mindsets. Just as Shams did to Rumi:

"I learned to challenge the world alone at a young age. Then I came to the idea that we should walk with the crowds. Then I concluded that it is necessary to walk with the crowd. Then I realized that the real march should be against the crowds ..." (Rumi).

So, that a person begins to walk on and live in the straight path leading to Allah upon realizing that they live in the reverse side upon the inversion of their life through the revolution of the heart and their previous life.

Their friends don't understand them and want them to repeat their old habits, but they refrain because they no longer enjoy their old habits. As a result of the slow turning of their hearts from their old friends, they are drawn to people who share their new understanding.

This is hijrah (migration) ...

The word hijrah evokes the words "export" and "exclusion" in my native language, Turkish. It means "to go out," "to emigrate," "to leave ..." You know, like when they say, "I quit drinking."

A person migrates from their old understanding, old beliefs, and old friends, that is Mecca within themselves to Medina within themselves ... Medina actually means "judicial locality, jurisdiction, city." The real name for Medina was Yathrib. Our Prophet gave it the name Medina at a later stage. Why? The words Medina / Civilization also evoke each other.

A person reaches the true civilization from the ignorance within them only by "the knowledge of the truth." The aggression in their dissatisfaction and greed leaves its place to peace. And they return to their heart with the provisions they've just learned. They break the misconceptions, patterns, concepts, and "idols" there and call it "Mecca al-Mukarama (Mecca, the Honored)," "The Cleansed Main Space".

This is just like the difference between our personal and particular mind, which is the WHOLISTIC INTELLECT, and the UNIVERSAL INTELLECT, which carries the intellect of the knowledge of the truth ...

The one who migrates from the particular intellect to the universal intellect tries to look with the intellect of Allah, not with their human intellect.

In other words, with the intellect of the One who sees the whole ... Because they know that they could at most see a small part ...

Let's call the universal intellect the whole intellect and the particular intellect partial intellect.

What I call the whole intellect is the cosmic consciousness. The will and consciousness in the main system, that is, the universal consciousness, and the partial/unitary intellect is the unitary will and consciousness that is available within each of us and that emanates from the cosmic consciousness, which is actually a single whole in each of us.

What we call the unitary mind is actually hypothetical. Because if there is an issue that everyone who works on the human brain and its perceptions agrees on, it is that everyone perceives the same subject differently and evaluates according to the "existing" conditions at the boundaries of their perceptions and formulates an idea by reaching a conclusion without considering the non-existent conditions ... Our unitary or individual intellect makes hypothetical judgments because it cannot see the whole picture. It only sees a part of the picture, but since it cannot see the whole, what it sees leads it to make mistakes. It subjectively interprets something it sees according to its own perceptions and experiences, what it was taught, and the predominant characteristics of the ego.

I usually use the following example: you know, computers come out with a new model every year; let's think of people like this. People's ways of thinking are formed according to their subconscious, characteristics, and weaknesses of the ego, physical characteristics, conditioning, upbringing, and social circle.

This DATABASE shapes the way people evaluate the events they encounter.

Experiences, conditionings, and how one is brought up show only the part of the scenery that can be seen from that person's window.

However, the "universal consciousness" that does not change according to the person is like looking from the roof, not from the 1st, 2nd, or 3rd floor.

It's like looking at a scenery from a bird's eye view and evaluating by seeing the big picture.

When I read the words of one of Allah's friends, I was very impressed: "Do you want to reach Allah, then know that the biggest obstacle between you and Allah is your intellect ..."

Maybe that's why Rumi says, "Without being called insane, one is not called a dervish."

Many things that feel right when viewed with a unitary intellect can be incredibly wrong when viewed with a holistic mind.

Then why is religion based not only on intellect but on faith?

The most important reason for this is that the intellect is prone not only to the right thinking and inspiration but also to the wrong way of thinking called "delusion." It pulls a person to the wrong path by showing the behaviors that are harmful to the ego and self as beneficial and the bad as good.

And this issue is a serious test not only for those who have just embarked on a path towards religion but also for those who have reached certain ranks.

Delusion shows something that does not exist as real, or vice versa.

It leads to misevaluation of the events and false choices.

So, when people act with a unitary intellect, they are open to all kinds of ideas.

This is where faith comes into play. Even if it does not make sense at that moment, one should choose to do what is right in the path of Allah with surrender and trust. This is a cognition with one's heart, not with one's particular intellect.

While faith is to trust and believe; delusion is to fear and doubt.

Within the framework of Islam, surrender to the ideas of the Messenger of Allah (PBUH) without suggesting an opposite idea and obey his teachings.

After that, seek out why that incident happened, what is the wisdom in it! Nobody's holding you back from seeking!

"O Ali, everyone approaches Allah from the gates of birrand good deeds! You be close to Allah with your intellect ..."

So, it should be thinking and comprehension that underlies human behaviors; not the conditionings or one's social circle ...

We are freed from conditioning through intellect, and from the veil of our egos through faith.

Even if we do not understand, if we always believe, we will have the true treasure that I have always talked about.

The True Story of the Irreligious and the Faithless

He turned to him and said, "The faithless has the better of the irreligious." He smiled and said, "Exactly, only someone worse could overpower him."

He said, "No. You didn't understand. Think of it this way: now give me the book in your hand and ask me to put it inside ..."

He was surprised. He said, "All right. Take it. Will you put it inside?"

He said, "Okay." He took the book and went inside, then his companion saw that he was entering one of the rooms on the other side of the house ...

Then he came back empty-handed ...

He said, "Yes, I put the book in the room inside and returned." He responded, "Okay. I believe you."

"What now? What does this have to do with faith or the irreligious?" he asked.

He replied, "Now, look. You gave the book to me and asked me to put it inside. So, I took it and told you that I put it inside, right?" He replied, "Yes."

"Well, in that case, you didn't personally see me put the book inside, you just saw me go inside and you believed that I put the book on the bookshelf, and you believed ... But you didn't personally see me putting the book there, did you?"

He responded, "Yes, but I trust, and I believe in you."

He responded saying, "Okay, let's start over now. I'm bringing the book back, and this time we'll go together, and you will see and witness that I will put the book in the library."

"Oh... well..." he replied.

He brought the book back and together they headed to the room where the bookshelf was, and he saw and witnessed him placing the book on the bookshelf.

"But what does all this mean?" he asked, confused... "Look," he said. "There is a state of duality in believing. There is Allah and you. Even if you do not see Allah, you trust and believe in Him, but you do not bear witness to Him.

Faith is like believing without seeing. Allah is closer to this, that is, the understanding of servant with the idea of servant and Allah, rather than the one lost in plurality ...

Yet ... the issue is not to remain faithful, but the state of "iqan" which brings the stage of bearing witness and described in the Quran as the state of certainty ...

If one approaches Allah, then there is Allah and the servant ...

Closeness is in this sense … There is duality …

But certainty is to bear witness to Allah. The one who eventually bears witness to Allah has gone beyond the stage of faith, disappeared in Allah, existed with Him, and bears witness to Him …

When we went inside to put the book on the bookshelf, you no longer have faith that I performed this action or in the sense of believing in me because you witnessed me putting the book on the shelf. You are now a witness, and you know that I did it because you were with me …

This saying, "the unbeliever has the better of the irreligious," actually means that the one who bears witness to Allah in a consciousness even higher than the stage of faith, who knows Allah, and who is qualified as faithless in this respect, that is, the one who goes beyond the consciousness of faith can lead a non-believer to the path of Allah … This is, in fact, the basis of Islam … What do we say? "Ashadu an la ilaha illallah …"

I Bear Witness That There Is Nothing[24] But Allah

That is, "I saw," "I see" … I only see Him in everyone, everywhere. I do not exist. I exist with Him … That's why I do things with Him. In short, "I am for Him" and He is doing things with me.

How beautiful Hazrat Ali summed this up.

One day, Hazrat Ali went up to the minbar and said to the congregation, "You can ask me anything about whatever exists from the bottom of the Throne of Allah down to the earth. There is knowledge in my chest (in my heart) like a deep ocean. The Prophet of Allah (PBUH) put it into my mouth from his dignified saliva and it is still in my mouth (wisdom pours from my tongue with his abundance). I swear by Allah, who holds my spirit in His hand of power, that if I were allowed I would tell people about all the knowledge in the Torah and

---

24 Thing: Creature, god, deity

the Bible, and everyone would support me."

In the assembly where Hazrat Ali made this speech, someone who wanted to humiliate him in his own way turned to Hazrat Ali and called out, "I have a question for you!"

Hazrat Ali said, "Ask me to learn something, not to challenge me and test me."

The man said, "You forced me to do this, O Ali! Have you ever seen your Lord?" he asked.

Hazrat Ali responded, "I do not worship a Lord I have not seen!" ...

"And how did you see Him?" asked the man.

Hazrat Ali replied, "The physical eye cannot see Him, but hearts see Him with the truth of faith (with the noor (divine light) bestowed by Allah). My Lord is One and Only, He has no partner. He is One, there is no second. He is the only One without any counterparts. He may not be limited by time or space. He cannot be felt by sense organs and cannot be measured by any measure!" Upon this answer, the man fainted.

Another incident I love very much:

One day, Hazrat Ali was asked, "Did you see Allah?"

Hazrat Ali answered: "I do not prostrate to ALLAH whom I have not seen." "Well, where did you see him?" Hazrat Ali gave the magnificent answer:

"Show me where He is not..."

"I haven't seen anything before where I haven't seen Allah." (Hazrat Abu Bakr).

"Even if the veil over my eyes was lifted, my certainty would not increase." (Hazrat Ali)

Wahm refers to hypothetical reasonings. That is, the difference between wahm and intellect completely determines the direction of our perceptions and comprehension.

We said that wahm is to consider the non-existing as existing and the existing as non-existing. We use our intellects in two ways:

- The worldly/virtual/artificial manner ... The dimension lived without thinking beyond death and lived according to worldly values.

- The faithful manner ... The dimension that also thinks about beyond death and organizes life in both worlds accordingly.

The intellect in the first dimension which I call the database which is subsequently uploaded with our egos (likewise, the intellect was created just like the ego, that is, they came into existence subsequently; this bears meanings such as a kind of deterioration [as a result of the combination of the dampness in the breath with the corpse] and reduction.) The spirit is out of command, that is, it is blown and resurrected unchanged and without any creation process.... The ego is a name, that is an Asma, created from the Spirit which is an Attribute. The conditions we are in, our education, things we were taught are the intellects that are "connected" with what we perceive with our five senses and guide us with our "worldly - that is, our physical dimension."

In fact, I explained this several times in my articles using the following example:

imagine a child born in 2014. Starting from the womb, this child is planned according to the conditions of the world in 2014 ...

From what they were fed from birth to their education "uploaded" to their comprehension through parents, friends, or teachers, everything that is currently accepted in the world has become the teachings "read" by their brains in their consciousness ...

Just like the difference between the child from an environment conditioned that "singing is bad" fifty years ago and the child conditioned with perceptions that "being a singer is the best profession"."The connected intellects" only enable us to build "a virtual world" with worldly values and with our senses and perceptions.

We all see the world from this window that we look through.

However, as it can be seen that everyone has different conditionings based on their "versions," these brains that are condemned to live with "so-called truths" will be far from reaching the "essential truths" and experiencing the true life.

Most succinctly, I can give an example as follows: our minds that we constrain with certain patterns can tell us what to do day and night without our awareness.

There is day and night, right? Yes, it is for this worldly measure and judgment. But how valid are worldly evaluations? Like everything else, there is a world that updates and changes itself. Yes, some measures are scientifically accepted, but then there are things that are not scientifically determined, right? There are too many of them … The smallest part of matter is an atom; this was once in force but now there are quarks, and they even advanced further and claim that there is no matter … So?

If even day and night lose their validity after leaving the atmosphere and leave their place to eternal darkness, then "eternal" lives cannot be earned even if "limited" lives are earned through these conditionings.

One day when I was thinking about all this, I saw this verse written at the entrance of a cemetery: "Every ego will taste death …" (Surah al-Ankabut, Verse 57).

This verse written on a plaque at the entrance of cemeteries actually says that we are "immortals."

However, the failure to sufficiently think about this verse leads to the failure to understand the deeper meaning in it and thus, conditioned us by the incomprehension that we are nothing beyond a bodily reality.

It was the body that died, but not consciousness, that is, the spirit. The ego experiences nothing more than a taste of a momentary feeling of death …

Why? What do we do when we eat a meal; first we "taste …" "To taste" food is one thing, "eating" is another thing.

When we taste something, there is a message of "eating a small piece." However, saying, "I ate my food" is very different, it means I ate the whole meal …

Here, it is also quite explicit and clear that Allah has chosen every word in the Quran very carefully, we will only "taste" death …

Or would Allah not say that every ego "will die"?

We were going to taste it. So actually, there was no such thing as death. Just as we have tasted this world for a moment, we will taste the feeling of death for a moment before we proceed to eternal life. Therefore, I should awaken as soon as possible to recognize and mature my spirit and essence, which is my mount in eternal life, without thinking I am limited to my ship in this limited life, my body.

The whole issue was actually in my brain …

My perceptions, thoughts, my imagination made me and each person another realm in the realms.

Just as there is a world outside of us, a space-time, each of us contains a separate world, a realm within us.

The Lord of the Worlds is also the Lord of the realm that I envision in my brain …

The issue was that; what I envision in my brain is not the same as what the person closest to me envisions in their brain.

Yes, we are all spectators in a movie theater, watching life as if watching a movie, but the point is that each of us has another life in our brains that we only see and live in that general universal film.

And when I actually see so much brutality and cruelty in the world and people just sometimes give up evil because of the fear of death, I admit that I say, "Fortunately, human beings don't know that they are immortal".

Anyway … let's get back to our topic.

There are three factors that influence the formation of human intellect.

•Ego.

•Sensual desires and wishes, bodily needs.

•Conditionings and learnings.

I think we more or less have an understanding of the conditionings and learnings. Let's now get down to bodily desires and wishes.

Eating, drinking, traveling, sleeping, sexuality, and anything that makes us think we only consist of the BODY ... Materialism ... The idea that we are bodies, that we are mortals, and that life ends with our death ...

Our ego is our feeling of "self." The idea of "I" is the ego ...

One will either follow the path of one's intellect or one's delusion, that is, their hypothesis, in which there are also ideas that come from jinni and demonic influences. You must overcome them with your will and intellect; otherwise, they will divert you from your path.

The subject of "ego" is very sensitive. With the verse above, "Every ego will taste death," it has been revealed that the ego is not actually the body, because the body dies, but the ego will only taste that feeling of death instantly.

Misunderstanding of the ego poses many problems. I will go into the topic of the LORD so that the subject of the ego is understood.

Likewise, our Prophet said (in some sources, there is a narration that was said by Hazrat Ali) "Man arafa nafsahu, faqad arafa Rabbahu."

Here again, the word "arafa" has been purposely chosen. Because "arafa" is used to mean "to know, to recognize."

There are stages of ego in Sufism, surely you have heard ... (Nafs al-ammara (the commanding ego), nafs al-lawwama (the accusing ego), nafs al-mulhama (the inspired ego), nafs al-mutma'inna (the peaceful ego), nafs al-radiyya (the pleased ego), nafs al-mardiyya (the pleasing ego), and nafs al-safiyya (the purified and perfect ego)).

And there is the acquittal of ego, which means cleansing the ego. Sculpting the ego on the verge of the divine truth ...

There are such words among people:

For example, when you smell the aroma of food, they immediately say, "Do not torture your ego, take a bite if you want to ..."

For those who might be very fond of certain worldly pleasures (eating, money, etc.), they say, for instance, "Their ego is quite high!.."

The expression "torturing the ego" is also misunderstood like other concepts …Since torture is to leave in the dark, it means to leave the ego in the dark. And to torture the ego is to do what the ego, which is our "divine truth," wants in the worldly direction … The word torture also refers to "putting something out of its place." This is either by reducing or increasing it, or deviating from its time or place. Even milk drank outside of its time can be described with the word "torture" (Al Mufradat). We have to struggle for the world process to return to the "essential" of our divine truth … This is a process that we must go through by turning towards the compassionate and doing what it does not want (in a worldly sense) … "The disciplined ego is "brilliant", says Cemal Nur Sargut …

And as Shams said:

"Be one of those who know their ego, not one of those who erase it …" But how? What does it mean "whoever knows their ego knows their Lord …?"

If we don't understand this, it's really difficult to try to keep our intellects from drifting to delusional influences.

If the one who knows their ego knows their Lord, let us examine what is the concept of the LORD…

THE LORD

Fihi Ma Fih ... "In It What Is in It ..."

Up to now, I have met many people who failed to comprehend the matter of the LORD although they are neither religiously ignorant nor view themselves as quite knowledgeable. As a person who did not have a grasp of this subject for many years, after really starting to understand it from the edge, it was very painful for me to see my own ignorance and to realize once again that we do not know Allah.

This issue is a subject that needs to be understood correctly, and if it is understood, it is a subject that can change your life. Because the most effective element in the formation of our "particular mind" that we mentioned in the above section is what we call "the ego" and it is the one that turns our lives into heaven or hell ...

We may be one step closer to understanding why and how things come and how they will be resolved if we can truly comprehend the subjects of "ego" and "Lord" even a little after reading what I will say below InshaAllah.

After you start to grasp these issues even from the edge, you can start to perceive that you, your loved ones, or those around you, and even the ones you have recently met are exposed to such issues from what they tell you about themselves or their problems, even without knowing them ...

Everything that you see and do not see is merely a version of the meanings of Allah's names and attributes brought to the realm of existence and dressed in a body.

In short, whom will you complain about and to whom will you complain? In a sense, this is the statement you read in translations saying, "Everything is Him and He encompasses everything."

Whether a saint or a thief, everyone you encounter is nothing but the manifestation (coming into existence) of the certain names of Allah.

The difference is there; they are from Allah, but not Allah. I will go into further detail about this below. Try to grasp what I am going to tell you, and after this truth, you will begin to see how you should think about your spouses, mothers-in-law, fathers, bosses, jobs, children, and all sorts of other issues that you have complained about in your lives. Once you understand the way of thinking, once you realize that what you have encountered and believed you are exposed to is the teachings about yourself, you will find that the way to deal with these lessons will result in defeating yourself, not the other person.

As long as we think that we (I) exist and there are others, neither will our tests end nor can we solve them. We encounter the same kinds of people and events under many different names until we realize what the real issue is.

"And there was only Allah. There was nothing but Him."

In recent years, we often hear or read the words of world-renowned physics professors and scientists: "We are all one …" "We are all ONE."

"The universe is an illusion, a dream …"

"A universe from nothing …" "A universe created-formed from nothing."

"Only one consciousness …" "There is only ONE consciousness, mind, INTELLECT." Such matters are now well expressed and accepted as a result of international scientific research. The problem is that those interested in these matters do not even realize that what Islam said hundreds of years ago has only just been scientifically expressed because they have not met the truth of Islam (if they know, then they are "covering" this truth).

For those who are not able to take Islam beyond worship, these matters are very distant from them.

When people I know and meet begin to talk about such matters and statements on the universe, they look at me in amazement when I say, "These are already available in the Quran, our Prophet said these."

While everyone is polarized and blames each other, they actually do nothing but attribute what they cannot see, because of their own ignorance.

That is why, whether claiming to be religious or not, we all need to get out of our own minds and take a step to get wise with the "ONE TRUE INTELLECT," that is, the intellect of Allah. Otherwise, we would not have done anything but destroy our own lives and eternity.

When I received an offer to write this book, I initially wanted the author of the book to be unknown for this reason; because I think that the knowledge that is so important can be inevitably ignored because of the judgments that each of you will make with your particular intellects. Not because of reservations.

Because you begin to think with certain stereotypes such as woman, or man, young, or old, learned, or unlearned, famous, or unknown, and because you fall into the traps of your ego, that is, your particular intellect, it tries to prevent you from gaining knowledge through deceptive thoughts ... I don't know how this happens. Because I went through the same phases about others, which I can still pass from time to time, albeit momentarily ...

Put aside what you think of people and concentrate only on the knowledge. If that knowledge seems meaningless to you, then you have found it meaningless with an unbiased view, and I support this.

But if you fall into your own trap and fall into other ideas, remember that the ego and the devil are already deceiving people with ideas.

This discrimination among people is due to the words of the devil, "I will not prostrate to him," which is his greatest sin causing him to be expelled from Heaven. Allah commanded all the angels to prostrate to Adam. However, Satan did not adhere to this, and because of his arrogance and deceit, he took the name "devil" that day.

One of the lessons given to us here is this:

We become devilish and fall into the duality called shirk as long as we see everybody as beings apart from Allah just like Satan saw Adam.

However, the matter is the existence of Allah, who is the One and Only, in the universe. Our Prophet and our Book described these so beautifully and intelligently; no one who newly understands these matters should think of themselves as inventors ...

Everything has already been said, those who newly understand it can only be explorers, recently discovering what has been in existence since pre-eternity.

Everything has already been created, those who recently discovered it are not the creators of that thing, but only the means to bring it to the earth ...

We all came into existence from nothing ... Our only existence is our nothingness. Because everything is the embodiment of His names ... "There was Allah and there was nothing with Him!" (Hazrat Muhammad [PBUH]).

What is the Lord?

In Verses 30 and 31 of Surah Al-Baqarah, it is said that Allah taught Adam all of His names, and this is the characteristic that will make Adam the highest of all created things, the "Caliph."

We mentioned the saying about the ego that exists in all of us, "Whoever knows their ego knows their Lord," to help you to understand your Lord by knowing your ego.

So, what is the Lord?

First of all, we need to pay attention to the following while examining the Quran. There is a very important matter that I think people who are interested in the Quran are overlooking, just as I did for years.

I must say that I really struggled with being as clear as possible here. Because the knowledge of Allah is such sensitive knowledge that trying to explain some things to someone who does not know the "details" of this knowledge without using Sufi terms, but by continuing to follow the rules is really like the edge of a knife.

The biggest reason I want to do this is because there are no books and dictionaries left that I have not consulted throughout the years to understand Sufi terms. However, people who find it difficult to learn those terms are missing the truth of the Quran, as I have missed it for years, and therefore cannot live their lives in the way that they wish to do so, they waste it in pursuit of meaningless things. Again, the same as I have done for years. Therefore, I wanted to try to write in a language that the current generation and those who do not examine these matters much can understand and in parallel with the scientific elements.

Allah knows the truth of everything. This is called Allahu Alam. My aim here is to say that we generally do not have the time to turn to any other way except "wishing for a resolution to our troubles in the world". In fact, our only savior is Allah, who is our everything, and to be able to address certain information regarding His prophet Hazrat Muhammad (PBUH) and His Book, the Quran.

Yes, let's go back to our topic and try to fix a big misunderstanding and misusage.

In the Quran verses, besides the rank of "Allah" (unseen-witnessed) indicated by the name of Allah, sometimes the names ar-Rahman (the Merciful), al-Haqq (the Truth), and ar-Rabb (the Lord) which are the names and attributes of Allah, and which express different manifestations of Allah are also mentioned.

However, Allah, the absolute Creator, is One and Only. Then why are His different names used in various verses in the Quran?

One of the many reasons for this is that Allah addresses us from His various ranks and that we can get answers quicker if we call on the name of His responsible rank in the events we encounter. (Because, as we have already stated, the name "Allah" does not come to the Earth … The universe is the reflection of His name, the Truth (the Muhammadan Light) …

Let there be no misunderstanding … Think of it this way, there is the sultan and his ranks fulfilling his orders in his presence. Let's say he has a grand vizier, qadis, muftis, and navy commanders. They are only the sultan's ranks fulfilling the commands of the sultan. They do not have their own existence. But, regarding any incident in the neighborhood, you apply to the being who is affiliated with him under his command, whose essence is him, and who is at that rank, not the sultan himself; and that is the qadi, right?

It is said, "Approach Allah with His beautiful names." In many books, I see that the beautiful names of Allah are listed only for the purpose of glorification rather than leading to an understanding.

"I was a hidden treasure. I wanted to be known …"

If we try to understand why these names were given to us while counting the names of Allah, we can understand the mechanism of the universe better.

Saying, "Allah is as-Sami (the All-Hearer), al-Baseer (the All-Seeing), and al-Qayyum (the Sustainer)" only brings us to absolve and glorify Him. Yet, Allah showed the angels, who said, "Why do you create Adam? We are absolving and glorifying you," Adam's counting the names is evidence when he said, "I know what you don't know."

We cannot praise Allah properly; we do not have the capacity … But there must be something beyond our praise, and the statement of " the angels glorifying and absolving" in the verse indicates that it is not enough to just try to praise Allah …

Beyond his glorification, Allah wills Adam whom He made superior to the angels to try to understand and know Him and to do this through knowledge; otherwise, would He say, "And Allah taught Adam the names"? In order to understand Islam in the real sense, don't we need to understand the SCIENCE in everything that has been created?

I get this from this message, and there is certainly more to it, because Allah's words do not end, and new beauties are understood like the first leaf of a bud opening at every comprehension.

That is why, while Allah lists His names in the Quran, does He not give us confidence, as He says, "Are you crying? Do not be afraid. I hear you. Because I am the All-Hearing, I hear everything, do not worry, I am with you ..."?

One day, one of my friends who was struggling to believe in a verse saying, "He sees everything" in the Quran asked, "Huh, so why is there always praise?"

May Allah be pleased with him, because he had really been a trigger for me to develop this understanding. Why were these names constantly counted?

I thought about it over and over, and one day while I was reading the Quran it dawned upon me:

When we get stuck, we want someone to lean on, right? We want someone to help us. We want to rest our heads on someone's shoulders. In fact, we basically want to be protected and taken care of in every relationship, we want to lean on that person and hope that they will take care of our troubles for us.

Yes. Actually, my Allah was doing this ...

"Do not be afraid. I see everything properly, My servant. I will take care of it. Trust Me because I have the power to do everything. Do not lose your hope, I am here. Even if you think that I don't see, I see what you are going through. Because I see everything and surround it with My knowledge. Your financial difficulties will be solved because I am the sole owner of property. Then, ask Me ..."

"Your responsibility belongs to me. You trust Me, trust Me completely because I am the All-Powerful ..."

"If your mother's love for you is a drop in the ocean, I love you as much as an unlimited ocean. So, feel how much I think about you, how much I love you, how much compassion I have for you, and trust

Me..."

When I lost my father, I felt broken.

One day my Allah sent me something I wanted so much that I never thought that it would happen, and that day I realized that my Allah was so rich. I didn't need anyone but Him.

I can humbly tell you this, from my own experiences. The fact that the matter of FAITH is so important is because He only wants TRUST from us. That's all. And that is again just for us.

With the characteristics of a mother struggling for her child the name Hannan (the Clement), Allah who is the embodiment of the name "Hannan" again invites us to reach Him only for our sakes.

Now, let's get back to our topic. The matter of Allah's characterization of Himself with different names and at different ranks ...

For example, Mansoor Hallaj said "l Ana al-Haqq (I am the Truth)." Many of us know this story, and we have already touched on it. What has he been through because of saying this? Those who could not comprehend what he really meant tortured him, and they did so in the name of "religion!"

Look carefully, he says, "I am the Truth!" But, this does not mean, "I am Allah." Why is that? Well, how much do we comprehend the main statement here without getting the message in the statements that we think are all the same?

What did we understand when Mansoor Hallaj meant to say "What you see in me is nothing but the names of Allah? His name of al-Haqq (the Truth). I already do not exist."

Or when Jibril (Gabriel) comes to Hazrat Meryem (Mary) to breathe his breath, Meryem (Mary) says to him, "I take refuge in the Most Compassionate from you." Why? Why does she take refuge in the name of Allah, "the Most Compassionate", but not in the name "Allah"?

These are topics that really require very long and detailed explanations.

I would like to mention them in our other books InshaAllah, but now that our topic is Allah's name the LORD and since the concept of the LORD is related to our ego, let's return to this subject firstly to know ourselves so that we can get to know Allah afterwards.

Surah Yusuf, Verse 39: Yusuf (Joseph) said: "O my fellow prisoners! Which is far better: many different lords or Allah—the One, the Supreme?

Here, Hazrat Yusuf (Joseph) talks about "lords who are different from each other" and says, "Is Allah, the one who annihilates all these lords better, or are the lords who are different from each other better?

Now, if you have noticed, he calls out to his fellow prisoners, that is, there is a "conviction" in this verse and there is an attempt to explain the means to get rid of this conviction.

Let's continue with an example. The Quran mentions pharaohs: "Yes, they lived once, didn't they?" Do not say so! Do not exclude yourself from the Quran again; otherwise, you will not be able to insert yourself and attain the hidden treasure. In the Quran, every name, every tribe, devil, angel, and prophet used in stories, is actually mentioning us. It guides us.

I have always tried to keep this in mind while reading since the day I learned it from Ibn Arabi (he explained it in one of his articles, which I read); otherwise, I would have thought of the Quran as a poetic book of stories which does not concern me and has no benefit in it for me, just as many ignorant eyes view it as such.

What beautiful and poetic words uttered by Rumi: "Even if a person remains in the world, he is both the pharaoh and Musa (Moses) ..."

Now, in Surah an-Nazi'at, Verse 24, the self within us calls out to us:

"(And the pharaoh said) I am your most exalted Lord ... "

Here is some crucial information to keep in mind; almost no rebel in history who is said to have rebelled against Allah claimed to have the power to create, to have created the earth and the heavens, etc.

Because if the rebel said that everyone would agree that this person is crazy anyway.

No. Almost everyone in history, including the pharaohs who rebelled against Allah, knew that they were not the creators. So, the one thing to remember here is that the pharaohs didn't claim to have created everything, etc.

The pharaohs and such rebels claimed that they were not creators, but that people should only obey their "kingdoms", that is, their "ruling" (as the owners of the property), and therefore, only follow their commands.

The word god means the one WORSHIPED. However, unfortunately, the failure to fully understand the word "worship" also led to discrimination.

I researched the centuries-old origins of the word 'worship'. I have even researched as far back as millenniums. And what I have found is that the meaning of the word 'worship' is used in almost every society as a synonym for "to work, to serve; slavery, servitude; to cultivate; obedient slave; to serve Allah; servitude to Allah …"

I mean, even if a person claims to be an atheist, they still worship Allah without knowing it. Because first of all, that person is NON-EXISTENT … They think of the names of Allah manifested in them as their individual selves and think that THEY exist. However, there is no me or you, but only Him. The atheist cannot comprehend this, maybe they don't want to admit it out of arrogance.

They cannot even control the breath they take; they are not in control of anything including their own existence. They are slaves to Allah by working in and serving Allah's system and His servants, that is, by working for and serving Allah even if they do not understand or want to understand this, and by existing in the world beyond their control.

Everything actually happens in comprehension. When people progress in comprehension, they move forward in life, and not remain standing in one place … It is said that when a person travels to their essence, which is the longest journey, it is as if they walked around the universe. Because everything is happening in the human brain, comprehension, i.e., within.

When we say, "I cannot worship or I do not worship, I do not believe, etc. ..." we are not aware that we are actually worshiping Allah anyway.

How helpless we are.

However, Allah says, "Leave it to me. Surrender. You're already Mine. Surrender." So?

What does SURRENDER mean?

This word, which comes from the Arabic root SLM, means ISLAM.

One day, when my friends from abroad asked me "What is your religion?" I responded, "I am one of those who surrender. I am one of those who try to reach Allah on that path," as I knew that their minds might have associated Islam with "Islamic terror" because of the manipulative incidents and pictures shown to them.

They gave me confused looks. "Surrender?" they asked. I replied, "I am one who surrenders to Allah". My Prophet Hazrat Muhammad (PBUH) and all the other prophets are also in my love and respect.

"How's that? Then, you are a Muslim!" they asked.

I responded, "Muslim means one who surrenders to Allah and attains salvation, peace, and redemption. Yes, I am the one making an effort on the path to be a Muslim, to surrender to Allah. But in your minds, you have a concept of Islam manipulated by the conditioning of the pictures shown to you, and this is done deliberately. I continued to say, "I am a traveler of Allah who tries to be a true member of Islam, not a member of the ISLAM, that you have in your minds because of your lack of knowledge on this subject."

We think of worship only as salah, fasting, and pilgrimage, but they are the obligations that are required to comprehend Islam, also for belief and faith, and that are invaluable if only we know the treasures they contain. In other words, even if a person does not comprehend Islam and is not subject to it, in a sense, they continue their compulsory servitude of Allah. Hence, a person is a servant, a slave, who needs breath, and yet is too helpless to even have control of a single breath they take. A person neither has the might nor the power to command the food they eat to go to their kidneys, not the stomach, and to make the water they drink go to the heart.

People are under the impression that they do not have an understanding of "servitude" and do not worship only because of their own lack of and limited understanding.

Every servant is in compulsory worship and servitude. In addition to this, Allah wants the servant to serve voluntarily for their own life and salvation, for the reasons I will explain in the following chapters. Therefore, He recommends Islam and asks people to believe.

"In voluntary servitude, there is love and affection for the Creator. Servitude refers to the most advanced degree of love nurtured towards the being that is served."(Surah Al-Baqarah, Verse 165).

The concept that we call pharaoh is the ego that wants to be obeyed and claims and ASSUMES that it is the only one with the authority. Pharaoh claims that he is a deity, in other words, that he is to be worshiped (as an idol) and served, but not that he is a creator. And he wants to have authority in the property of the body granted to human beings.

Since we do not properly know the name Allah and do not try to understand the religion of Islam knowingly, we make sentences like "There is a creator, yes, but I do not believe in religion ..." or one that I have heard a lot: "Yes, we are all a part of Allah. Allah is the universe, etc."

Here is the real problem, I think, and because I did not understand it for years, I had to suffer and burn severely for I was deprived of such a truth for so long. If I had known this reality much earlier, I would have experienced long before how Allah made it easier for us in both lives (this world & the hereafter).

Our Prophet is the person and prophet with the HIGHEST comprehension of Allah and His every rank. He is "Salamun qawlan min rabbin raheem" (Surah Ya-Sin, Verse 58). The main reason why the word Islam is so important comes from its connection with the word "Salam (peace, greetings)". Our Prophet is the one who brings us the Salam, that is, the news of Allah, in this realm created for the sake of the rosy face of our Prophet. There is a meaning in this verse, "O Muhammad, you are the greeting of your Lord to these worlds ... Allah contacted His people through you." Therefore, anyone contacting the Prophet contacts Allah. He is Allah's greeting to us. Such a magnificent truth and beauty is my Prophet. Don't mind them and say "Salam!" They will know the truth soon! (Surah Zukhruf, Verse 89).

Isn't that why there is no other religion, namely the way, other than ISLAM, in this universe whose existence is based on our Prophet, who is Allah's greetings to the worlds? While everybody is the manifestation, image of our Prophet, and he is the manifestation, image of Allah in the mirror, what else do the people who carry the names of Allah do other than greet each other and carry the greetings of Allah? Islam is not that, but what? Everyone bows to each other in the Kaaba ... In that beautiful house, which is the manifestation of the divine essence, just like in the heart. They are the names that originate from the attributes of Allah alone, which remain with everyone when their bodies and souls are stripped. In this case, is not the one who sees anything else the devil? In this case, what happens to a person, who sees something else, other than being expelled from heaven?

Allah says that He will fit into the heart of His believing servant ... That heart is the place where Allah, who describes Himself as "the light of the earth and the heavens", reflects in His humble servant with His light ...

Some of us continue to misunderstand the saying that there is no difference among prophets. Yes, there is no difference among them in aspects such as being chosen by Allah and made free from sins, but there is a difference in "comprehension and experience". Because they each also represent the rising ranks and stations of Islamic understanding in order to mature the Islamic understanding that started with Hazrat Adam. In the Quran, there are examples and accounts of incidents related to every prophet starting from Adam for them to mediate in explaining the degrees of comprehension each servant will go through.

And the Prophet of Allah (PBUH), who is the last prophet, is the highest of all prophets and servants in knowing, comprehending, and loving Allah.

And yet let's not forget that the day we realize that we cannot fully comprehend Allah, we begin to proceed in comprehending Allah. This is impossible in our capacity. For this reason, we say "Al-Hamdu-lillah (li Allah)", that is, "Praise belongs to Allah" and "Laa uhsiy sana-an alaiyka anta kama asnayta ala nafsika," as our Prophet said.

This means: "It is not possible for me to eulogize[25] You; it is not possible for me to glorify You. My Allah, I eulogize and glorify You however You glorify and eulogize Yourself ..."

Surah ash-Shuraa, Verse 11: "There is nothing like Him." (Station of Transcendence.) Hamd (Praise) is the highest form of eulogizing and glorifying. You praise both in joy and sorrow. Gratitude is in times of blessing and is not continuous (Imam Rabbani).

In order to evaluate the painting of a painter, it is necessary to be at least as knowledgeable about painting and its techniques. Otherwise, this cannot go beyond an ignorant comment. Allah is the owner of unlimited knowledge, power, mercy, art, and beauty ...

Basically, none of us can glorify Him, this is impossible. For this reason, we say "Praise belongs to you, my Allah ..."

Since Our Prophet has the highest comprehension of all people and prophets, he is the prophet of all creatures who knows this best. He had a comprehension and integrated lifestyle, by Allah's leave,

---

25 Eulogize: To praise, to glorify. Praise and glory be to Allah who sends all blessings whether seen, unseen, known, or unknown, who shows us the path to salvation, and who honored us by allowing us to be from the ummah of Muhammad (PBUH) whom He loved very much (Imam Rabbani).

into the Muhammedan understanding with all ranks starting with the transcendence of Hazrat Musa (Moses), the immanence of Hazrat Isa (Jesus), and the divine unity of Hazrat Ibrahim (Abraham) …

Actually, the statement, "We are all a part of Allah" which many people speak unknowingly, should be considered as follows:

• The essence of Allah and His essential attributes[26] (These attributes belong only to Allah. He has not bestowed upon His servant …)

• The names of Allah and affirmatory (fixed, permanent) attributes[27] of Allah that He has limitedly bestowed onto His servant. (The features bestowed by Allah, similar to which are found in His other creatures, but exist in Allah in an infinite and perfect degree).

Our Prophet emphasizes the Oneness of Allah and says: "Do not contemplate (do not think) about the essence of Allah, you will fall into sin."

Here he says: The essence of Allah is not a power that any of us can comprehend. We are beings of limited comprehension, and His essence is far beyond our comprehension.

Then he continues: "You contemplate the creatures of Allah (that is, the beings that are mirrors of His names and attributes)."

This is where we make a mistake. Surah Ikhlas also mentions the indivisible ONENESS of Allah. Then, it continues by explaining the matter of tawhid (Oneness), that is, His attributes and names, His creatures are a reflection of ONENESS. To understand this matter is

---

26 The essential attributes of Allah: a) Wujud: existence; Allah exists, and His absence is unthinkable. b) Qidaam: The existence of Allah has no beginning. c) Baqa: eternity, having no end. d) Wahdaniyyah: oneness and having no equal. e) Mukhalafth-un lil hawadith: He does not resemble His creatures. f) Qiyam bi nafseehee: Allah does not need anything. Everything needs Him.

27 The affirmatory attributes of Allah: a) Hayah (Life): Allah is always alive. b) Ilm (Knowledge): To know; Allah knows the past and the future, everything that is hidden and apparent. c) Sami' (Hearing): To hear; Allah hears everything. d) Basar (Sight): To see; Allah sees everything. e) Irada (Will): Allah wills, and He does whatever He wills. f) Qudrah (Power): To have power; Allah has infinite power. g) Kalam (Speech): To speak; Allah owns words. He announced to His prophets. The Quran is the word of Allah. h) Takwin (Creation): To create, Allah is the creator. He created everything in the universe …

so important for Islam that anyone who fails to understand this makes the mistake of saying "We are part of Allah.".

Hazrat Ibrahim (Abraham), Hazrat Musa (Moses), Hazrat Isa (Jesus), and Hazrat Muhammad (PBUH) are narrated to us using numerous stories to explain these matters to us in comprehension by gradually ascending the ranks. The understanding of tawhid (Oneness) begins with Hazrat Ibrahim (Abraham), Hazrat Musa (Moses) represents transcendence (the existence of Allah that we cannot comprehend), Hazrat Isa (Jesus) represents immanence (the manifestations of Allah that we see everywhere and in every existence), and it is accomplished in the Prophet with a spectacular comprehension by adding on all these listed, that is, both the stages of transcendence and immanence, as well as Oneness.

When our Prophet asked what Islam is, it is stated that he received answers such as "salah, fasting, and zakat" and confirmed them, but said, "Islam is first of all Oneness".

That is to say, when we say, "We are a part of Allah," we mean that we are mirrors not to Allah's transcendent and indivisible essence, but to His names and attributes; by doing so, we basically say: "The meanings of Allah's names and attributes have come into being in us."

In a sense, when we say that Allah taught Adam His names, we can understand that Allah said to Adam that everything that exists in the universe is the embodiment of the meanings of the names and attributes that He "wanted to be known with".

Allah, who is One, has become apparent (visible) in the realm of existence by the embodiment of different characteristics with the meanings of His names and attributes in each of us. As if He has a unitary existence, we think our own existence, which originates from Him, belongs to us.

"Open your eyes! Whoever is in the heavens and whoever is on the earth belongs to Allah. Even those who worship other than Allah; they do not follow what they associate with Allah, but follow their assumption. And they do not say anything but lies." (Surah Yunus, Verse 66).

In many other verses of the Quran, avoidance of ASSUMPTION is mentioned for various reasons. (When I try to explain the tawhid and the situation that covers this matter in the chapters on the universe, its creation, and its characteristics, we will see together that the scientific data recently discovered are the same as what the Quran describes).

This rank where Allah becomes known to His creatures through the meanings of His attributes and names, that is, the rank where He descends to the realm of existence (which we also call the realm of witnessing, that is, seeing, being ready) is called the rank of lordship.

It is impossible to think and comprehend the essence of Allah and His essence may not be known as a characteristic. And we must not forget the hadith of our Prophet and understand it correctly[28].

Now, in light of this information, let us come to the name LORD to the rank of lordship.

The second most commonly used name in the Quran is Lord, the most commonly used being Allah...

In addition to the meanings such as "to discipline; tutor," the name Lord "religiously" refers to "the one who creates and encompasses the whole world" as well as many other meanings such as "the one who is responsible for you, who educates you, who helps you, who guides you and who disciplines you." And when it is said the Lordship (rank) manifesting from His divine essence, it is understood that it is not only the state of disciplining and possessing but also Allah who is the only power that has everything.

In everything we see in the universe, what we see is the meanings of the names of Allah (also called the shadow) that became apparent and

28 The word "hadith" in Arabic originates from the root "h-d-s." Etymologically, it means "new as the opposite of old; adventitious; recently occurred." By word meaning, hadith is "what is subsequently generated," and news may be referred to as a "hadith." Hadiths are divided into two as Nabawi and Qudsi. In addition to its meaning "saying," it also refers to incidents, happenings, news, artworks, and short stories about our Prophet in Arabic. These meanings are used interchangeably. In the Quran, it is mentioned in 28 places in various derivatives such as "hadith" and "ahadith," and there are known to be 40 authentic hadiths.

took shape. In Sufism, it is also expressed as the meaning of the names wearing a garment.

It is said that Hazrat Muhammad (PBUH) was the first prophet to say that the existence of the human is also based on Allah's names and attributes ...

The meanings of the names that we know as the beautiful names of Allah exist in every single unit, and by intensifying, these names unveils the creature called the human.

In recent years, together with the quantum, scientists have proven that everything we see is actually one thing, that everything depends on unity in oneness, and that it comes into being out of nothing, that is, probably without knowing, they have scientifically proven the understanding of TAWHID (wahdanniyah; oneness) in Islam. Our Prophet stated that this world we see is a "dream". Scientists have now accepted this fact. It has been scientifically proven that everything we see is an illusion and a dream.

Can we say that our Prophet's prayer, "O my Lord, show me the truth of things (In Arabic, ASHYA is plural of THING)," means that the truth of everything in the universe, including us, is the meaning of the names of Allah and we are advised to pray to learn this truth?

Everything we see, everything we think comes into existence through the meanings of the names of Allah called "Asma." Asma means names. "Husna" means beautiful. All the names of Allah are beautiful. Because they all exist by their opposites, and all of them are put into action for different purposes and form this magnificent universe.

The distinction between good and bad, the difference between good and evil is in question for those of us with a subjective view, who cannot see the whole and look at it with the ego.

How well Ibn al-Arabi describes it.

We cannot know the existence that Allah does not want to be known anyway, but the existence and names, which Allah stated as "I wanted to be known," wanted a body of their own ... They wanted to see themselves ...

They say, why did Allah create us? Did He need our worships?

Let us listen to this with quotations from my dear Ibn Arabi ...

There are two types of manifestations of Allah:

• Unseen manifestation

• Visible manifestation

The unseen manifestation (the ESSENCE specified as HU/HUWA) is the manifestation that we cannot imagine, we can only "feel" Him ... We know that He is with us at every moment, He embraces us ... Such a wonderful feeling.

The unseen manifestation, on the other hand, is the manifestation of His attributes that He shares with His people and the reflections of His beautiful names and attributes.

In the pre-eternity, Allah places a name (or a few names of His as Essence, as in Himself) in each of His servants from His unseen manifestation into the heart of every human being as limited with a certain capability. That name is you. So, that name wanted to wear a garment and see itself and Allah predestined this to that name. That name is buried in the earth of your body, it is waiting for you to become a diamond deep in your heart, to be discovered, and to bring you to Allah ...

In fact, Hazrat Pir describes this as follows:

Names want a body suit. They first go to the name al-Qadir (the All-Powerful) and say, "Give us an image of existence..." The name al-Qadir says that it is not capable of this, and recommends that they go to the name al-Irada (the Will), and maybe it can help. They gather and go to the name al-Irada. The name al-Irada says it does not have the power to do it alone and then refers them to the name Allah where all the names are united ... And when the names go to the name Allah, they say, "Let us move away from you and attain the ability to love you." And with the generosity of Allah Almighty, each of them is given this chance and a separate garment and image.

As each name gets a garment, they begin to tell the discrepancies of each other to their faces. Because every name has its opposite. Then, chaos and quarrel broke out among all the names. Thereupon, Allah, the Most Glorious sends Hazrat Muhammed (PBUH) ... Hazrat Muhammed is the cleanest mirror Allah has ever looked at. His heart reflects all of the names of Allah as gathered and in the most mature state as in Allah.

Mehmet Ali Bulut stated in his magnificent book titled Decipherment of the Spirit that it should be contemplated whether the prophets and the friends of Allah mentioned in the book, all those superior people are free from sin because Allah willed so, or because they defeated their egos with the contribution of their wills and revealed the names on the path to Allah; this statement increased my love and respect for all prophets, particularly our Prophet, and the friends of Allah ... Love including will and remaining attached to Allah and His love in selections at all times is, above all, a respected and admired struggle with the ego ...Yes, when Allah sent our Prophet, all the names gathered in him in harmony with their opposites, and thus, each name sees its beautiful state in him; then, Ease, Peace, and Islam among the names begins ... Each name learns to see only the manifestation of Allah in each other ... As long as your heart makes an effort to reveal the truth of the name bestowed upon you from the unseen realm of Allah as in Allah and not as in the worldly side of your ego, that essential manifestation revealed takes all other tribes within you under its control. And as your heart converts into an inner heart, this divine light that manifests in the mirror of your inner heart ensures your enlightenment and your entire body and all your organs (names) enter into the control of the essential manifestation in your heart ...

Although you came as Adam (Spirit), Eve is created from you. Your ego is created from your spirit. You become a Creature from the Truth ... Your names become visible from His attributes. When the murshid al-kamil (the perfect teacher) gives you "breath" with the Muhammedan light, your heart just in the middle of the body, that is, the Moon of your body world divides into two. The divine light of the sun hits the Moon and while you think your ego is the owner of everything, Eve (ego/whim) returns to Adam (Spirit), that is, to the attributes from which the name came about, and the separated Adam and Eve are reunited in you. So, ARAFAT is this comprehension. The day on which you come to this eternal truth is the eve of the day before your eid. Your ego attains "nothingness" in your spirit, and Rahman (Compassion) (attribute) covers the Throne of Allah, that is the heart.

Unless we reach this level of comprehension, we handle the treasure bestowed on us in our dirty mirror of the heart and in line with our egos, and thus, we become incapable of voluntarily reaching Allah. As long as we rule the names given to us not by the morality of Allah, but by the morality of our egos, we will be the fire to our torment. This is why our Prophet came to "complete the righteous morality", that is, to direct us to the morality of Allah ...

Our ego is a property of the body that has become apparent from the attributes of Allah. Those attributes belong to the essence of Allah, they are from the Essence (HU). In other words, we think that we found existence separate from Allah when we were not separate from Allah. The devil can only deceive Eve, the ego, but not the Spirit, that is, Adam. That is why our Lord, who directs us to our own name, continues to give us opportunities to reach Him in ourselves and from there to Allah while educating us with the manifestations of other names.

We, on the other hand, continue to live with those whom we call "my sibling, my parent, my spouse, my boss, my in-laws," unaware of our beautiful name that actually disciplines us and that will take us back to Allah once we find and understand it ...

We are just mirrors. We are not the same as our names. Islam is the journey to find our origins in the box of the body, and the journey of returning to our origins.

You know yourself as a friend of Allah whose name has disappeared in the name of Allah, and by His means, you will return your name to Allah not only from your name but from all the names of Allah. Amanah[29] belongs to its owner.

On your own, you can turn to Him only from your name. With the help of the perfect teacher, these friends of Allah who, by proxy, bear the reflection of our Prophet who is personally the reflection of all the names of Allah (they only completely manifest in our Prophet in their mature state; no other person can have it to this extent), Islam is, to reach Allah from all beautiful names, which are the doors, and it is, on the one hand, the path to be a drop, that is, a Servant (Creature), by reaching the sea as a drop in His sea and on the other hand, it is the journey of being human living in that Sea (the Truth).

The ego (from the attributes) and the intellect are subsequently "created," brought into being. The ego is the names, but its essence is the spirit, that is the attributes. Therefore, if the ego is returned to the spirit, one MIGRATES from ego to the spirit. The origin of the migration lies here. The ego gains identity with the manifestation of Allah's attributes and names and the manifestation in the property of the body and this comprehension of personality is called the ego.

That is why everything is benevolent, good, and beautiful. What we call bad or ugly is actually nothing but the "degrees" of what we call good and beautiful. And this distinction exists for someone who does not have a holistic view. What is ugly for one person is beautiful to another, what is good for one person is not that good for another person, because we have fragmentary views.

When someone cannot marry the person they want, they see it as an evil, while another person considers marrying someone they want as good, but over time, their point of view changes, and everyone sees the good in what they experience. That is why everything is beautiful, benevolent, and good.

"… He 'alone' has the Most Beautiful Names …"(Surah al-Hashr,

29 Al-Amanah in Islamic is the moral responsibility of fulfilling one's obligations due to Allah and fulfilling one's obligations due to Allah's slaves.

Verse 24).

Angels, who are stated to have a structure of divine light (noor), and the jinns, who are said to have a structure of fire (naar), derive their existence from the Beautiful Names of Allah.

In fact, human beings are a combination of the meanings of the names and attributes of Allah.

"And [mention, O Muhammad], when your Lord said to the angels, "Indeed, I will make upon the earth a successive authority." They said, "Will You place upon it one who causes corruption therein and sheds blood, while we exalt You with praise and declare Your perfection?" He [Allah] said, "Indeed, I know that which you do not know." And He taught Adam the names - all of them. Then He showed them to the angels and said, "Inform Me of the names of these, if you are truthful." (Surah al-Baqarah, Verses 30-31)

It is said that every being we see is a composition of the meanings of the beautiful names of Allah. To fully understand this, we need to understand exactly what a composition means ...

Composition means superposition. We even use the Turkish word "merkep (donkey)" for the animals, "to ride"; the origin of the word is "mount; vehicle."

In other words, the fact that we are a "composition" of the Beautiful Names is because we are loaded with the meanings of Allah's names as if we are a mount and because we are bodies carrying the meanings of His names and attributes. And since we have no existence other than His names, human beings have no existence except for a composition of the divine names. All beings are bodies that bear the meanings of Allah's names. Not more than that.

The differences among people such as temperament, physique, talent, and weakness are because the names of Allah are dominant in various degrees in every human being.

The properties to reveal the functions and activities, and provisions of the Beautiful Names of Allah, which are the names and attributes of our Lord, is called the stage of Lordship (rububiyyah) of the manifestation of Allah, and Allah's name/attribute referred to as LORD refers to the fact that He has the degree of Lordship.

So, the name of Allah, whose essence is referred to as Allah and who has Oneness, in the stage of names is Lord. This stage is called Rabb al-Arbab (the Lord of all lords), Rabb al-Alamin (the Lord of the worlds). And He is the Lord of all.

However, since the weight of the meanings of Allah's names is different in every person and some names are more dominant in each individual, these dominant names also prevail in you by "pointing to your ego." And this is the composition of the beautiful names arising from the different combinations of names carried by each person, which we call the Particular Lord. Your name of existence in your heart originating from the divine essence is your purpose and your sirat al-mustaqeem (the straight path). It is your choice and the crossroad of destiny to go to Allah, to guidance, or to go astray by abandoning yourself to the devil.

The names in each of us are from Allah in nature, but they are from the Particular Lord in terms of their composition.

I don't know if you paid attention, but they are called friends of Allah; Ahlullah, the people of Allah ...

We, who do not have any existence of our own and who carry the names of Allah as a capacity, but who are under the authority of the combination and weight of some of those names, can only understand the concept called the ego after finding the meanings of the names dominant in us and the meanings of the names with weaker authority in us ...

So, in a sense, as the Particular Lord, therefore this is expressed by the words, "the one who knows their ego knows their Lord" ...

Some people are impatient, some people are too compassionate or even too emotional, some people are irritable, some people have the ability to write, some are very strong, stingy, etc. ...

Since we are under the registration of the names that have weight on us and we cannot control this situation, we react immediately and say things like "What can I do? I followed my ego. How do I know? I could not resist my ego ..."

Basically, what happens is that the names of Allah, which are dominant in our spiritual balance, make us do what they want by recording us.

What we call the Particular Lord is one of the recommended methods to objectively write down our positive and negative aspects of our personalities and to understand which names are dominant or less influential in us in order to get to know our personalities more closely.

If we look at the advice of the friends of Allah, we can better understand and reveal the characteristics given to the manifestations of the names in us, if we serve the creatures of Allah day and night, which is the best method of moving towards our names rather than investigating what names we bear.

In fact, the system of our life and existence has been created intelligent enough to lead us to that path, in other words, to our own reason for existence and to Allah as long as we do not do what is required of our names and as long as we engage in activities that oppose them.

The name of the Lord does what it wants ... There is no distinction between good and bad at the point where it operates. Moreover, it performs every activity based on a purpose and wants anything to be when it says "be!"

When we are born, we set out with these forces, with our being that we call "personality" and which we think belongs to us ...What we generally call "My Lord" at the first stage is the composition of the meanings of the names of Allah, which has weight over us.

But if you pay attention, there is a situation referred to as the matter of the ego and its 7 stages[30]: For example, in the commanding ego

30 Nafs al-Ammara (The Commanding Ego): This is the ego that commands evil and enjoys this.

(an-nafs al-ammarah), we are not in a position other than being the instrument of our egos. Eat, drink, etc.; it rules us in the way it wants because it is the resultant of Allah's names.

I am very impressed by Ibn Arabi's narrative about the issue of "the ego who commands evil ..."

All the names of Allah are beautiful, our question, "why do negativities happen to us?" may also be clarified with this explanation in addition to the difference in measures caused by the weights of the names ...

Allah says, "... and I breathed into him of My spirit, ..." (Surah al-Hijr, Verse 29). So, not His spirit ... This point is worth contemplation ...

Allah is One ... An indivisible One ... He is Ahad ... There is no oppositeness ... We live together in the "unity in the multitude" reflected on us from the divine light of our Prophet, like different seeds in a "pomegranate".

Hazrat Ibn Arabi says that there is a trinity in our creation; the divine essence of Allah, His breath which He breathed into us with His command "Be!" and our name that reveals in us ... This trinity, this meeting explains our creation. That is why we read some of our prayers 3 times and 3 is an important sign.

Allah kills us with every breath and revives us by breathing into us again every time we breathe. That is why, with every breath, there is a new resurrection, a new comprehension, and a new chance at life, says the beautiful friend of Allah.

The meeting of the pure spirit with the ego, and the ego becoming the breath of the one who is blowing into a cleansed reed flute makes

Nafs al-Lawwama (The Self-Accusing Ego): This is the ego that regrets when it does evil, and asks for forgiveness.
Nafs al-Mulhima (The Inspired Ego): This is the ego that gets inspiration from Allah.
Nafs al-Mutmainne (The Ego at Peace): This is the contented ego.
Nafs al-Radhiyya (The Well-Pleased Ego): This is the ego well pleased with Allah.
Nafs al-Mardhiyya (The Well-Pleasing Ego): This is the ego which is well pleasing to Allah.
Nafs al-Kamila (The Perfect Ego): This is the distinguished, pure, clean ego.

us pure ...

"And I do not seek to free myself from blame, for indeed the ego is ever inclined to evil, except those shown mercy by my Lord. Surely my Lord is All-Forgiving, Most Merciful." (Surah Yusuf, Verse 53)

As we begin to realize this situation, Nafs al-Lawwama enters and we try to control our ego in some way, because we begin to apprehend the nature of the actions that we carry out with our bodies, and we realize that we need to correct them.

Our understanding of self-discipline and overcoming the negativities in our ego gradually arises, and as a result of these 7 stages, we cleanse our ego and break its authority on us. In this process of uprising and cleansing, we gather the beautiful meanings of the stages of ego on ourselves, move away from negative meanings, identify with our spirit, and walk on the path to reach Allah.

Just as the lack of or excess of minerals in people's bodies determines their bodily structures and determines their strengths, weaknesses, and abilities, the name that weighs less or more than the other names of Allah in our spiritual body determines our spiritual orientation.

When Yusuf says, "Worship Allah, who removes these godly rules, instead of the lords" in the verse, he conveys to us the message to break away from the control of the meanings of Allah's names that are not in balance in us and that control us because they exist in different weights, and to orient towards the name Allah where all names are in the same balance.

What we need to do is to recognize these records, which are essentially our ego and which we think are in our own "personality," to understand our deficiencies and weaknesses by learning the intensity of the meanings of names in us, and to perform the actions and worships required to balance these deficiencies and weaknesses.

Sufi masters do this by recommending that people pronounce the missing names in certain proportions, to practice dhikr, and carry out the behaviors pertaining to those meanings. For example, if your stinginess is intense, they will recommend that you recite the names of Allah with the meanings of generosity and recommend that you practice deeds for good and sharing.

Unless we do these things and do activities such as reaching the name Allah and trying to make up for our deficiencies, we cannot truly reach the path of approaching the name Allah. We become blind to our souls, captive to the desires of our egos ...

Islam shows us the methods of attaining Allah and the Truth. In other words, to meet the sea of the name Allah, where all the names are in balance, with the Truth in yourself, when you are a drop ...Even if you are a small drop, the drop that reaches the sea is now from the sea ...

Islam provides it … Sufism tells us this … However, the superior conscious side from the other teachings is that it enables you to live this with your living being, with the Truth, and among the people … Otherwise, it is easy to retreat and live alone on a mountain ... The issue is to return to Mecca like the Prophet who came from the Ascension, the Prophet who found peace in Medina, and to live with the hereafter in the worldly life. (Since it is not possible to attain a "station" beyond a certain point in comprehension in some Far Eastern teachings, this is the most important reason for a consciousness increased after a period of seclusion, which starts from a level of unhappiness even lower than from where it started after returning among people. Dr. Mustafa Merter explains this very well in his book Dokuz Yüz Katlı İnsan (Man of Nine Hundred Floors) where he shares his experiences …)

For example, they say, "Do not torture your ego!"In fact, torturing the ego is to give it what it wants. Doing what it does not want is a blessing for it. And torturing the ego, leaving it in darkness (as you remember, torture in my language Turkish means darkness) is to help it reach the divine light by continuing to do what it wants.

The predominant combination of names prevailing in us is our Lord, who forms our personalities, and is not separate from Allah.

Only because the names exist in different intensities within us, they differentiate us from other people, and when we say, "my Lord," we sometimes call those names of Allah, although we do not notice.

Psychiatrists also know that the subconscious of a person wants what it wants immediately (control), and that subconscious is basically our composition of beautiful names, and this is perfectly normal since it is our (Particular) Lord.

The goal is to reach the name Allah. The prayer to reunite with Jamalullah (the Beauty of Allah) basically expresses this wish.

The "middle path" mentioned in the Quran can be the path we will reach by the equal manifestation of these names. If you look at the Sufi masters, you will see calm, peaceful, and balanced people. This is because of their efforts to get out of the control of their own egos and reach Allah.

That is why the dhikr of the name Allah is very important.

To sum up, the issue is to reach the divine records by getting out of the recordings of the predominant beautiful name, namely the godly recordings, and to reach the united name, Allah. And this was explained by our Prophet so clearly and briefly, "Adopt the morals of Allah ..."

Many physics professors and scientists abroad talk about the fact that everything is one. There is only one consciousness, and they say everything is actually one, even though we see differences.

In fact, this is the matter of tawhid (oneness) that was mentioned centuries ago in Islam.

Each of us are beings composed of the meanings of Allah's names. This makes us dependent on ONE source.

And for this reason, the word "creation", which is written as the correspondence of the word "halq[31]" in translations and interpretations, may also mislead us in the way we understand the concept ...

"Halq" is the word that is translated as "to create" in the Quran and

31 In Turkish, halq means "people, public" and, "to create."

that is generally used for this meaning … Allah "creates (halq)." And this is how it is mentioned in the verses …

Why?

Let's give an example of the concept of creation: Let's say someone creates a pencil. There is a pencil that is formed in our understanding of creation, and there is its creator, isn't it?So, there is a duality. There is the one I have created, and there is me.

But Allah has "created (halq)" us.

In fact, the verb "halq" is also "halq" in Turkish (my language) …

We think of the concept of "creation" as "creating out of nothing" in our own comprehension … However, some of the friends of Allah express that Allah did not create (halq) human beings out of absolute nothingness, but out of relative nothingness …

Allah, of course, brings into existence from nothing … He is capable of everything … However, what is meant here by the word "halq" is the same explanation with the understanding of oneness and the oneness of Allah …

When we understand the word "creation" in its meaning in our languages, we give ourselves an independent being "separate" from Allah … In fact, in a sense, we fall into the same mistake as the devil where he considered Adam separate from Allah …

In other words, duality comes naturally, and we think that there is us and there is Allah … By attributing to ourselves a being "separate" from Allah, we fall into a hidden polytheism …

However, we do not understand that we say, "La ilaha; neither me nor he, she, it, that exist," "Illallah; it is only Allah who exists, there is nothing other than Allah" (we say that everything around us that is the manifestation of His names and attributes is only a sign of His existence) …

However, in the universe and in our existence that we think exists, there is nothing other than Allah. And if so, how can we say, "to create?"

If you look at some of the interpretations of the Quran, the word "halq" is translated as "to create." This can directly make us think that we are separate from Allah. We think there is I and He, whereas there is neither I nor you, but only He.

The only thing in us and everything is the embodiment, attiring of the meanings of His names.

The words Satan (Iblis) and Garment (Elbise) almost evoke each other. The Devil is the one who sees One as Two, and he thought that Adam was not a being that Allah breathed from His soul, but a being "separate" from Him by being stuck on the apparent mud and not what is inside that garment …

However, expressing how Allah brought us into being with the word "creation" leads one to the concept of duality unknowingly. If it were so, it would be He, and our being. However, what we think is our own existence is the form of His names that came out in our absence. So, there is no duality. There is only Him. Everywhere there is only Allah with the manifestation of His names and attributes.

This is a reality expressed in the word "halq" in the Quran. Becoming HALQ from al-HAQQ. As long as we think ourselves separate from Him, dedicating individuality and being unitary to ourselves and failing to understand that what we think as ourselves is nothing but the composition of His names, we cannot grasp the fact that everything is actually ONE which the physics professors have understood through scientific determinations in recent years, and we fall apart from Him.

This is tawhid (oneness): No one and nothing has existence beyond the shadows, protrusions, or embodiments of the meanings of Allah's names. And when we are "marginalizing" each other, we are not aware that we are becoming Satanic, we are committing the same duality Iblis did, and this is the reason for us being expelled from the Heaven, that is, from Peace.

In short, we are the carriers of names and attributes glorifying, that is, swimming in the sea of Allah's names and attributes … The Sufi masters use the expression, "the attiring of the names," for this purpose.

"Everything is One." In recent years the world started to thoroughly understand Quantum physics, this is the understanding of tawhid (oneness) that our Prophet intended to explain to us in the Quran centuries ago.

When asked about faith, our Prophet stated that it was impossible to enter the Heaven as faithless. And he added, "You are not considered to have faith unless you love each other ..." The practices of a magnificent religion such as Islam do not yield the desired results because we do not understand and because most of us do not try to truly understand.

Because, also in the Islamic states, Islam is generally focused on the station of shariah, that is, the physical requirements; there are almost no efforts in the stations of tariqah, haqiqah, and marifah. It is, of course, correct to live the religion in the station of shariah because as Hazrat Abd al-Qadir Gilani says, "Unless we perform what is apparent, we may not reach the hidden. And what is requested from us again is to have a grasp of the deeper meanings called the hidden. Otherwise, our physical worships do not descend to our hearts."

"To Allah belong the east and the west, so wherever you turn you are facing ⊠towards⊠ Allah. Surely Allah is All-Encompassing, All-Knowing." (Surah al-Baqarah, Verse 115)

Even if it seems difficult to understand, Sufism basically describes the methods and explanation of orienting towards Allah.

It is not possible to separate Islam, the Quran, and Sufism from each other ... The QURAN is the essence of Allah. It is the station where all differences are removed.

FURQAN is the attributes of Allah. It is the manifestation where differences occur. Al-Furqan is the 25th surah of the Quran. Furqan also means, "the one that distinguishes the Truth from the superstition. The word "test" also originates from this understanding. If Allah willed, He would have created all of us free of sin like the angels. But He equipped us with the meanings of His names and attributes and showed us whether to use them for good or for evil.

When "tests" are in question, there is always a routine answer. Allah tests us. He wants to see how His servant will behave.

Allah, of course, tries His servant: "And know that your properties and your children are but a trial and that Allah has with Him a great reward." (Surah al-Anfar, Verse 28)

The word "fitnah" is a word derived from the Arabic verb root F-T-N. It has meanings such as "to melt in fire; to allure; to deprave; to try to make someone change their mind." And even the word "cunning" meaning "dissuading" originates from this meaning.

It is used to give numerous meanings in the Quran. Some scholars, like Seyyid Shariff Curcani, described the word fitnah as "something that leads to reveal the tendency of a person towards good or evil" based on the meaning, "to subject to fire to distinguish fine gold from imitation."

So, this word "fitnah" or "test" attracts attention to the positive side of fitnah by its meaning. In fact, its use in many Quran verses to mean "test" refers to this.

Fitnah is the name given to the big fire started by goldsmiths to distinguish gold ore from copper.

Even if we do not realize it, there are opportunities in every incident that we encounter to allow us to cleanse ourselves from the evil within us.

One cannot become ripened before burning or else one remains unripe. One cannot mature without suffering. People do not think or question. But they understand that every moment is a grace to thank for through these burnings. Once they were turning towards Allah with pain, now they turn towards Him with praise and glorification. Because they became aware that every MOMENT given to them is a blessing.

Tests are for Allah. They say, "Allah tests His servant." This is, of course, correct. He wants to see how each servant will behave. Yet,

Allah still tests, cleanses, and prepares every servant for the hereafter again for His servant; He is so merciful …

So, they say, "Allah says that He wants to see how His servant will behave …" Doesn't Allah, who knows everything, who is the owner of yesterday, today, and tomorrow, and who is from all eternity, know how His servant will behave?

My beautiful Allah of course knows it. He already knows what we will do in timelessness, in the MOMENT. The main point is FOR US! Because we are here to see what we choose and why we choose. Almost every child taking an exam thinks they studied really hard, but the exam results ensure that they witness THEIR own status … Otherwise, the teacher always knows the capacity of the student, it is the student who does not know their capacity … Allah shows us to ourselves through these fitnah and tests. Take a look around you … Each one of us considers themselves immune, everyone thinks of themselves as princesses and princes … Who knows themselves? Allah keeps us, witnesses, to our egos through all these tests. It leads to those we claim that we would never do, our judgments, the incidents to "open" all our locks "locking" our beings gifted with these extraordinary powers… We are here to reach our truth by becoming the "opener," that is, al-FA-TIH(A), of our physical locks, our ego locks. We are here for our own conquest …

"Rather, man, against himself, will be a witness." (Surah al-Qiya-mah, Verse 14)

He is cleansing us from ourselves. So that only our golden side remains. In order to melt down our copper. So that we could be pure servants. Purified and valued. They say that diseases remove sins. So, Allah wants to cleanse His beloved servants "here," "while on the earth," because in our lives in the hereafter the cleansing process will be tougher.

Do not consider it a suffering, Allah protects us … That is why He is cleansing us.

FURQAN

The differences in the universe are expressed with the concept of "furqan." Furqan[32] comes from the same root as FRK (difference). What forms the difference and diversity between the creatures brought into being in the universe is the manifestation of the meanings of the names in different products/resultants.

We are all equipped with the names and attributes of Allah and therefore, Allah who is referred to as Rabb al-Arbab in Sufism, is the Lord of all of us; He is the Lord of the Lords. The Particular Lord, on the other hand, is the composition of beautiful names arising from the manifestation of the meanings of the same names and attributes of Allah in each of us at different weights.

Composition of Beautiful Names

So, your Lord and my Lord are, of course, the same, but the way the meanings of Allah's names and attributes exist in you is different to another person. And what comes into existence is the meaning of Allah's names and attributes, just like everything else in the universe; but

---

32 Furqan: It is the infinitive form of the verb meaning farq or tafriq, that is, to differentiate, to distinguish. In general, "farq" is used for those recognized by the intellect while tafriq is used for those recognized by senses. "Furqan" also means the one who disjoins, "mefruq" (disjoined); by these means, the conclusive evidence that solves and concludes important cases, miracles are also called "furqan." Based on this meaning, one of the names of the Quran is "Furqan." (Elmalılı Hamdi Yazır).

some of those names are more intense or less intense in each of us. This is called the "composition of beautiful names" in Sufism, and before understanding this composition constituting your ego, it is difficult to discover our deficiencies and abilities.

Here is an example:

There is Abd al-Qadir Gilani, a friend of Allah. With many karamats, he is one of those permitted by Allah to help us when we need help.

Did you notice his name? ABD AL-QADIR ...

Abd means servant and Qadir means might ...

His name means the servant of Allah's name al-QADIR. He is, of course, the servant of Allah just like all of us but, as we briefly mentioned in the section about Ana'l Haq, he is a friend of Allah in whom the name al-Qadir stood out in the intensity of Allah's names ...

This means that the weight of the name al-Qadir is excessive in him than what he is capable of is because of the manifestation of Allah with His name al-Qadir in him.

For example, who are those people whom we call saints (friends) of Allah?

They are the servants of Allah in whom the meaning of the name al-WALI, one of Allah's beautiful names, manifests ... that is, the meaning of Allah's name al-Wali comes into light in their existence.

Every person has a different "mixture of beautiful names" and all opposite names of Allah manifest in every person at different ratios; all these result in different characteristics which eventually lead to the formation of the human ego.

So, its essence is the Lord composition.

Therefore, "Rabb al-Arbab" is the Lord of the Lords, that is the Lord of all of us, and the Particular Lord is our personal Lords referring to the beautiful name of each of us and the composition of beautiful names.

This saying of our Prophet or Hazrat Ali is very important for us to recognize the weaknesses and capabilities based on these weights and deficiencies of our egos.

It is crucial to understand this matter, or otherwise, a person may not correctly determine the weaknesses and capabilities in their personality profile, and they may not orient it correctly.

Since, in consequence, it is the manifestation of the Lord, the manifestation of the Lord in your ego wants its wishes to materialize immediately. And just like we have just mentioned, it is also known in psychology that the subconsciousness wants its wishes to materialize immediately. This is the root cause of it.

The LORD wants His wish to materialize immediately; there is no distinction between good and evil, because, under the name Allah, there is a name just across, so everything that happens is GOOD.

Let's think of it this way:

If we are making an analysis of our bodies. We say that our iron levels have decreased, or potassium levels have increased, and we take vitamins because of a magnesium deficiency, etc., right?

Yes, this physical analysis is a determination required for us to restore our "physical health" by knowing what is below and above the limits, isn't it?

Now, think of the same situation for your spiritual bodies. Actually, it is not complicated as it is perceived, and I don't know if it is really possible to continue on the true path before solving this issue.

Just like restoring our health through the prescription given by the physician after having our analysis done and taking the nutritional supplements, the depiction of murshid (the one who guides the spirit, that is, makes it mature), the doctor of our spirit, is a guide required for us to gain our spiritual existence and our truth.

Since they passed through the path to reach Allah by themselves, those who approach Allah and ripen, those who reach Allah know that path, its details, threats ahead, and the particulars; and thus, they can guide the disciples who want and decide to walk on that path. Because this path is the one that is the straight path that is called Sirat al-Mus-taqim, and it is a path where one can easily get lost.

In the Quran, terms like "sabil, siret, sunan" are used every few verses, and these terms meaning "the path and the journey" indicate that we are only guests in this world and the destination we need to reach is Allah.

We think that the only way to thank Allah is through words and good behavior and good deeds. This is also true but still, a great praise is to contribute to the manifestation of the meanings of the names (beautiful names) and attributes bestowed by Allah in us both through those we listed and those we comprehended scientifically and to allow them to come into existence by this way.

We do not know that we are moving away from our own salvation while displaying behaviors beyond our control based on the weight of the names within us and before we apprehend that when we say, "my ego," we say "my Lord" at the same time.

The most important way to discipline your ego is to get help from a friend of Allah who may identify the ruling meanings of the names in you and which names are predominant and which are inferior in you.

They will show you the names to balance the uncontrolled weaknesses and the deficient qualities you are suffering from, and they will help you reach the name Allah which is your main target by balancing your predominant ego.

Anything told in the Quran under the prophet stories is for this purpose.

There are 28 letters in the Quran and 28 prophets. Each one tells us what we will encounter during our climb to discipline this ego and how to behave in certain situations.

Unless you exceed the records of personality, no matter who or what you turn towards, that is your god and your Lord.

For example, if your weakness is gambling or if it is love that you turn towards, this becomes your Lord. In short, anything that is in the form of desire occurs with the mixture (composition) of beautiful names created in you by Allah and constitutes your hell.

This is explained in Surah al -Infitar, Verse 8 as follows: "In whatever form He willed has He assembled you."

Colors already exist. We get different colors when we mix yellow, blue, and green. Different colors when we mix red, purple, and black ... The color that we get is nothing more than different combinations of an existing being, so it does not have its own structure.

This composition in a person constitutes the spirit, and it constitutes their ego.

And the only difference in the ego, the spiritual structure in human beings is the different combinations and manifestations of the meanings of the names and attributes.

If one gets results directed towards their ego when they put their ideas into practice, then they think of their spirit and existence as a separate body, a separate existence.

(We are born with this composition and our personality; ego develops under the influence of this composition. This spirit – energy – composition is formed as a result of the composition and although it seems like an independent spirit, it is not separate from the Absolute Spirit – the Holy Spirit. But we can say that it is a degree of the Absolute Spirit.)

Another explanation of the statement, "those who know their egos know their Lord," is, for example, when one is afflicted with an illness, they begin to have a grasp of Allah's name, ash-Shaafee (the Healer), and restore their health with the manifestation of that name, or they understand the name "ar-Razzaq (the Sustainer)" through sustenance; it is to understand that the abundance and shortage in life, all contradictions, anything that happens is the locus of the manifestation of Allah's different names ... In short, knowing the Lord means to know Allah through His names and to know Him at this degree ... However, one should remember that the name Allah covers all the degrees of manifestation of Allah, and it includes the degrees of the essence ... However, "to know the Lord" in the name Lord that belongs to the degree of lordship is to know Allah at the degree of His beautiful names.

So, there is the name (or it may be several names) (HU) coming from the divine essence in the hearts of all people, and our fundamental objective is to reach that name and then, the name Allah. When we reveal that name, all the tribes, that is, the names in us enter into the domination of that name ... To recognize and see their truth, people need two types of mirrors to be able to understand their beautiful name which is the treasure buried in the earth of the body. One of these mirrors is 'a devil'; it appears with the contrast of the name in that person. For example, a person's temperament that we do not like is the manifestation of the name that is contrary to the name in us. On the other hand, we see the most mature and most perfect version of our name in al-insan al-kamil (perfect man). So, the ego may proceed in two directions by turning towards the world/devil or to the Most Compassionate. If it matures and moves to higher degrees, the face of the ego turned towards the spirit reaches the purified ego degree and disappears, and only the Truth, the spirit is left in the person.

When each explanation is taken into consideration, what is basically noticeable is that we are surrounded by incidents on the path to reach our own beautiful names by clearing the negativities in our egos. Because Allah manifests through everyone as our eternal teacher and allows us to reach our names in the pre-eternity. Since this process is easier and less painful in this world, Allah wants to cleanse us in this world, and He never gives up on us. He creates thousands of people and incidents to educate and discipline us and helps us in every moment. Yet, we are not even aware of the purpose of why we came to this world ...

The Quran basically wants to tell us about ourselves, not others. Why should we care about others before finding our own essence ...

How do they impact us? We should first find out if we think and live properly.

We should find the salvation first, and then, we can thrust out our hands to others for a true and sound salvation. Anyway, the one who discovers themselves discovers the universe ... The Quran tells us that submission, that is Islam, which is the journey to Allah, is a path and a teaching consisting of stations of comprehension and not an inherent label written on our identity cards.

On that path your "ego" rebels against you. Our egos are like satans imitating us. We read about the riots of the "tribes" in the Quran ... We consider them as stories of thousands of years ago ... However, "the tribes" are the meanings of the names predominant in us that act in the opposite direction and keep us from turning towards the true path ... Those rebellions are the beautiful names that do not want to enter the dominance of the beautiful names of Allah within us and that try to lead us towards transgressions.

Hazrat Ibn Arabi, may Allah be pleased with him, uses a marvelous expression while describing salah and says, "When we stand to perform salah, we act as an imam to the tribes within us and the angels surrounding us; they follow us while they perform their salah." We will analyze the salah with congregation as mentioned in the Quran with an interesting description, but I should mention under this topic that "congregation" does not only refer to the "people outside ..." Let's stop searching for everything on the outside ... We cannot know the outside without turning towards the inside ... The first congregation is to line up the tribes, names, and meanings, our intellects, hearts, and thoughts within us (while performing salah in congregation it is said to stay closer otherwise the devil will pass through us; preventing the "devil" from passing through our feelings and thoughts when we stand for salah is one of the deeper explanations), to UNITE the tribes within us, and to stand for salah before Allah ... There are beautiful names of Allah such as al-Jalal (the Majesty), al-Mutakabbir (the Greatest), and al-Jabbar (the Compeller). Do not misunderstand, these names are not bad. All the names of Allah are qualified as Husna, that is, "very or the most beautiful." The difference is related to the manifestation of the names in a person, and the direction and intention of their action based on the intention of the person, and depending on the destructive intention, the names may be destructive with their powers. The narration in the statement, "Prayer is the weapon of a believer," is very suitable for this situation; just like a weapon, the meanings of the names exhibit their powers and actions in the direction of your intention with their power …

This is where intellect and faith step in. And they invite to Islam the tribes in our egos that are trying to rebel, that is, to surrender and to the straight path called Sirat al-Mustaqim.

Your bodies are a locus for the meanings of Allah's names. The existence in you is nothing more than the existence of Allah. The only difference is that the name that prevails in you is not the name Allah where all names are in a balance and covered (which is also called al-Ism al-Jami' [All Comprehensive Name]), but the name al-Jalal (the Majesty) because it is more intense and dominant than other names. To balance the name al-Jalal, increasing the activity of its balancing name that is its contrast in your spiritual body through the dhikr of that name is one of the procedures followed … (For example, your murshid tells you to perform dhikr of x numbers of al-Jalal and y numbers of the name Allah.)

So, what represses the uprising within you is the balance of the names. This is one of the openings of the "middle way" recommended in the Quran and the statement, "neither overdoing nor underdoing."

While the poison of a snake can kill us, isn't the antidote that can resurrect us also made from the poison of the same snake?

It is the same. The difference between them is the MEASURE …

One of the names of Allah is al-Qahhar (The Subduer). We also have this name, but if we use this name to do evil we will become devastating; however, if we use it to devastate the evil within us, we will enter the path of becoming human.

Just like this, Allah actually has no bad names. They are all beautiful. What matters is our intention as we turn towards it, and how we use our bodies and existences for the manifestation of that name.

Islam regards intention. The matter of testing lies here ... "Allatheena itha asabat-hum museebatun qalu inna lillahi wa inna ilayhi raji'un." (Surah al-Baqarah, Verse 156)

This verse, in fact, summarizes the matter ... This verse is written on coffins at funerals. I am going to share its interpretation:

"Who, when disaster strikes them, says, Indeed we belong to Allah, and indeed to Him we will return."

Of course, the interpretations may be partially explanatory but in a book like the Quran that is dressed in many layers, it is impossible to say that we reach the meanings that we should understand "in the essence" through interpretations ... Now, I am writing down based on the information I get from the Arabic word roots and the books of the friends of Allah:

When disaster (trouble, an unpleasant incident) strikes them, they say, "Indeed we are for Allah (that is, for the manifestation of the meanings of the names and attributes of Allah), and to Him, we will return!"

I have read Hazrat Ibn Arabi saying that the Sufis utter this verse when they face trouble and that the trouble may be removed after some time. Allahualam. Allah knows everything.

But the main point is that the essential understanding that is generally not given in the interpretations - I don't know whether this is because it is not possible to give it in such a short explanation – unfortunately takes us to the point that Islam limited with interpretations may not find its true place.

Trying to understand and criticize Islam by only reading some interpretations would be a grave error.

While each verse bears tens of meanings, this is nothing more than an unjust judgment. Then, who would such a judgment harm? Of course, it harms us. Because this beautiful book that facilitates both the worldly life and the life in the hereafter is our greatest treasure that we fail to see although it is just before our eyes.

We are for Allah. Every creature is nothing more than the form of the names of Allah that occur in different weights.

The meanings of the names have found a body, and the Quran, from time to time, calls this the world or the city. While saying "in that city," etc., it also refers to the names that want to establish their own sovereignty. Unless those names meet the opposite names that balance each one of them or unless they are reflected with manners in their essences, they would become your pharaoh.

Don't say that the pharaoh lived hundreds of years ago, and it has nothing to with you. Do you know what pharaoh means?

According to the Islamic scholars, PHARAOH (fir'awn) comes from the word "far'ana" or "tafar'ana" meaning ARROGANCE and PRIDE. The plural of the word is FARAINE. Due to this meaning of the word, arrogant and cruel people are referred to as "tafar'ana'r raculu." Apart from these, this word is widely used to mean "the one who misguides, infects, and damages others."

Pharaohs wanted to make their people admit that they were the Lord. Yes, this is also among the predominant beautiful names that exist in us. And let's see why Islam is to reach Allah …

Because the beautiful name "Allah" is the beautiful name where all the names are in balance and are covered. In religious orders, this beautiful name is intensely used in dhikrs, and this spiritually elevates a person. But if the beautiful names given to someone as dhikr without knowing that person's composition (mixture) of beautiful names and which names are predominant in that person, then they put an even heavier burden on their ego in the direction of that name. This is something like the imbalance after working the muscles on the right arm and leaving the muscles on the left arm weak.

So, in consequence, for an independent and unconditional intellect, we should first try to be freed from the conditions of our "egos" that constitute our partial intellects (fragmentary/subjective intellect) and "to become wiser with the intellect of Allah."

We can succeed in adopting the manners of Allah and becoming wiser with the intellect of Allah by removing our relative existences between us and Allah.

If you eliminate the veil of your ego, only your spirit is left ... Then, the divine light of Allah directly manifests in you. Remember, every veil deprives one of the sun ...

Our teacher Cemalnur Sargut says that ego is female, and I think it is in reference to hawa (caprice). Every Adam is created with his Eve (an opening to the fact that we are all created with our partners), that is every soul is created with its ego ... And when one reaches its caprice (that is, Eve) to Adam, that is the manifestation of Allah (the spirit), the ego qualified as female becomes so beautiful that it becomes HOURI. Houri, the most beautiful state of the ego ...

If your ego reaches the "breath," then it becomes brilliant ...

Remove yourself so that only the Creator is left ... Then, the blessings fall upon you from the Sama' ...

CHILDREN BORN FROM THE SAME MOTHER

"Life takes attendance ...
And from the class, you avoid the most ..."

-Deniz Erten

Squall

One should remain at WAW ...

And Allah says: "Everything created is my family, please my family so that I will be pleased with you ..." We were in Madinah. The call for salah was recited announcing that it was time for salah.

We were at the Masjid an-Nabawi (the Prophet's masjid), we stood up and began to prepare.

Just then, an Arabic girl holding her baby in her arms arrived at the section where we were. She was looking for somewhere to perform her salah among the crowd. We signaled to her and made room. She quietly snuggled with her baby.

We waited for the call for salah, and once it ended, we started to perform salah.

She slowly placed her sleeping baby on the salah rug and performed salah with us.

The baby who was sleeping silently like an angel began to cry as if she was short of breath as soon as her mother put her on the floor. It was as if she was squalling (crying) from the pain of being separated from her mother although she did not exactly know what was happening.

This was the first time that we were experiencing something of this nature.

We were in the salah, and we immediately refocused remembering that we were before Allah.

After finishing our salah, the Arabic girl picked up her baby. Right then, the baby suddenly stopped crying. She restored her previous angelic state and was silent once she returned to her mother's heart, arms, and scent.

Now, we started to cry.

Because we understood …

We were like that baby placed on the floor away from the arms of their mothers. We were separated from the grace and love of Allah and placed on the floor. Maybe, this was one of the reasons why our Prophet said, "I was made to love perfume." The scent of a mother is the scent of heaven, and it was the only thing that pacified us. And the arms of our mothers.

That day, I thought for the first time of our Prophet saying, "All my concern, worry, and sorrow is my people that I left behind after me …"

And even during the Ascension, he thought of us and cried, "My people … My people …"

One day while I was thinking of all these, I wondered what UM-MAH (people) meant. Although I heard it a thousand times before, although I thought I knew it, it was one of the thousands of words and concepts that I didn't know the exact meaning of. I immediately checked the meaning.

And at that moment, a wet fire fell into my eyes from my heart that was aching as if it was burning.

Do you know what UMMAH means? The children born from the same mother.

"While everything was sacrificed for the humans, humans make themselves suffer hardship." (Shams Tabrizi)

We came to this world like an incomplete painting. Our other halves, our essences, that is our twins, are behind the curtains. Maybe, just as it was proven by science, people fail to see the whole picture of the person before them whom they think they see when they look with their eyes. And our brains complete this.

So, each one of us came to this world incomplete. To become complete. And to reach our essences and truths behind the curtains. Even though we evaluated every incident we encountered as bitter or sweet, basically, they were the opportunities to complete what was missing in our incomplete paintings.

Each one of us carries the meanings of Allah's names. Some meanings are less in some of us while some are more ... Every incident that we encounter is an opportunity for those names and meanings to reach maturity in us and for the missing ones to become complete.

We don't, cannot accept some incidents and people. We say, "What kind of a person is this?" But they also bear the names of Allah, and their meanings just like us. They bear the same names in different weights. That is why we consider them strangers, we consider them "apart" from ourselves. And they also think of themselves as "apart" from us. Such irony ...

However, every person and every incident is a part of us because every creature that we see is only a reflection of Allah's names. In Sufism, it is explained that this life is a mirror. Actually, each person reflects us and tells us about ourselves. And as we keep on rejecting those meanings, they continue to appear before us in the form of different people and incidents bearing the same meaning and contents. They pursue us until they make us accept their existence in us.

Just like you may not pass to a higher grade or level unless you succeed in the make-up exam of the lesson you failed. Although the teacher of that lesson changes every time, you cannot progress to a higher grade before understanding the fundamentals of that subject and passing the exam of the lesson. And the comprehension of people is like a ladder. In every climb, you get cleansed from your previous state and ascend towards what you should be. And the Ascension (Miraj; from the same root as urooj), which literally means "Ladder," refers to ascension in comprehension. Whoever climbs the ladder in their spirits, they approach towards Allah and recognize the universe in the same extent.

When we regard everything around us as a manifestation of Allah and a body carrying His meaning, then we begin to see whoever we see around us, our spouses, in-laws, children, or employers, as teachers and discipliners helping us to get our diplomas. They are the means chosen again by Allah for us to reach "maturity" which is the purpose of coming to this world and to complete our missing parts.

Look around you. Look at the recurring problems in your life. Look at the people always making you go through the same thing although they have different names. They are only our discipliners.

If one has never-ending financial problems, then they are quite likely to be fond of money and property more than they should. If one has never-ending problems with their child, then they are likely to be keen on their child as if worshipping that particular child.

If the problems with the spouse do not end, one is very likely to exceed the limits of a sense of ownership in their ego.

We are all rapped over the knuckles where we have weaknesses or deficiencies. Just like Yunus carrying the straight wood for 40 years and not the crooked ones. What is referred to as wood is the ego. Once you remove the curve of the ego, it is so nicely chipped that the artwork hidden inside is revealed. He was trained at the hands of Taptuk Emre. "Taptuk" means "consented." Do you see how the training leading to consent is?

The names of Allah and their meanings assume bodies and provide us with the training sent by Him.

Let it not be misunderstood, think of it this way: Everyone in our lives is like the teachers in the schools abroad that we were sent to who carry the meanings of our parents and who were chosen by them. Each one of us goes to different schools with different abilities and skills and takes different courses. We have teachers providing different trainings.

Every one of us takes courses to attain certain objectives when we come to this school, and we pursue a diploma by maturing those abilities and objectives.

So, isn't the school of life something similar to this? We were descended on earth when our homes were near Allah, and we wanted it. The purpose was to fulfill our objectives, reach maturity, be cleansed from our deficiencies, and return to where we came from in the most beautiful way.

While returning to where we came from, we should therefore be thankful for everyone who had been a teacher to us through the problems they unknowingly caused. Because if we leave here with that incomplete picture, we will eventually have to complete it somewhere. And this completion process will be more painful than we think of it here.

It will be more painful because our perceptions are "limited" in this world. As per our testing, we are allowed to hear the sounds, feel objects, and tastes to a certain extent; otherwise, we would not be in denial. The pain we feel here is at a minimum due to our limited perceptions. Likewise, so are the beauties.

But when we pass to the other realm, all our perceptions will reach their actual extents. Then, the limitation on the pleasure and pain of our mistakes or happiness will be removed. I think of this every time my heart is torn out. Think of how your heart will be torn out there, what would it feel like?

Again, that is why they say, "Did you fall ill? Be grateful, Allah is removing your sins. He is cleansing you in this world. He loves you so much that He empties your sins in this world and cleanses you. He does not leave you to the hereafter ..."

The friends of Allah said, "O my Allah, You didn't give me any trouble today. Don't You love me?" They became friends with Allah, and because they know that trouble is the means to maturity …

Allah called us INSAN (human).

INS-AN … Ins at the MOMENT (an) …

He said, Ya sin. That is, "O insan (human!") Why?

One of the meanings of INSAN is "affinity, closeness." It means the one who establishes a superior affinity to Allah than all the other creatures. So beautiful …

But another meaning of INSAN is "the one who forgets." Why? When we were separated from Allah and sent to the World meaning "below," we chose to be one of two openings of the word insan.

And if we have chosen "to be the one who forgets" instead of "the one establishing affinity to Allah," then it means that we have accepted to return to our essence without "remembering" and completing our deficiencies.

Allah made a deal with the spirits of all humans to return until the Last Judgment Day. We all PROMISED.

And Allah asked on the Day of Alast: "Am I not your Lord?" (ALAST: Am I not, BAZM: "Assembly of Discourse" in Farsi).[33]

And we answered, "Yes, You are our Lord."

But then, we treated ourselves, others, and other things as our Lord. We forgot that the existence in us and everything that exists is only His existence; we forgot and broke our PROMISES.

Human, who is entrusted with the "Amanah" which no living thing dared to assume, neither remembered the Amanah nor the promise.

Qalu Bala is the time when people acknowledged the oneness of the Almighty Allah and affirmed His Lordship. Bazm-i Alast is the meeting where this deal was made. In narrations, it is said that Allah made a pact with all people who will return until the Day of Judgment and their spirits and descendants, and this is referred to in the Quran as

---

33 Bazm-i Alast is the original expression that refers to the occasion where Allah gathers people and asks, "Am I not your Lord?" There is no literal correspondence to this term in English and it is translated as the "Day of Alast."

follows: And 'remember' when your Lord brought forth from the loins of the children of Adam their descendants and had them testify regarding themselves. 'Allah asked,' "Am I not your Lord?" They replied, "Yes, You are! We testify." 'He cautioned,' "Now you have no right to say on Judgment Day, 'We were not aware of this.' Nor say, 'It was our forefathers who had associated others 'with Allah in worship' and we, as their descendants, followed in their footsteps. Will you then destroy us for the falsehood they invented?'" (Surah al-A'raf, Verses 172-173)

Yet, human is so precious that, before Allah, all the living things admire Allah's love for people so much that all living things strangely resemble humans because they all want to be like them … If we consider people we see around and the incidents we go through apart from Allah, then we will have adopted ourselves and them as "gods." So, the "god" in la ilaha (there is no god) refers to this. It rather means "god and thing."

And then, Allah, whose oneness we witnessed and admitted in the pre-eternity, whom we witnessed that there is nothing but Him, and for whom we said, "Ashadu an la ilaha illallah" (I bear witness that there is no god but Allah), creates incidents to remind us of our promises because we have forgotten our testimony that "there is nothing but Allah."

They say that Allah asked this question a couple of times. We may be directed to this question at every moment and in every incident we encounter. Only Allah knows the reality. Allahualam …

While getting something done for us, when we say, "If Ahmet helped me, I would now be appointed …," "My daughter needs to find a job. Can we find an influential contact?" "I don't have an influential contact to have the job I want …" "What am I going to do, there is no doctor to treat my illness?" Allah actually continues to ask us questions.

You say that you are hopeless. And even when you witnessed that everything belongs to Me.

I bear witness that there is nothing but You. Then what? Who is

Ahmet that you ask to arrange your appointment? His instrument. Instead of asking from Him, I rely upon one of His servants.

While I am only surrounded by Him, who can give a job to my daughter? When everyone is His shadow. Of course, He gives. Why didn't I ask directly from Him? Why didn't I trust Him due to the delusion in my mind? Why was I mistaken?

I am looking for a remedy; He is the owner of remedies. The name al-Shaafee (The Healer) even belongs to Him. Where and from whom am I asking for a remedy while the one I should ask from is Him?

I am unaware that I adopted lords. While there is only Him, I forgot, and I think that there is something apart from Him. And meanwhile, He keeps on asking me: "Haven't you suffered enough? Am I not your Lord? Why don't you ask from Me?Let Me pick My instrument. Trust Me and surrender!"

We forget. We placed Him somewhere above in our heads and we forgot that we are surrounded by Him. Everywhere and everything is only Him and His.

Or we judge others!

Judgment ... why is it bad? People say, "do not judge, you will experience the same thing," but they do not exactly know why they say this.

Judging is to give a "verdict" on a matter. Therefore, it is to close oneself to the "opposite" of that matter. Just like qada (decree) in the concept of destiny. There is no escape once it occurs; we will live through it, and it will be our destiny.

Yet, Allah allowed people to commit sins so that His names al-Tawwab (the Accepter of Repentance), as-Sattar (the Veiler of Sins), and al-Ghaffar (the Most Forgiving) will be active. Otherwise, His names would not have activity, and this would lead to an imbalance. However, there is a balance in contrasts. When we say, "this is how it is," about a matter, we step on one of the mines in the universal mechanism. And we activate that mechanism. Closing ourselves to the existing contrary of a matter is like denying the name of Allah that gives existence to that matter.

All of Allah's names are available in us. And the more of His names we manage to activate in ourselves and the more we can reveal them in the direction of Allah's consent and not our egos, that is when we start to be the "human" meaning "the one who is close," and not "the one who forgets."

Judging is like "to tear." The names of Allah that exist in us, but we do not activate come to us and try to emerge by kind of tearing out of our chests, bodies, and brains.

That's why we will definitely be torn about the matters we judged. And this incised, torn site will give us great pain whether it is our children, a loved one, or ourselves.

We conditioned ourselves. We locked our brains with a judgment. And we rejected that incident or person before noticing the name of Allah in that incident or person. So, until we experience and admit what we have rejected, we summoned that pain without noticing and knowing.

Nothing that we see outside is independent of Allah. But we think what happens is because of any situation or person, and this is our biggest mistake.

The way to release the meanings inside in a manner worthy of Allah is primarily to accept that they all exist in us with their opposites.

"How lucky is that person who sees their defects. Whoever sees a defect of another, they purchase that defect and find that defect in themselves." (Mathnawi, II, 3034) "I learned about humans. Then, there are the good and the bad among them ... Afterwards, I learned that each human has good and evil in themselves." (Rumi)

They asked Jesus:

"What should I do for Allah not to respond to me with wrath?"

"Then, do not respond to anyone with wrath," he answered. The narration about the "stoning" (the story of Mary Magdalene), which kind of means a person has the right to judge another only if they have never committed a sin, ties our hands, and gently and wisely tells us that we do not have the right to talk about someone else by ignoring our own sinfulness and we are helpless …

Do you know how I see the relationship of the servant with Allah? Like the relationship of a mother and her child. Allah already explained His love to us in many verses and hadiths by comparing His love with the love of our mothers. And He willed to explain to us how much He loves us and how much He shows mercy to us as well as His compassion. We are not actually rising against Allah.

Just like we do not rise against our mothers … We are just trying to prove our existence. We exist! Just like a child trying to prove their existence to their parents by saying, "I also exist! I also exist!"

The attempt to prove one's own existence by saying, "I also exist!", to make this accepted, and to be honored is nothing more than our ignorance. We are trying to tell Allah that we are also here just like the effort we put in to make ourselves accepted just as we do to our parents.

A hadith says that the spirit is blown into the baby in the womb after 120 days. That baby lives in the spirit of the mother and "shares the spirit" of the mother for 120 days. Therefore, although people think that they do not understand their mothers, as years pass by, they begin to resemble their mothers. And this should be the reason for this; shared spirits.

Then, the baby whose spirit is formed also with those taken from the mother comes into the realm of existence with their own spirit.

Allah wills that His servant whom He equipped with His names should resemble Him. In Sufism, this is called "adopting the manners of Allah." I always compare this with the happiness of parents when their children resemble them.

During pilgrimage, there is a state of entering into ihram. This is not just a formal ceremony or clothing; it is basically putting on an understanding. While in the state of ihram, you may not harm any servant of Allah, even an insect. Because you live with the feeling that you have adopted the manners of Allah. That is why battles are forbidden during the sacred months. Ihram is to get equipped with the manners of Allah, and what is requested from us is to adopt the manners of Allah while we are living in peace.

So, the situation in each one of us is no different than this. The corporeal umbilical connections with our mothers are cut after birth, but our umbilical connection with Allah never ends.[34] How? Allah calls us to the following in the Quran: "Hold onto the rope of Allah."

The rope of Allah takes you out from Allah's name, ar-Raheem, to the realm of existence like a human being coming from the womb (raheem) of the mother. While studying the meanings of the name ar-Raheem, I thought that it might not be a coincidence that the name from which Allah brought the creatures into the light was called "ar-Raheem." And when I learned that the place where the meanings of the name ar-Raheem will be revealed in the broadest manner will be heaven, I began to think in astonishment and excitement about what was further revealed with the saying, "The heaven is under the feet of the mothers."

Maybe because of this, the songs about "mothers" have more of an emotional impact on us. Such a magnificent beauty. Such a magnificent intellect.

Quantum mechanics has scientifically proven that the creatures are interconnected, and each creature is "connected with ties" to each other and to a single consciousness (in fact, it is the effort of every creature to prove the piece of a single consciousness that belongs to itself).

That is why it is said, "One should remain at WAW." Take a look at the shape of the WAW; like a baby in a mother's womb …

This is why I cherish Rumi, may Allah be pleased with him, and repeat … FIHI MA FIH. "In it what is in it."

---

34 It is said that at the moment when our Prophet passed away to the hereafter, he said, "my abhar has detached." Abhar means baheer, that is "the most radiant, the most apparent," and it is said to be "golden yellow" which is the color that connects us to this world and mentioned in Surah al-Baqarah.

For example, you become a guarantor for someone. What did he do? He fled! And you became indebted. The properties of your son which he acquired through hard work are suddenly seized. Your daughter lost her job, your spouse was defrauded, or your car was stolen.

Even if we cannot see when we look, the material losses incurred by a family member, a loved one, or ourselves are actually Allah's mercy although we don't know.

Allah directs the bodily damages to the properties with His compassion and shows mercy to His servant, yet we, the servants, fail to see the wisdom and compassion there and complain.

I know that we are in a great chaos of understanding. All of us. Our "evil selves" that are commissioned "to deceive, to show one as two, to dislike" are in charge every moment and they drag us to make us think that Allah has forgotten about us.

But while Allah talks about His compassion for His servants, He explains His compassion through various examples. For example, He describes the development of a child in the womb of the mother in Surah al-Alaq, and there are such fine meanings here.

The prominent physicists of the current world proved a theory called the string theory years ago.

The string theory is actually the very same as quantum physics. But what attracted my attention here was this:

According to the string theory, matter is neither solid, liquid, nor gas. As you go down to the origin of matter, you reach the atom, and then to sub-atom particles. At the farthest point reachable, there are the strings as a form of energy that are neither solid, liquid, nor gas.

Everything in all universes consists of these strings.

• According to the string theory, strings are the particles that move in the 11th dimension.

• According to the string theory, if we were able to see the 11th dimension, we would not see matter as separate but only as the interactions of the strings with each other.

Everything in the universe consists of "strings" and energies. And interestingly, they are connected to the main source and each other with a "rope."

The concept of the Rope of Allah (Hablullah) mentioned in the following verse in the Quran, in fact, explains this theory. Just like Allah, the Most Merciful and the Most Compassionate, mentions in various statements – may it not be misunderstood – and expresses by associating His love to us with the love of a mother, He grows, feeds, and protects each one of us in His "womb." We should just not forget that we are still and will forever be in that womb regardless of "the virtual images" deceiving us outside, and continue to live with that peace and happiness …

"And hold firmly onto the rope of Allah all together and do not become divided. And remember the favor of Allah upon you - when you were enemies and He brought your hearts together and you became, by His favor, brothers. And you were on the edge of a pit of the Fire, and He saved you from it. Thus does Allah make clear to you His verses that you may be guided." (Surah Ali Imran, Verse 103)

As narrated by Hazrat Abu Said el-Hudri, the Prophet of Allah said:

"Hablullah (the Rope of Allah) descended to the earth from the heavens is the book of Allah."

When a baby is born, they are transferred from the form of living and feeding in the womb to the "world life format," and the first time when they breathe in the worldly "breath," not the mother's, the oxygen in the worldly breath burns their lungs. And at that moment the newborn baby begins to cry.

That is why the friends of Allah advise not to take that worldly breath into your lungs too much, otherwise, if you take the world inside too much, you will burn and cry like that baby.

We are fed with the breath of Allah. He protects and guards us with his name al-Hannan (the One who shows mercy) and His other names. He knows that we will suffer when we are separated from Him (in terms of consciousness), and He wants to remove our mistakes out of His mercy. Therefore, He gives us unlimited chances which we consider as trouble and evil, but which are good in purpose and result. The purpose is to protect us from ourselves; the purpose is to warn, not to scare.

He does not need our protection. He does not need our worships. He does not want us to feel hopeless or alone.

Does a mother want her child to be sad?

The words imam, ummah, and ummi are all selected for this reason, and not by coincidence.

The word IMAM comes from the root UM. UM, that is, mother.

We have already mentioned that IMAM means "the one who calls the lost children of Islam to the path of peace with the compassion of a mother."

One trusts in and surrenders to their mother but cannot surrender to Allah. I am writing it this clearly. Allah asks for FAITH. And FAITH comes from being ASSURED.

Is there any fear left in the one who is assured?

Your mother won't do anything to harm you; doesn't she want the best for you?

Does she want you to be hurt?

I am asking so that you contemplate, think. Think because Allah loves a thinker.

The devil who wants to surround us from left and right, front and back with fear says, "You no longer have a job. Huh! Let's see how you will provide food for your children?! Go ahead, steal!"

What do we do? We complain about why we are going through something, and we reproach Allah unknowingly and unwillingly.

Will your mother upset you? Just BE ASSURED and SURRENDER for once …

With a great genius as if to summarize this scientificness with poetry, it is stated, based on the statements associated with the Quran and the hadiths, that all the creatures and the universe will be affected by the sin of one, and the mussels at the bottom of the seas will hold us responsible for one sin.

Because the selections of each one of us affect the destiny of each creature in the universe. And again, everything in the universe will be affected by the thawabs of one of us, and even the mussels at the bottom of the seas will feel grateful for a thawab of one of us.

The worst enemy people could ever encounter in their lives is again themselves. There is, in fact, a battlefield in a person; both Mecca and Madinah are in a person. People need to migrate from themselves to themselves. They need to be EXPORTED from themselves. That is exactly why it is called; HIJRAH … Just like it is in QIYAMAH, get out of yourself, get outside, and migrate! Hijr, which has meanings such as "export", "outside", tells us to migrate from our false perceptions in life, from the friendships and relationships that feed our egos, from our egoist comprehension, from our understandings and beliefs that harm us, and from our conditionings. From the short temper and the primitive ego within us to our Madinah which is disciplined, and which has found the civilization that comes from existing with Allah … ("Madinah" means "civilized" and our Prophet named this city Madinah which was previously called "Yasrib.") HIJRAH is the representation that we may not find the true civilization unless we reach our city of Madinah that bears the civilization of Allah from the primitive ego within ourselves …

We, actually, need to concentrate on ourselves, not others.

Tolstoy says, "Everyone wants to change the world, yet nobody thinks of changing themselves."

If everyone changed themselves, the world would change anyway.

We should be determined to be ready and waiting with all the names of Allah's attributes to complete this true picture remaining in our essences and ensure that they get into our areas of activity. For this reason, the dervishes who enter the path of Sufism are told to do things that they do not understand with their current comprehension as they proceed onto that path but which they start to grasp as their comprehension increases.

For example, Shams sent Rumi to a tavern and asked him to get him some wine. Why did he do this?

Because everything that we reject is again from Allah.

As long as we reject that, we attribute a separate existence to it, and we kind of take it as a "god." And we fall into the sin of considering Adam separate from Allah, which is the cause of Satan being called the devil, and we do not even notice that we demonize, that is, we do not notice being deceived and being expelled from heaven. Anyone whether on the path of Allah or not will return to Him. Both have the SIRAT meaning the PATH. They are both on their paths. There is no escape. Whoever we are, the destination will always be Allah. But one of them is the "Sirat al-Mustaqeem," which is the straight path towards the target, and the other one is the path of the misguided. Both heaven and hell belong to Him. There is nothing apart from Him …

Therefore, we should always be careful about what we think and speak. For it is also mentioned in the Quran, that a good word is like a tree or a seed. That seed is attached to the soil with a strong root and its branches spread in every direction. However, a bad word is like a tree without roots; so, the more shoots we plant in this world, the larger the forests we have in the hereafter.

"Have you not considered how Allah presents an example, [making] a good word like a good tree, whose root is firmly fixed and its branches [high] in the sky?" (Surah Ibrahim, Verse 24)

Hazrat Ibrahim Khalilullah, that is the friend of Allah, asks his mother: "Mother, who is your lord?"

"Your father."

"Who is his lord?"

"The pharaoh."

And when he asks, "Who is his lord?" his mother shushes him.

Then he breaks all the idols, hangs an axe on the biggest idol, and says, "Since these idols are gods, then this big one killed the others."

So, the word Rabb (Lord), everything that we consider to be apart from Allah and we idolize, will consistently come our way until we break it and get freed from its recording and being a servant and slave to it without noticing. However, there is nothing except for Allah. There is nothing but the creatures of flesh and bones that Allah brings before us to complete our deficiencies, to admit our failures, and to reach maturity, and the incidents that make them become causes.

Allah is in communication with each of His servants and He will, of course, do this through His servants. How will He do it? Are you expecting to hear a sound from the skies? It is said that Allah awards His servants through His servants, and He also sends punishments to His servants through His servants.

Are you a victim of a theft? Concentrate on yourself and not the thief. That theft is from Allah, and it is nothing but the universal mechanism returning a mistake you made in response to an action (or it is a test from Allah to move up a rank) … Think of what you did to someone. Forget about the thief, I mean, remove the means. And when there is only the Creator that is left, you won't lose your temper. Who else will you be angry at except for yourself? Allah has mobilized His names and sent you the "response" you deserved for what you did. That's it! Why do you care about the thief? That is between them and Allah; you should think of the reason for calling that thief. What did you do and to whom? Or what are the weaknesses that you cannot defeat in your ego that make you experience such things?

If you try to evaluate the happenings independent from the underlying causes, you are no different than a person trying to remove a poisonous plant in the garden by only pulling out the leaves. When evaluating the happenings, you need to think about WHY did that happen to you. In other words, your focus should not be on the person who broke into your car and stole several items and hate that person, but to think of the possibility that this is a response to something YOU did (or, depending on the care, your parents, or a family member) by remembering that this came from Allah. Because people fight against the superficial appearance of the incidents. However, unless one goes down to the root and eliminates the root CAUSE, that poisonous plant in the garden will continue to grow. To remove the shadow, you need to fight against the body, not the shadow …

"What is the underlying cause of this experience?" This is the only question.

Maybe it is a judgment, maybe an insult, perhaps something you did, maybe something your parents or your grandfather did to someone's child. So, because of all these, to cleanse your entire family starting from 7 generations before you and to cleanse yourself to remove this energy from yourself, that is, you need to do tawbah istighfar, meaning to ask for Allah's mercy, and to put this tawbah istighfar in action not only verbally but also in our comprehensions. Various Islamic procedures are recommended to achieve this (to ask for blessings, ransom, etc.). When you do this, the energy that leads to this problem will be completely removed from its roots.

First, remember the first condition of being Adam; to comprehend our non-existence. Unless we disappear, the pain we suffer in this realm of a dream to be effaced is beyond comparison to the pain we will suffer in the hereafter; the pain here is nothing. Out of His mercy, Allah wills that we accept His names and complete our missing parts.

It really upsets me when people refer to Allah, who placed the quality of a mother struggling to protect her child among His names with the name al-Hanan, as "the One who treats with anger, tortures, and casts into hell."

Yes, because Allah loves every one of His servants and protects them, to the extent of the harm done by a servant to another servant, that servant will, of course, get a response that will make them sustain torture; yet there is still a mercy to that wrongdoing servant even in that torture. The purpose is to direct that servant to the true path. Does Allah discriminate among His children? Does He not want all of us to take the right path?

Maybe that child cannot continue their studies because they lost their father, maybe their mother is getting re-married, and they begin to have quite different problems with their future stepfather. How does it make you feel to cause them to be dragged to wrong paths when they may become good people?

Surely, if it is not Allah's will, the father of that child neither dies nor becomes permanently disabled ... The point here is that the destiny of all creatures in the universe simultaneously changes with one incident; this must be one of the things expressed by the saying, "Allah is in a new glory every moment." Everything is restructured through a single incident. There is certainly good in every evil, but knowing that not only do our faults affect us but also all the creatures in the universe and the fact that they will complain against us for this should keep us away from making mistakes, right?

There is surely still compassion under all the trouble or rage we incur which we think Allah made us experience but which we actually incur due to our actions or as a test. We do not know Allah. We evaluate Him and our experiences based on our presumptions; and this leads us - I am ashamed to say, may Allah forgive me – to have experiences for which we blame Him and misleads us to think that our experiences are related to Him being wrathful.

Try to handle three of your children and see how you get lost in the judicial system and notice how you are questioned by your own children. Yet, Allah thinks of the good and the subsistence of the entire universe from the human to the larva on the leaf and to the ant with an uninterrupted justice, without getting tired, and with all His power, and thus, He makes us experience activities and incidents in this direction.

However, as Einstein said, "We cannot solve the problem with the logic that led to the problem." We cannot see the whole picture by looking with the human mind, by looking with our state which is still a segment of the picture, not the whole picture. Surrender steps in just here. "You cannot see; I see, and I know. Then, surrender to me; consent to Me manifest in you, to become apparent in you; then see how my name al-Hakeem, which I call wisdom, that is, everything is required and thought-out, reveals in you."

If we cannot see this, it is because of our ignorance and prejudice.

Human beings cannot know themselves without making mistakes; they cannot reach the rank of humanity; so, let's make up with our mistakes, draw the necessary lessons from them, host them for once, and send them off to not to repeat them.

If Allah did not love us that much, if He did not care about us for us, He would not have mercy on us; put everything aside, would He want us to be pleased with Him?

If Allah were enraged and desired for us to burn in hell why would He want His servant to be pleased with Him?

"…Allah being pleased with them and they with Allah …" (Surah al-Bayyinah, Verse 8). Once Allah is pleased with you, it is more difficult to preserve it, and the first thing to do is to be pleased with Him just as He is pleased with us.

"Allah keeps firm those who believe, with the firm word, in the worldly life, and in the Hereafter. And Allah sends astray the wrongdoers. And Allah does what He wills." (Surah Ibrahim, Verse 27)

"... Allah is pleased with them, and they are pleased with Him ..." (Surah al-Mujadilah, Verse 22)

Come on, overcome your ego, and pray for your greatest business rival. Come on!

Come on, pray for your neighbor's daughter who has begun to reach the peak of happiness when your daughter is less happy. Come on!

Come on! Pray for somebody who has caused you harm to be guided by Allah. Come on! Is it that difficult? It is so difficult, isn't it? Why?

Isn't the real Muslim one who cannot sleep when their neighbor is hungry?

In fact, when I, you, we pray for our neighbors and when we are delighted with the happiness of others even if we are unhappy, and when we ask Allah to increase their happiness, the angels saying "Amen" to our prayers say: "Let Allah give tens of, hundreds of, thousands of this happiness to you." They say "Amen" after our prayers. That's why people going to Mecca and Madinah say "Amen!" loudly because the one who teaches you this knows that the unseen angels accompany you in addition to the visible people and the prayers of hundreds of people are hundreds, thousands, tens of thousands of times more effective with their participation.

In comparison with other doctrines, one of the best sides of Islam is that it brings arrangements not for "individual" development and maturation but for "collective development and comprehension." It is advised not only to pray for your own welfare but, as a method for the acceptance of prayers, to pray and have concern for all humanity and later pray for yourself by descending rank by rank.

Actually, you do not know that you do good for yourself even when you think you pray for others. Angels beg Allah, cry for you, and say, "May Allah give you so much more in return."

Every good that Allah makes you contribute to is in fact a favor for you, not for that person.

A beggar comes to Hazrat Aishe's door. Hazrat Aishe gives him a Date (something available in the home) and as he leaves, he says: "May

Allah be pleased with you."

Our Prophet says to Hazrat Aishe, "O Aishe, respond to him saying, 'May Allah be pleased with you too.'"

Why?

Be sure that it is not certain who helps whom in this universe. You suppose that you help somebody, but you become a pharaoh. We could, at best, be the intermediaries carrying the good sent by Allah to one of His servants. And we must be thankful to Allah and then to that person for being chosen as a mediator to send Allah's property to Allah's servant.

Property belongs to Allah, the servant belongs to Allah; He could have chosen another person as a mediator for goodness, but if He has chosen you, you must pray to Allah for the other servant who caused you to be chosen as a mediator.

"One who does not give thanks to the servant of Allah is regarded as someone who does not give thanks to Allah…"

Anybody for whom we are chosen as a mediator by Allah to deliver goodness is one of our beloved ones. Actually, they help us, as Allah wishes so, without even realizing… Just because of this, may Allah be pleased with them.

Therefore, "Do not rub it in with vanity." says the verse. As I say, we live in reverse order. How ignorant I am. How very ignorant!…

This is why it is said that if you want your prayer to be accepted, pray for as many people as you can while praying, and we include "ummat al-Islam (the community of Islam)." Because everything and everybody existing for energy participates in the prayer although we cannot see them.

My Allah permitted me to perform the salah right beside Kabaa on the night of Qadr. I wished for it so much that I had an inner voice saying, "My Allah accepted my prayer."

Then, I stopped and quickly repented. Who was I?

I felt boastful like a person whose prayer was accepted, and I said,

"My Allah, please forgive me." And later I remembered giving my food to a beggar on my way to Kabaa.

Maybe it was his prayer that caused me to obtain my wish. Maybe, it was my grandmother's prayer that she had said, "If Allah wishes it will happen" when I asked her, "Pray for me grandma, pray for me to perform salah close to Kabaa tonight."

Or it was the prayer of a family friend's daughter who said, "May Allah predestine you with what's in your heart. May Allah accept your prayers," when I told her that I will pray for her sister, who was experiencing some difficulties, that night.

Maybe it was one of them or all of them.

The important thing was that it was made possible for me to save up money or collect stamps or cars (collection) in this world, or to collect prayers.

I had to collect prayers. I had to collect prayers from different people through my actions which I sometimes voluntarily do with love and which I sometimes do in order not to be defeated by my ego and to defeat it I had to carry out those actions in order to receive prayers, the best thing ever, and become close to Allah with a prayer which is the main purpose, not for a provision.

Allah began to give Moses' (Musa) tribe famine because they were not content with nor appreciated what they had. People only know that they are equipped with treasures when they lose them. This is unfortunately how it is. Unless the ego is disciplined, people are controlled by their weaknesses and bad traits, and one day, they lose what they have by going astray. Look at the people who have lost their wealth and health and you will see that they either failed to sufficiently give thanks or unfairly reproached Allah or they were mistaken by saying, "Nothing would happen to me." They inadvertently called for that distress.

Let's repeat saying that you cannot stay at home for 40 days. We understand the landmines in the system unexpectedly when we are being confined to that house...

When Moses' (Musa) tribe went astray and was disciplined with famine because of ingratitude, Allah who is ar-Ra'uf (the Compassionate) and ar-Raheem (the Merciful) suddenly began to send them food again.

Moses (Musa) was surprised and asked Allah decently: "My Lord, you sent your blessing again, thank you my Allah. May I learn the reason?"

Allah answered: "I would not have provided but a donkey was living among this tribe. It was very hungry, and it was nothing but skin and bones. It prayed so sincerely that I couldn't hurt it..."

Maybe I was there through the prayer of a dog that I had fed on the street.

Allahualam.

My Allah knows the best.

So, we do a favor for ourselves, with each kindness we are chosen as a mediator.

This ego ...

You have certainly heard that Allah created the ego and Allah burned it thousands of times in the fire because it said ME. But every time that ego continued to say, "ME ..."

Islam is the religion of jihad (holy war; literally meaning struggling) ... This is true.

However, jihad is a word specifically chosen in the Quran. You engage in jihad with your ego, you engage in jihad by using your knowledge, your properties. You engage in jihad at the risk of your life when necessary. You also engage in jihad when settlements become impossible, when your adversary makes an attempt against your life, and when you are obliged to.

Our prophet Mohammad went to Abu Jahl who denied him many times in order to summon Abu Jahl to Allah's path by speaking and agreeing and to peacefully invite him to Islam. He had never preferred to engage in war or bloodshed. Moreover, as he delayed the decisions of war to the utmost, some of our Prophet's companions occasionally consulted and conversed with him.

But have a look at how our prophet spoke. They were victorious on the way back from the Tabuk Expedition, but his companions were too exhausted. Our prophet said after the victory, "We are returning from the little jihad to the great jihad." (Aduni Kesful Hafa, 1, 425)

Our prophet referred to, the "Tabuk Expedition" that he had joined with his most crowded army as the "Little Jihad."

His companions were confused and when they asked, "O Messenger of Allah, our war has just finished, how could we afford a new war?" He answered, "The true fighter is the one that fights against their ego …" (Tırmıdhi, Jihad, 2)

"The greatest jihad is the one that is against our ego …"

The vanity and pride coming from winning a victory waits in ambush. Also, the feeling of superiority because of feeling strong. And no war could be as tough as the one that is against one's ego. Because people can be cruel towards others, but they are always merciful to themselves.

Our Prophet Mohammed rode his sacred camel and he entered Mecca with humility. To keep away from arrogance, to remember that the true winner is Allah, and to avoid nourishing his ego.

The winner is Allah, and we are the intermediates.

The only thing that enforces people to use strength and brute force is "scientific insufficiency and ignorance." That's why the pre-Islamic period is called the "Period of Ignorance." The matter that prevents faith or the basis of misapplications is ignorance.

In Islam, conveying the truth through science and the method of relying on an invitation to Islam is called "engaging in jihad with knowledge and the Quran."

A person cannot conquer the hearts with any weapon even if they capture the bodies. "Invite to the way of your Lord with wisdom and good instruction and argue with them in a way that is best …" (Surah an-Nahl, Verse 125). The one who is underpowered "scientifically" wants to forcefully express their anger.

When we say knowledge, we first think of the knowledge related to Allah and the basics of faith, and Imam Azam (the greatest imam) called his book about the basics of faith as "the greatest Islamic jurisprudence," that is, "the greatest knowledge."

"So do not obey the disbelievers, and strive against them with it [i.e., the Quran] a great striving." (Surah al-Furqan, Verse 52)

Allah orders His Prophet to engage in the great jihad. He wants him to put in his greatest effort while fulfilling his task and inviting people to Islam. The war order came after immigration, and many other subjects are with the invitation aspect of this verse.

"On the Day of Judgment, the ink of the scholars and the blood of the martyrs are weighed; the ink of the scholars weighs more than the blood of the martyrs ... (Suyuti, el Camiu's Sagir, nr 10026; Ibn-i Abdilberr, Camiıl Beyani'l-Ilm, nr 139. There are others attributing to Hasan Basri).

The one who learns the knowledge of Allah already begins to comprehend oneself and the universe.

It is said that the sleep of the scholar is more beneficial than the worship of the ignorant.

"Everything has a path. Heaven's path is knowledge." (Muazdh Ibn Jabal) "If one enters a path intending to gain knowledge, this means that Allah has incorporated them to one of the paths leading to heaven. Angels, pleased with the seeker of knowledge, place their wings above the seeker. Those in the skies and on the earth and even the fish in the sea seek forgiveness for the scholar." (Narrated by Ahmad Ibn Mace, etc.)

Even guns have a range. However, the words, the location where the truths will reach, and time neither have a limitation nor an obstacle.

"... Be devoted to the worship of your Lord 'alone'"—in accordance with what these prophets read in the Scripture and what they taught.

(Surah Ali Imran, Verse 79) Rabbani means the one who knows Allah by striving with the knowledge of Allah and worship …

The basis of all evils in the world originates from ignorance. Abu Jahl is pointed out as an enemy of Islam because of ignorance. The one who wants to reach Allah must primarily try to reach the divine light of knowledge from the darkness of ignorance. And the first thing for a person who departs for jihad is to research the truth of the visible through knowledge. The scholar who does this gradually begins to see Allah everywhere with the appearance of the name of Allah in them and they are inevitably surrounded by Allah, the Guardian, with a sense of mercy. Allah knows the best.

As for the word "qital" which means to fight: "Fighting has been made obligatory upon you 'believers', though you dislike it. Perhaps you dislike something which is good for you and like something which is bad for you. Allah knows and you do not know." (Surah al-Baqarah, Verse 216)

When it is said that Islam is a religion of jihad, as the word and concept of JIHAD is not understood, bloodshed is the first thing that comes to mind and people are made to think of battle and war which is not recommended in Islam unless necessary and things reach the point of self-defense.

JIHAD in the Quran rather speaks of a person's struggle towards their own essence. JIHAD comes from the root of the word JAHD and JAHD means struggling, making effort, striving (there is a mutual exertion in JAHD; one side is against Islam, and the other side struggles in favor of Islam).

Hence, our Prophet said 'jihad-ul akbar' for jihad with your ego. It is not easy to struggle with habits of many years, false teachings, and your undisciplined ego.

On the other hand, there is the word QITAL meaning war, battle, and used in the Quran, and action states like qatele are mentioned in the Quran …

As mentioned in the verse above, if Allah has predestined war at some point – that the word 'war' leads to unpleasant feelings in one's mind - there is the statement, "it has certainly some good in it that we cannot comprehend".

In the verse above, "to battle" is expressed with the word "qital" and "qatele" means 'they killed'. "Qital" means mutual fighting to death. As seen, qital is a special form of jihad which occurs at the point where it is necessary to fight with the heart and soul. Although jahd is a general concept, it is a special form of jihad where one risks one's life while jihad is done with knowledge, property, etc.

It is obligatory at the point where it is required. To battle comes from the root "SAV," meaning to repel an attack, and it is a kind of defense against mutual attacks.

When the killing of Muslims started and tyranny became extreme, Allah commanded defense. War was predestined because people were persecuted. Since it is easier for the people of Allah to battle compared to the jihad with their egos, our Prophet called the jihad using swords as "jihad-e-asghar (the lesser jihad)."

During a war when Hazrat Ali lifted his sword, a denier spat in his face and Hazrat Ali lowered his sword, and he released the denier. That beautiful person described as the lion of Allah said to the denier, who asked "why didn't you cut off my head, Ali?" "I cut your ego's desires and wishes with the sword of my tenderness and my knowledge. Look what have you become?" Then, the denier became a Muslim from then on. That sword, Zulfiqar, is a sword known as the sword that sacrifices the ego and Hazrat Ali is the meaning of this.

When angels asked Allah, "Will you create a being that sheds blood?" Allah stated that He had taught Adam all the names and he knew the matters that angels did not know.

Right here, another meaning that we can understand when we think about it is that a human being tends to cause bloodshed because of their ignorance, however, is it possible to prevent a creature from causing bloodshed by teaching knowledge and through discipline?

A Story from Mathnawi

There is a story I love very much in Mathnawi.

The sultan of the era made a painting competition between the Turks and the Mongols. Each team was given opposing walls separated by a curtain to prevent the two teams from spying on each other. Each team started to paint not knowing what the other team was painting. The Mongols drew such a beautiful picture that was filled with striking colors; green, and purple. Their expression of color was remarkable.

The Turks, on the other side, just sculpted the wall that was given to them. They sculpted and sculpted...

Something interesting happened when it was time to lift the curtain... The picture the Mongols had painted with those magnificent colors was reflected on the wall that the Turks had sculpted with care.

The picture reflected on the sculpted wall was so beautiful that a masterpiece emerged.

Our Prophet reflected the truth of Allah and His infinite meaning to the whole universe like that sculpted and immaculate mirror that has reached purity. And Allah's will to see this is the reason for our existence.

So, to become just a mirror and to understand that there is nothing beyond it. And to reflect just like a sculpted and purified mirror is only possible by finding our essence.

The one who reaches their essence understands that they are "created" with what they "deserve."

V.
ISLAM

"Religion without science is blind, and science without religion is lame"

-Albert Einstein

Religion is a Path

"Basic meanings" lying in the depths of Islam were removed from our consciousness for centuries. Are we innocent? Never... So, to speak, our inclination to investigate these truths because of 'our worldly troubles', contenting ourselves assuming that we understand only the physical and material dimensions of the religion and the beliefs that are imposed on us that "Religion is another thing, science is another thing" have resulted in lost lives and unhappiness...

The perception of two concepts being different was successfully reflected to us, except for the orientation from one to another, with the feeling that we must choose either science or religion.

Matter is separated from meaning, the physical world from the hereafter, human from human, and religion from religion.

What happened next?

Self-destructed societies that lived in pain while history was repeating itself.

And now, many "false truths" dictated to us under the name of science during our academic lives as well as many distinctions I listed above began to lose their validity especially with quantum physics entering our lives and with Allah saying, "You caused enough pain for yourselves, yet you could not learn," and certain "unchanging" fundamentals of science are ruined with new scientific discoveries, particularly during the last 300 years.

However, for some reason, many new scientific findings still remain undisclosed to the public.

The laws that science cannot explain their reasons have come to the surface even more. However, those explanations were available in religious understandings.

The laws of Allah (sunnatullah) must have been these. There were so many of these…

When many things done in this basic distinction both in the name of civilizations, countries, and humanity, so to say, "have blown up in society's face," the non-negligible existence of the centuries-old explanations imparted by the fundamental teachings lying in the truth of religion regarding those things that were unexplained was revealed.

It is clearly indicated in the Quran that "The religion next to Allah is Islam." So, I really find using the word 'religions' strange …

Even though religion is stereotyped and presented to us as a distinctive concept, it sums itself up quite clearly.

The word 'religion' is an Arabic word, and it is accepted to be derived from the word 'deyn', which includes meanings such as 'responsibility', 'debt to be paid at a certain time'. It also means 'customs/tradition', 'reward', 'subservience', 'sovereignty', 'provision', 'decree' and it has many more meanings.

The word 'religion' in the Quran is used to express Islam as well as other beliefs. But the word 'religion' specifically refers to Islam. It is clearly stated that the concepts of Islam and religion have the same meaning and the religion brought by all prophets is Islam. (Surah Al-i Imran Verses 99 and 85, Surah ash-Shuraa, Verse 13)

Beyond that, the word religion in the Quran carries different meanings in terms of Allah and servant, and aside from the many meanings such as "Allah's decree, His questioning, His dominance" it also covers concepts such as "surrender, obedience, and worship" in terms of servant; thus, religion is basically the PATH that regulates the relationship between Allah and His servant.

"Path…"

I have met many people who say, "I believe in Allah, but I don't believe in religion". It is surely each person's own life, own beliefs, but it is the same thing for me to say, "I do not believe in religion" as a cliché without knowing what one is believing or not and to say, "I am religious" without knowing what religion is.

When I ask, "You don't believe in religion, or you say that's what religion requires. Ok, I understand, so what does religion mean?" There should be an answer I need to get, right? But my questions were mostly unanswered, there wasn't an answer. Maybe, you don't know either, right now while reading this book or you haven't investigated what religion is. Because we, human beings, prefer grinding what is offered to us without questioning instead of developing it.

Religion means PATH.

PATH …

The Quran is the only divine book that has undistorted Arabic. It is not something that I say just by looking at the verse on this subject; you can comprehend it only if you examine the Quran.

"Innad Deena Indallahi Islam …" (Surah Ali Imran, Verse 19) "… Indeed, the religion in the sight of Allah is Islam …

So, "The path (religion) in the SIGHT of Allah is to SURREN-DER." Before explaining this concept, let's see why religion in the sight of Allah is Islam.

Why should Allah, owner of the land of the universe, have more than one constitution when every country has one constitution?

This is such a constitution that it is never behind time; on the contrary, it updates itself in all time zones, with the miraculous words and narratives it contains according to the time lived in.

So, you don't need to issue a statutory decree, etc. When you investigate, among all the possibilities, you find that it is equipped with a special A'Rabic, that is, RAB-IC (Rab means Lord).

Each prophet mentioned in the Quran was sent with the highest knowledge on what the people were developing and interested in at that time so that they could attract attention in their times.

During the period of Hazrat Moses (Musa) there was 'magic'; during the era of Jesus Christ (Isa), it was 'health and healing'; and during the period of our Prophet Hazrat Mohammad (PBUH), it was poetry and lyrics… Yet, religion is such a beautiful word and so scientific and poetic at the same time, it is impossible to describe or imagine that it is a human production.

This is described in many of the verses in the Quran.

Surah Yunus, Verse 38: "Or do they say [about the Prophet], "He invented it?" Say, "Then bring forth a surah like it and call upon [for assistance] whomever you can besides Allah, if you should be truthful."

Yet, the people who assume themselves as Muslims thinking that Islam is something "gained at birth" and because it is written "Muslim or Islam" on their identity cards and who deem themselves entitled to go to heaven just because it is written so and consider others as non-believers are enough to indicate that this matter is not essentially understood.

Let alone being born a Muslim, we are not qualified as humans when we are born! Each of us are mortals when we were born and the word 'mortal' is a concept given primarily for the body's external surface, that is, because of our being from flesh and bone.

Besides this, the word 'mortal' is related to the word 'bashir' that means "herald" and it also contains the meaning of 'bearer of herald'.

All of the prophets, primarily our Prophet, are referred to as 'mortals' in the Quran.

Being a human is a candidacy and a process. This process proceeds towards the positive or the negative. While the word mortal is usually used in a positive context in the Quran, human is used in statements involving criticism ... In some explanations, it is expressed that although humans have the characteristics to become "khalifatullah," the mortal is capable of revealing all of the divine names ...

I understand from this subject which may be explained in further detail, but which will still never end that what we need to understand for now under this section is that being a mortal, a human, or Adam are not the same. Allahualam ... I am interpreting this sign only based on the Quran.

If you investigate, you can have a better comprehension of how the words mortal, Adam, and human are used in the verses. Although these are used to substitute each other's meaning in translations, this may lead us to have an insufficient understanding. It is already unbelievable that each of us considers ourselves a caliph. If the universe is filled with Allah's caliphs, why is humanity in such a terrible state? This is only an expression for "candidacy" ... If only each of us would be a "caliph of Allah (khalifatullah) ..."

However, I will try to display by my own comprehension of how evaluating the Quran just with the interpretations prevents us from understanding the Quran as required; that in many interpretations, it is impossible to consider these concept differences due to the unlimited content of the narrations and each word; and to be able to truly evaluate Islam and the Quran, it is required to first try to understand these meanings on the surface from the original language of the Quran and then, to get a roadmap to understand the other meanings ...Remember again that this language is not the Arabic we know but, it is a special dialect of the Quraysh language and it is the language of Allah... I didn't understand Arabic when I started studying the Quran, but there was something about it that when I combined the verses with my inner voice, the meanings gradually began to reveal in my consciousness...

Of course, it takes effort and there is no end to this... Understanding this infinity even with my limited comprehension makes one confront the insufficiency of the word "infinite" for Allah.

As I say, when you read this Book by trying to understand that it says, "O, human" when saying "Ya Sin," you will experience that there is an external power calling you "O, human" and that infinite power reaches your body and even your marrow by shaking you all over.

It is a Book that is current in all ages and beyond the ages. Its narrative is valid for all of us at any moment. Once again, television news has been broadcasting the violence against women. Mind-boggling murders and attacks... I thought of the people who say that the Quran was descended for the people living in that era in Mecca... Today, the unbelievable murders of or violence against "the daughters" of many mothers are no different from the Meccans burying their daughters alive. Although the numbers of the years have changed, the contents are the same. So, what is needed is to feel and keep the Quran and Hazrat Muhammed (PBUH) who brought peace and safety when materialism, unfairness, injustice, and violence were about in that era of Mecca (like this period we and the world are experiencing), alive. Quran is a self-revealing book as long as you make an effort and intention. That's why Islam is a religion of intention... Intentions open all doors.

And when you intend to understand this Book produced by Allah and you wish to be taught by Allah, you will hear this: "Rahman allamel Quran."

"The Most Merciful taught the Quran" (Surah ar-Rahman, Verses 1-2)Allah says in this verse that, "He will teach you. And He taught it. You will experience this inshaallah.

Why? Because Allah does not break His promise.

"This is the promise of Allah. And Allah never fails in His promise. But most people do not know." (Surah ar-Rum, Verse 6) Yes, He does not break His promise.

And when you live this, you will think: "Then which of your Lord's favors will you both deny?" (Surah ar-Rahman, Verse 45)

As long as the servant of Allah wishes; it is always narrated that regardless of whether that servant is somewhere all alone if they ask for knowledge, knowledge will be delivered to them whether through another servant or in other ways. You have surely heard the hadith that "Allah gives wealth to whomever He wills and knowledge to those who want it."

We struggle for wealth, but how much effort do we make for knowledge?

However, wherever there is effort there is wonder ... And wherever there is bother there is Ahmad (Hz Muhammad [PBUH]) ...

I have a lawyer friend named Özgür who spends half of the year abroad and the other half of the year in Turkey. Although he believes in Allah and the Prophet, he doesn't perform his worship, but he is a really charitable person and he has a very good heart, really good...

One day when he visited me in my office while we were talking about the truth and religion, as usual, he said: "Deniz, you are peaceful, there is something you are taking shelter in, and yet my problems do not end that I could turn to Allah!"

I smiled, I even laughed. I asked, "Do I really look carefree to you?"

"I don't know. I mean, you are not aggressive, you generally smile, and you are peaceful. I don't hear you complaining. I don't know, maybe it is because you perform salah and worship", he said.

I asked curiously: "What kind of troubles do you have?"

And he told me about the unexpected financial problems he had been experiencing lately.

"If I make the slightest amount of money, I owe ten times as much, if not for me, for my family. I constantly have financial difficulties. If I didn't have these difficulties, I may turn to Allah too, but I must struggle with financial difficulties that I'm not sure where they come from. This also causes me to have anger issues, you know? Therefore, I am always angry and nervous. Because I don't deserve these difficulties!"

We all tend to think we don't deserve the troubles we encounter. Because our egos are 'untouchable'. It is always another who is mistaken, deficient, bad; and we are always as clean as a whistle.

However, everything we experience has been especially chosen in order to tame and domesticate our animal sides, otherwise, how could we mature?

I understood why he was experiencing financial problems. And why he was aggressive. We are all tested from our weaknesses. In fact, it was his own financial weaknesses and dependencies that created the troubles and unless the moral weaknesses in his spirit are resolved, the reflections of these weaknesses in the material world would not be solved.

We, unfortunately, go on a pilgrimage or go to Umrah after we solve worldly problems, after the circumcision, education, and wedding of our sons. We turn to worship after solving our household problems. We always make the same mistakes; however, if we firstly turn to Allah and try to educate ourselves on this path, each of the problems will be removed from us one by one.

He turned to me and asked, "Do you never feel desperate?" I said to him, "I felt like I could feel desperate from time to time, but it was momentary. Then, I say, 'My Allah I know You immediately succor especially for broken, sad hearts.' I don't merely believe in this Özgür… Believing would fall short, I know, beyond belief, that He is with me. I know that He won't break His promise. I know that He is the only true friend. While you have friends whom you cannot reach, there is a true friend whom you can reach whenever you wish. There is Allah talking to you in every moment. He always hears and considers you. How can I feel myself lonely and desperate? Allah answers me even by showing me writing on a TRUCK passing by, talking to me anywhere and in every moment when I ask a question. Allah speaks to me through a phone call from an unexpected person when I am bothered, conveying a message that eases my pain… When I am confused, I open the Quran, Allah answers my questions directly with the verses that I come across."

Then, "Look…," I said. "I want you to do something even if it doesn't have meaning for you Özgür. Just perform ablution, an ablution cleaning not just your body but also your mind and heart… And take the Quran.

Think about your situation and open the Quran with a sincere intention. Allah will speak to you directly. You will see, if Arabic is difficult for you now, firstly start with Mathnawi. Is Mathnawi not carrying the word of Allah to us conveyed by the last friends like other friends of Allah? Today, go home, perform ablution, ask Allah your question, and open Mathnawi with faith and turn to Allah with a simple heart… You will have an experience."

I am neither an oracle nor a superior person; on the contrary, I am a weak servant. But I knew that He, who is the owner of all might and mercy, would never leave anyone turning to Him in the lurch. The next day, while I was browsing Mathnawi with my mother, the phone rang.

It was Özgür. I answered the telephone, he was crying…

"Deniz", he said trembling. My eyes were filled with tears, I looked at my mother.

"I did what you said. I performed ablution; I took Mathnawi from the bookshelf. I turned to Allah and asked: "My Allah, why don't my financial problems end? Why does my fury not end, what should I do?" Then, he was quiet.

I was listening to him quietly shedding tears… "And I am reading you the page that was shown to me," said Özgür.

These were the writings on the page: "If I am free, why all this rage? Is Allah's mercy not greater than His fury that I am still furious?"

And later, he read a narration about the damage of pursuing material values and getting caught up in temporary pleasures.

We both cried.

Allah who calls you specifically by your name… Such mercy and affection… We all experience many things like these events, and I have experienced many other situations in this life. We all experience because mercy rains on each of us in every moment.

I wanted to do my part as an ordinary person by making an effort to become "nothing" by means of this book. Surely, you will appreciate it. Although we think differently, if we can serve to develop different ways of thinking at least, we may already hit the road of reaching holistic purpose, because Allah has already united us with our differences.

The Quran Is Beyond the Ages

The Quran is such a magnificent Book that it narrates the past on the one side while it narrates tomorrow and today on the other side.

This splendid Book communicating with the reader interactively is not simple Arabic. As it is 'Rabb'ic it is also available with interpretations in Arabic countries.

Quran is the biggest sign that Allah does not discriminate among His servants… If a person wants to turn to Allah with a clean heart and unconditionally, the Quran opens itself to them… What magnificent justice.

Rely on your Lord and be sure that He will enable you to read even if you don't know how to read because this is why the Quran is Rabb-ic and therefore, it was written clearly for anyone seeking Allah, not just for the people of a certain area.

Take Quran in your hand with an intention of asking any question even if you think it is foolishness and related to a worldly concern. Suddenly you will see that Allah speaks to you through a neighbor that has come to your door, or a passenger in the vehicle you get on while going to work or school or a friend, or through a title in a book…

Allah is in dialogue with us at every moment and anywhere, and we are in contact with Him only when we are in need or we want something … Just in our moments of prayer … But He still does not close His doors… He answers our questions with almighty mercy… He protects us at any moment and guards us with a mother's love…

Everywhere is filled with His signs and His signs are in everything…

And with this magnificent Book, He tells us about the universe and ourselves like a mother relaying life's truths to her child with tales and pictures in order for the child to comprehend what she conveys.

When this Book begins to conquer you, it will become impossible to drop it from your hand … There are many things in it from science to art, love, adventure, adrenaline, mystery, and secrets that you will want to be fully submerged in it…As the doors of Allah's kingdom open to you, you will realize that the paths going to Allah pass through the path leading to your inner self … You will fall into nothingness when you think you exist, and then you will fall into your nothingness again supposing that you are Him …

This is such a Book that nothing, except for the words of Allah, can contain such a miraculous narration with invariance over the ages and with unlimited knowledge …For instance, the verses interpreted as; Allah asked us during the meeting in the pre-eternity called Qalu Bala, "Am I not your Lord?"

It is said that this happened in pre-eternity… "Then Allah taught the names to Adam and the angels prostrated before Adam," says the Quran.

This event occurred in pre-eternity, and we are those who forget named "human (insan)" which means "the one who forgets" … I have thought about this event quite extensively.

And one day, something happened … "Allah taught Adam the names …" We have been learning the creation bearing the meanings of Allah's names from the Sun to the Moon, planets, stars, from cars to phones, television, from trees to dogs since we were born.

On the day I thought of this, I was thinking how the Quran has been timeless and how it contains the terms of each era.

I stopped at that moment.

"Allah taught Adam the names..."

Past time has passed in the presence of Allah ... not in our sights... We mentioned it in the chapter about time.

Then ... Maybe, when considered from our side, Allah was teaching Adam the names ...

In other words, ...

Maybe ... Yes, yes ...

Our Allah was "currently" teaching us the names and we have not yet been created!

Our Prophet's saying about this world's being a 'dream' was maybe connected with this...

Maybe we haven't yet been created... We have been in the rehearsals of ourselves. Maybe we have been raised in our cocoons to become butterflies ...

And or perhaps we have been created and the names were taught to us in pre-eternity... Maybe it was one of them, maybe ALL of them...

It was both yes and no. "Yes, and No," just like in the story of Hazrat Ibn Arabi ... These are the two words I learned from what I experienced...

What is a miracle if not this? Allahualam ... Allahu Akbar ...

TAWHID AND CREATION

Now, let's look into the basic and fundamental comprehension in Islam without which one cannot exactly be a 'believer': TAWHID...

I want to note that it is easier to say, "I am a Muslim" with many mistakes and the wrong comprehensions than saying "I am a Mumin (the one who believes)." The main goal is to proceed on the path to becoming a Muslim who is a Mumin, because these two concepts are connected, yet they are not the same.

You can find a short explanation about this at the end of this section.

Firstly, I share a few answers in the hadiths that our Prophet gave when he was asked about creation.

According to the statement of Jabir Ibn Abdullah who was one of the companions having narrated the most hadiths, our Prophet's answer to this question;

"O, Allah's Messenger! May you tell me the first thing that Allah created before everything?" I asked. He replied as follows:

Here, I want to address a matter before revealing the answer given by our Prophet.

Above all, is this; there is no other matter except for us. Although we think that 'there are other people' and we are being tried through them, in fact, there is just He and you. Everyone else is nothing beyond the 'means' Allah chose in order to mature you through you and for the dialog between you and Him. This is faith, that is, duality. The belief that there is Allah and you. Allah has allowed duality at least instead of multiplicity. However, the real aim in Islam is "certitude (iqan)," in other words, to have "certainty (yaqin)." This concept is basically (fana fillah), which is a state of annihilation in Allah, to abide in Allah (baqa-billah), and to understand that it is 'He' in you and to live accordingly. In other words, it is unity.

We will delve deeper into the matter of "certainty" which is mentioned in many verses, particularly in Surah al-Fath in the Quran and, with Allah's permission, together we will examine how much we have misunderstood some concepts…

The first thing we must understand about the Quran and Islam is not to ask, "what is this?" when looking at our Prophet's hadiths or Quran verses whilst depending on our individual intellects.

We must look by getting our intellects out of the way because each person's intellect is restricted with their own perceptions and conditionings. If we achieve this, Quran will readily speak to us and open itself to us. Indeed, there have been things that we were wrong about, haven't there? Not only do our intellects know the right things, do they?

Trust, intention, patience, and surrender are the desired things. If we can just achieve this, we can understand that the whole universe has always been speaking to us and helping us without doing much.

I know from myself; we don't like listening. Really. In fact, I think since the main point is listening rather than talking, Rumi introduced Mathnawi by saying "Bishnav," that is, "Listen." Just like saying that a book starting with the command "Read" can only be explained by saying "Listen."

As a friend of Allah says, "The only obstacle between Allah and us is our personal intellects. If we get it out of the way, only the Creator remains."

So, if we get back to the answer of the Prophet of Allah to Hazrat Jabir's question about the creation and existence, he answered it as follows;

"O, Jabir! First of all, the first thing Allah created is your Prophet's divine light. That divine light was wandering around with the power of Allah anywhere He wished. There wasn't anything at that time. Neither the Slate (Lawh) nor the pen, neither heaven nor the fire/hell existed. Neither an angel, sky, earth, sun, moon, jinn, nor a human existed.

When Allah wished to create the creatures, He divided this divine light into four pieces.

He created the pen from the first piece, He created al-Lawh al-Mahfuth (the Preserved Slate) from the second piece, He created the Throne (Arsh) from the third piece. He again divided the fourth piece into four pieces:

He created Hamalat al-Arsh (the bearers of the Throne) from the first piece, the Chair (Kursi) from the second piece, and other angels from the third piece.

He divided the fourth piece into four pieces again: He created the sky from the first piece, the earth from the second piece, and heaven and hell from the third piece.

He then divided the fourth piece into four pieces:

He created the divine light of the believers' insight/consciousness of faith from the first piece, He created the divine light of their hearts which consists of marifatullah (knowledge in Allah) from the second piece, He created the divine light of acquaintance (the divine light of La ilaha illalah Muhammedur Rasulullah) consisting of oneness (tawhid) from the third piece." (SeeAjluni, I/265-266)

In another hadith, the Prophet of Allah (PBUH) expressed it in this way: "Allah ordained, 'I created you from My own divine light and other things from your divine light.'"[35]

Now, in summary, it is understood from these hadiths that it is narrated in Islam in this way:

Allah first created our Prophet from His own divine light. He loved

35 Ahmed, Musned, IV-127; Hâkim, Mustedrak, II-600/4175; Ibn Hibban, El Ihsan, XIV-312/6404; el-Leknevi, el-Asaru'l-Merfu'a, s.42-43; Kastalani, Mevahibu'lLedunniye: 1/6; Krs. Acluni, Kashfu'l Hafa, C.1, 262265-266.

him so much that He then created the whole universe from his divine light.

So, what is the meaning of 'divine light (noor)', which we frequently hear about in the Quran? The word divine light (noor) means light, sparkle (cosmic light). We have explained it in the section titled Sound. What is light? KNOWLEDGE. Because every energy is knowledge. The divine light of Allah is "ilmullah," that is, "the knowledge of Allah," and the essence of everything consists of knowledge. Life is also present with the knowledge, with the divine light.

This word originates from the same root as the word derived from the word stem ZLM meaning acting against the truth and justice and the word "zulma," that is "blackout, darkness, black, being dark," and the word "zalim (cruel)" means "the one who is left in the dark;" the word "jahil (ignorant)," which is derived from the root JHL and also called "jahila," means "didn't know."

The people qualified as ignorant are the ones who are stuck in the dark, deprived of the divine light of the knowledge of Allah which is the basis of all knowledge...

Therefore, the cruel people's biggest cruelty is against themselves. This is the reason for the expressions in the Quran such as, "You have wronged your egos, you have wronged yourselves." Being against the truth as used in the word cruelty is the contrariety to the beautiful name of Allah who creates them, who is the reason for existence and proper living, al-Haqq (the Truth) which is the only reality and knowledge present in each person.

One will reach their truth only when they perform what is required by the dominant beautiful names created in them by Allah.

They will otherwise be sentenced to unhappiness and pain in a life that is deprived of His own light and knowledge of creation for they cannot take out and reflect the treasure hidden in them.

This is the main rule. None of the creatures in nature, except for the human beings, try to resemble each other. The cow does not act like a rooster. They all become indispensable by displaying their own reasons for existence. This is the purpose to proceed on the path of Allah with the reason for our creation and to understand the universe serving us in that sense.

Unless we behave in this manner, so to speak, we will be "punched" by the universe because of ourselves.

A cow trying to become a rooster may neither be a cow nor a rooster. It will neither be appreciated nor accepted.

For this reason, people's efforts to imitate each other, both intellectually and in terms of activity, as a result of deceptive likes in the worldly system with their individual intellects and with herd mentality under the name of fashion or trends will prevent them from being the stars of themselves.

Let's come back to the magnificent truth without wandering away from our subject. The thing we must understand with our Prophet created from the divine light of Allah and this understanding of the universe created from His divine light is that everything is basically an image, a light belonging to Allah, that is, knowledge, every one of us, and everything …

And that is why everything coming from the oneness is connected to that whole, just like a body. All of the organs are connected to each other, and they interact with each other.

The concept of "wahdat al wujud" in Sufism, that is, "the unity of being," actually refers to this.

This oneness and unity is so strong that the whole universe is affected by the sins and rewards of each one of us due to this connection, like the domino effect. Thus, every single creature other than us may complain against us or pray for us.

Because we are all connected and unified although we do not know it.

This matter, which is clearly explained in the knowledge of Allah, and recently, scientific developments have proven that we are all connected with an energy field. However, this argument recently proven by science had been told in the Quran many centuries ago.

We are all light particles coming from the same divine light, that is, light and knowledge.

Pieces scattered from that divine light.

Being scattered from one source makes us connected to each other although we think that we are separated.

This conception is succinctly called TAWHID in Islam and our Prophet was telling us that understanding this was essential for Islamic understanding.

One of the major dhikrs, "La ilaha illalah" says this... La ilaha... There is no deity... Neither You ... Illa... Just... Allah...

There is Allah...

Everything you see is His divine light. Everything that you think exists and you worship, beginning with yourself... That is, you do not exist; understand it! There is His hidden divine light in you.

If you do not realize that divine light and head towards the world, even if you have that potential you become empty; the world rises above you, and you become coal. However, if you look for that potential inside yourself and discipline it, you are saved from becoming coal and become a diamond, both are from the same material.

You can neither get angry, reproach nor otherize anybody. Because they have all been scattered from Allah's divine light. You see Allah in each of them.

When Allah's Prophet (PBUH) asked, "What is Islam?" his companions gave answers such as "Islam is salah, fasting, almsgiving." It is narrated that he told them that these were also correct but only true when they are with tawhid which is the fundamental understanding of Islam.

Then, what is "tawhid"?

Tawhid briefly means seeing Allah anywhere and in anything, making Allah ONE.

Actually, our Prophet had the last word when he said, "You cannot enter Heaven unless you have faith. You cannot truly have faith unless you love each other" (Muslim, Abu Davud, Tirmidhi) to clarify and express that we all come from a single source, and we are fundamentally connected to each other.

"And hold firmly to the rope of Allah (adhere to Islam) all together; do not become divided. Remember the favor of Allah on you; when you were enemies and He brought your hearts together and you became, by His favor, brothers. And you were on the edge of a pit of the Fire, and He saved you from it. Thus, does Allah make clear to you His verses that you may be guided." (Surah Ali Imran, Verse 103)

And although it does not contain the word "ikhlas" (I will talk about this in our other books detailing surah analyses in the future), even rereading, and trying to comprehend the surah "Qul Hu," which is called "Surah al-Ikhlas," as much as possible is like reading one-third of the whole Quran. Our Prophet, saying this, mentioned that the concept of tawhid in this surah is such a great and essential occurrence in the Quran.

As I indicated before, our prophet was ummi, that is, he is the mother of knowledge; he is the mother of the "Haqiqa Muhammadiyya (Muhammadan Reality)," the only knowledge of truth.

The divine light coming from Allah has been a mirror to him through infinite knowledge and it is reflected in the universe from him.

In fact, it is just like the Moon that does not have its own light and reflects the light coming from the Sun.

For this reason, in the Quran, the Sun also refers to the meaning of Allah, divine truth and knowledge, and the Moon, on the other hand, refers to the meaning of our Prophet.

As a matter of fact, SHAMS, who came and told Rumi to forget all that he knew when he had deep knowledge, also means the Sun. In fact, he was called Shams to express a person bearing the knowledge of Allah.

In the Quran, not only each word but even each letter is a verse, a sign, and even each letter bears completely different meanings and symbolizes different meanings. (Even, in history, for instance, in the Ottoman era, when you investigate names like 'prince shirts' were coined and these were caftans or other clothing items, with letters or pictures that are the symbols of verses, that is, the signs were embroidered or printed alone or with numbers for the wearer to be honored with the protection of those verses). This is really interesting … As a verse is a sign and letters are the verses, even carrying them on your person is a kind of shield against negative energy and powers … There are statements about the secrets of letters such as (Alif Lam Mim, Ta Ha) which are also called Huruf Muqatta'at (meaning disjointed or disconnected letters).

So, the illiteracy of our Prophet whom we call illiterate is actually the unlimited knowledge that we explained above … Therefore, this is the humor and irony of Allah to those who try to think he was ignorant due to the conditioning that he was illiterate …

There are many literate yet ignorant people. You know, the first name of Iblis was Azazel. This is also a verse and sign to those who are willing to understand.

Everybody is ignorant, no matter how much they know, unless they have the knowledge of truth. It is because of Allah's jest that scientific data and bases that have been believed for centuries change and are disrupted by another experiment…

It is stated that our Prophet's illiteracy is both a wisdom by Allah and to show that it is not an obstacle before revealing that infinite knowledge there as well as to avoid rumors of quoting from other 'religions' (in fact, the concept of so-called other religions is nothing other than beyond the teachings of Islam in those ranks).

"The example of those who were entrusted with (observing) the Torah but failed to do so, is that of a donkey carrying books. How evil is the example of those who reject Allah's signs? Allah does not guide the wrongdoing people." (Surah al-Jumu'ah, Verse 5)

Referring to Torah, those who are aware of the book but who do not act with their knowledge are compared to a donkey carrying books. They just carry information, not the STATE that information must be turned into. So, they were qualified by the depiction of a "donkey," and this is also criticism for us.

Unless knowledge begins to be experienced, transforms into a STATE, and results in being a "knowledge bank" and becoming "wise," it is nothing but a burden.

For this reason, the Prophet of Allah (PBUH) said, "I take shelter in Allah from useless knowledge." Some terms such as "To practice with one's knowledge" are expressions in support of and parallel with these expressions.

The required knowledge is not the so-called knowledge but the one digested and turned into a state. And the basis of each knowledge is the knowledge of truth.

The fundamental problem for most of us is this; we are usually Muslims "in name," not "in our hearts."

May we ask for the "ilm ladunni," that is, the "knowledge given by Allah" which is the "deen (path) by and in the sight of Allah."

One who begins to comprehend the knowledge of Allah, ilm ladduni, truly begins to live. They begin to comprehend the reason for their own life and creation, not the lives of others, and begin to put it into practice and sparkle just like a star. Each of us is already a star.

(The word Hadid "HDD," being an adjective derived from the word meaning rage, also means one who is enraged, rude, and harsh. Its other name is IRON.)

Moses (Musa) who had basic knowledge and was trying to understand the knowledge of Allah, thus wanted to befriend Khidr who had the knowledge of Allah, and learn from him.

The ilm ladduni is a term that we frequently hear in Islam and Sufism.

It is the knowledge that we must demand; actually, we already have it inside ourselves, but the main point is scraping it off and unearthing it like finding a treasure. However, this treasure is not far away, like in The Alchemist it is hidden in our gardens, that is, in our "hearts."

In Turkish, the word "ladun" is a concept that ensues the word "ind" that we try to identify with words "in the sight of, by, before." And the "ilm ladduni" means the "knowledge by Allah, before Allah," and it also means the divine information and intuitive truths inspired to people.

To reach this knowledge, it is not enough for one to be a scholar, but rather for one to reach the religion by Allah, it is necessary to reach near Him. We have spoken about this topic before… Reaching the sea from a drop… or benefiting from the knowledge of people who have reached Him. Here, in order to understand the truth of Islam, reading the books of people that we call "friends of Allah," "saints," that is, "who reached Allah and attained the goal of reuniting with Allah while living, brings us to the true knowledge near Allah, not to the religion that is falsified by meaning in the presence of servants.

The person who takes information from Allah like Khidr and who is a friend of Allah finds peace and is ready at any moment. Because they start to benefit from the knowledge of Allah that is beyond time and space and that surrounds everything.

It is stated that the river KAWTHAR (kawthar is a word from the same root as the word "kasrat" and means abundant good, abundance, nondepletable lineage, family, people, a river or pond in Heaven and it contains concepts such as message, Quran, knowledge, station of intercession) represents the knowledge of Allah. One turning to that knowledge is said to have come to the infinite knowledge.

Even, the Surah al-Kawthar we read during our salaahs is very interesting. Our Prophet's sons passed away. He was insulted as being cut off in terms of lineage.

As I say, the world perception is too bitter. The reason that makes a person wealthy and eternal is not blood ties and lineage but the knowledge ties, spiritual ties, and lineage. For this reason, it is even said that the section for good deeds of the Book of Deeds, where both good and bad actions of people are recorded, will remain open.

Because the rewards contributed by those who reach knowledge and good through that person will continue. We suppose that our lineage continues with the properties and offspring because of earthly deception.

That is why our Prophet is eternal and his influence will always remain because his lineage is the true knowledge and Islamic offspring.

Think of this if you do not have a child. Be sure of this. Everybody that you raise with the spiritual tie not with the blood tie in the way of Allah becomes your offspring.

The earthly glasses make you see near visions far and make you see far visions near. We are already here for this test. Values have been replaced; we will be liberated from our state of "slavery" on the day we realize this.

Only the one who is a servant to Allah will become the master of the universe. On the other hand, that person may not go beyond being a slave for other people and systems and may not attain their own freedom.

Now, let us identify the topic of TAWHID explained by the Prophet of Allah (PBUH) with new data and with science ...

If we unite all the information regarding the concept of tawhid and our being ONE and as we also know from quantum physics, each factor is fundamental and each of them is equal, and the mechanism does not run even in the absence of one.

Before Adam was sent to earth, it was narrated in the Quran that everything had been deployed in proper places by Allah so that he could live there.

Even the finest detail was thought of without allowing for any coincidences.

Many things can be said about this topic; even the distance of the Sun from the Earth is perfectly satisfactory and the extent of the Sun being our source of life while it might be the end of us are the signatures of a magnificent design and intellect …

Even we cannot understand the importance of life pertaining to Allah, who is al-Hayy (the Eternally Living One), life is like the summary of the universe.

We underestimate animals. However, they are the manifestation of Allah's name "al-HAYY" in the MOMENT …

In the author's native tongue, Turkish the word, "animal" is "hayvan" pronounced "hay-v-an". Hayy (Allah's name) +v+an (moment).

It has now been proven by scientists through scientific determinations that life does not consist of coincidences. On the contrary, it has been calculated in detail.

This is magnificently summarized in Surah al-An'am, Verse 59:

"And with Him are the keys of the unseen; none knows of them except Him. And He knows what is on the land and in the sea. Not a leaf falls but He knows it. And no grain is there within the darkness of the earth and no moist or dry thing but that is written in a clear record."

Here, while Quran identifies the earth with the human body, tawhid says that helping each other in the human body is actually present on the earth and we must turn towards it. Quran says that helping each other is essential in the world, not fighting, and actually, when we comprehend the understanding of tawhid we recognize that it is ourselves that both help and are being helped.

Here, the aim is to be "us," not "me."

Personal development suggests getting yourself out of the way and not minding what others do; let sleeping dogs lie …

Spiritual development consists of both personal and holistic development. The aim is not to become a god, but to be one in Allah.

And for all these reasons, as we are fundamentally a single body, we harm ourselves when we harm others.

Surah Az-Zalzalah, Verses 7-8:

"So, whoever does an atom's weight of good will see it. And whoever does an atom's weight of evil will see it."

This is a chain reaction; the whole universe but first ourselves begins to suffer from our single action. Because an opposite action must be formed in order to neutralize it. That return will be towards the source of the energy itself, that is, towards ourselves.

While water flows downwards from a waterfall, pure light energy of that water flows upwards. As we cannot see this event, we cannot comprehend it; this is the same for all energy sources and movements.

Any kind of energy released will go back to the source from where it was released. If it is negative, then in equal measure; if it is positive, then by increasing so much more. This is Allah's mercy.

"Has He not commanded that I will take ten steps towards whom takes one step towards Me. I will run towards the one who walks towards Me".

"Then, do not lose hope thinking there is no permission to appear in the presence and choose love; this is what all the prophets did," says Rumi.

Understanding the language of this universe founded on love and affection is not a source of fear and necessity, it is, in fact, the source of love and pleasure.

Therefore, there is no compulsion in religion. The actions done under the name of worship are not a burden, but a union, meeting, love, being loved, taking shelter, and a feeling of trust.

Everything in the universe serves human beings; air, water, the sun, and the stars ... Everything. And this is the same for the human being. When we get hurt or injured, our whole body is mobilized with heart and soul in order to heal that wound or injury. Beyond our control. Without even our realization.

Our body is the universe, the cosmos. It is a sample of the universe. So, it is said, "Everything in the universe is within a human being". For all these reasons, remember that if someone hurts us the whole universe will rush to help us. This will be instinctive, because each of us, is a universe and a small part of the universal body at the same time. All universal creation will dress our wounds without us knowing...

For our existence, the Sun, the Moon, and all planets perform their duties perfectly.

Although for years, they imposed the thought that "the strong extinguishes the weak" based on various people with disrupted spiritualities and animal selves, it has now been scientifically proven that this is untrue in the current status of the world, it corrupts the world, and it is not the truth itself.

People's harming each other is forbidden in all religions. "Believers are like a body in mercy. If the body's one side falls ill, the whole body becomes ill; Muslims also must have mercy on each other!" (Bukhari)

When our Prophet said, "the person who is not merciful, compassionate and affectionate cannot be faithful," the Companions said, "O Prophet of Allah (PBUH), we are all merciful and affectionate." He uttered, "You must be merciful on all creation, not just on humans." (Taberani)

"All creation from an ant to an elephant is Allah's family. They keep quiet here; they will speak on the Day of Judgement." (Rumi)

However, the teachings of the world are formed to separate people and to dignify some while oppressing others.

Considering that injustice belongs to Allah is really a way of getting yourself out of the way. Both denying Allah and dedicating the visions you see as injustices are a paradox; such a double standard.

It is surprising to see the people saying "Oh, may Allah help them!" when they see someone who is in need. Insensibility that seems sensible!

Why will Allah help, why did He give to you? You will help on Allah's behalf...

Allah sends what He gave you to His servant through you.

His names are scattered on each creation. They will support each other. In Kaaba, when you remove Kabaa, everyone looks like they are prostrating towards each other, doesn't it?

Why? Because each of them bears Allah's names, and so, each of them bows to another. Each of them is an embodiment of Allah's names. They do not have another existence ...

Separating Allah, ordaining in Surah Qaf, Verse 16, "And We have already created humankind and know what their souls whisper to them, and We are closer to them than their jugular vein," from ourselves, attributing existence to ourselves and divinizing ourselves, expecting help to descend from the sky by considering Allah as an authority in a station in the heavens... How strange!

Notice that this verse is very important. Allah refers to Himself as "ME" in the verses where He speaks to His Essence. But He says, "US" in the verses where He acts with His names. This may be both associated with modesty and as a reference to the abundance of His names.

We understand from the verses in Quran where Allah refers to Himself as "US" Allah acts in the world with His names. Each creation is a reflection of His names. From an angel to a jinn, to the human, animal, and plant ...

Saying "We are closer" may refer to His beautiful name in YOU, that is, your Lord. He is your Lord and the Lord of the Worlds, that is, the Lord of the Lords. He is also the Lord of all Beautiful Names.

Since the universe is nothing but a formation of His existence, consisting of creations embodied at different stages, keeping hands off by saying, "May Allah help!" is a miscomprehension.

You are the hand of Allah who sends help. Use that hand...

May Allah help!

We do not think. We both hold Allah responsible for the injustices in the world and we say, "So, you think only Allah can help you; come on, don't leave it like this!"

Unfortunately, this is bad news. We are all responsible for the injustices that are going on.

If we had only thought of the literal meaning of the saying, "The one who keeps quiet before an injustice is like a silent devil," we would have understood.

The word injustice (literally translated as "the absence of Haqq [the Truth]) we use it in the meaning of unjustness, it is the deprivation from Allah, as the name implies. Does not the word Haqq both being a name of Allah and representing the justice awaken us?

The philosophical perspective of "the strong live in this world, the weak are condemned to fade away" which was instilled in us for years is no longer valid in the current world. This belief has begun to expire from the animal world to the human world, and even from corporate structures to countries.

The most powerful national economies, the biggest companies, and the systems where the bigger eats the smaller and which are considered indestructible have one by one experienced a crisis.

The number of powerful animals is decreasing despite protection and the weaker ones mostly continue living. Animals such as dinosaurs, whales… The rule "big fish eat small fish" has started to be advocated by scientists with the theory that ill and weak ones are exposed to this elimination. As for the natural selection, the secrets of justice and divine wisdom continue and the ones which do not have the capacity to survive are basically eliminated[36].

This help is also essential in Islam. Since TAWHID and ONENESS are fundamental and helping each other is recommended. Both with the concept of worshipping and ritual states.

For instance, with the word "zakat" (almsgiving) derived from the

---

36 2 religious laws and 2 laws arise from 2 attributes of Allah:
1. Al-Irada (Will): Takwini Sharia - the justice and wisdom in the laws of the universe.
2. It is Tashrihi Sharia from the attribution, al-Kalam (Speech). This is the verse of rules which are mentioned in the Quran and are a requirement to be followed by people. Justice, wisdom, and compassion are again essential in these laws. (Risale-i Nur)

root of "z-k-y" meaning "to increase, to rise, abundance, to be pure, clean, good, straight, proper, and fertile," this help was made a "rule" under the name of "fardh (obligatory)," and it has not been left to conscious choices. And it is important to perform it frequently that it is referred to in the verses along with salah which is a fundamental worship fulfilled daily and multiple times during the day...

"And establish salah and give zakat ..." (Surah al-Baqarah, Verse 43)

"...And the establishers of prayer [especially] and the givers of zakat and the believers in Allah and the Last Day - those We will give a great reward..." (Surah an-Nisa, Verse 162)

"And they who are observant of zakat." (Surah al-Mu'minun, Verse 4)

There is a hadith about zakat, that "Zakat is the aqueduct, that is, the bridge of Islam."

When I investigated and encountered this for the first time I astonishingly thought:

"Life is helping one another, not a struggle..." (Said-i Nursi)

So, a friend of Allah has summed up a scientific matter, for which many theories had been produced for years and of which the truth was understood years later, with the knowledge of Allah ...

"I wonder how the atoms in the food resulting from that manifestation of help apparent in the whole universe fight to feed the body's cells with eagerness. Such a battle that is! Maybe, that help and running is assistance with the command of Allah Kareem." (Lem'alar, 118)

Day by day as I gain a better understanding of the words by our Prophet, "cry a lot," I inevitably cry more because of the information I encounter ...

In these investigations that I started by working on words, I am at the point where my own words fall short ...

What can be said?... Subhanallah.

THE CONNECTION BETWEEN AL-BAQARAH, AN-NUR, AND TAWHID

From now on, I will present you with my thoughts that resulted from some of my findings by adhering to the previous section ... None of them are from erratic thoughts but they are all based on word etymologies, concepts, and sources...

In the Quran, there is Surah Al-Baqarah.

When we look at the name of this surah carefully, we can see that the words BAQ (BAK, as spelled in Turkish, meaning LOOK) and ARAH (ARA, as spelled in Turkish, meaning SEARCH) are wisely hidden.

This surah carries many meanings for us like all the other miraculous surahs in the Quran that we all try to understand something to the extent of our comprehension.

Because of my character, I try to be especially attentive to words. I like to use different words and, as the phrase goes, to 'play' with them in my songs that Allah predestined me to write and compose.

When you investigate the meaning and essence of surah Baqarah, you become increasingly amazed...

When Allah begins to pull back the curtains of the secrets in the meanings of the words one by one, you realize that evaluating the Quran insensitively as if "it was sent to an old civilization and ablution was given for cleansing" is such gross injustice and ignorant comprehension...

The Quran reminds me of Alice in Wonderland. As you enter the Book, so to speak, it absorbs you and you set out on a journey.

A journey from yourself to your own truth …

This journey that we have set out to reach Allah is called "sayr-u suluk." The path to reach the Truth passes through a journey to the inner self.

It is called "sayr-u suluk." "The path followed …"

And on that path, one passes through unbelievable phases, miraculous, attractive states, and lands….

Just like in Alice in Wonderland…

Deniz is in Wonderland…

It can't be a coincidence that the word religion, the word "tariq" in the tariqa, the word "suluk," and the word "sirat" both mean "the path" with their different aspects.

When a traveler of the path of the Truth reaches the Truth, they become a Saint, the one who has reached the destination. They have united, they have met the Truth. And the essential thing is to reach Allah …

The word salah is Persian.

In the Quran, this word is used in the singular form as "salah" and in the plural form as "salawat." Now, let's look at the content and meaning of this word and concept:

When we investigate the Arabic dictionaries, we see the root meanings of the word such as "to incline, to turn towards, to attain, to reach; connection, to connect; support, to support; to lean/rest (in order to support); spine and thigh bones holding the creature upright, straight back, and spine …"

There are more details of this, but we will condense this comprehensive subject with a few topics within our section …

To incline, turn towards, reach, and to connect are such special expressions… In fact, we say we turn towards Allah, we reach Him, and we connect with Him at least five times a day when it is time to perform salah... So, using the word 'salah' and trying to feel this meaning makes our orientation towards Allah more meaningful... As we are not even aware of the meaning of 'salah' that we use it as an ordinary word, saying the original form of the word at least makes us think a little more...

There is a topic that I cannot pass over without delving further into it... That is the expansion of the word 'salah' regarding the "spine and thighbones ..." These two bones hidden in this word will attract more attention in the upcoming chapters when we talk about 'salah,' and it will amaze us all as this word refers to the spine and thighbones...

The spine consists of 33 vertebrae (bones) and it holds secrets about its connection with vibrations on the raising of consciousness that I will share in the chapters to follow and I believe you would be interested...

Besides this, "thighbone" one of the meanings of salah opens doors to different secrets...

The Quran mentions Hazrat Yaqub (Jacob) ...Hazrat Yaqub, may Allah be pleased with him, is the father of Hazrat Yusuf (Joseph) ... The word Yaqub (Yakubu in Hebrew) means "subsequent, successor" and it comes from the root of the word "heel..."

And now let's talk about the narration about Yaqub and the thighbone... We are told of Yaqub wrestling with an angel in a narration based on the Torah... I continue without mentioning implicit meanings here in order not to distract you ... It is narrated that the angel understands it cannot defeat Yaqub and hits its head on Yaqub's thighbone... It is also said that Yaqub's thighbone dislocates while wrestling with the angel and for this reason to this day Israelis do not eat the nerve on the thighbone ... Because it is said that Yaqub was hit on the nerve on the end of the thighbone ... (Torah, Genesis 32).

It is interesting that even the architect of the Eiffel Tower, Maurice Koechlin, was inspired by the thighbone while he was drawing the project of the famous tower ... The tube-form thighbone, the lightest and the most resistant bone in the body was an inspiration even for the

Eiffel Tower with its steady architecture despite its delicate structure …

I, of course, don't think this is all … I think it won't be realistic not to search for a symbol or sign underlying this situation that serves as a model for such a famous structure.

I was surprised by the thighbone not being mentioned along with the brain in the reviews about the human brain and its evolution and the energy distribution in the body

As one of the meanings of the word "salah," the thighbone had a great meaning since I knew that we produce electromagnetic energy from the thighbone and the nervous structure on it through our certain movements during salah and we try to activate our spiritual bodies …

Particularly the fact that this circuit starting from the heel, which is related to the name of 'Yaqub', and passing through the brain ends between two eyebrows, which is the location of the third eye while prostrating made me think that I needed to examine the matter of electrical activation even further …

This neural net beginning from the heel, passing to the thighbone and then to the coccyx, and proceeding to the brain through the spine was very meaningful for the word "salah" which also means to CONNECT …

My feelings about the efforts to form an electromagnetic NETWORK and field by activating certain parts of the body through certain movements in order to connect our personal computers to Allah became more intense …

Now, getting back to our subject, we can say that with salah, if we are talking about Allah's salawat we describe the situations such as where He turns towards, protects, and cleanses His servant, etc.… Our Prophet's salawat is him supporting and testifying for his people who turned towards Him and asking for their forgiveness, and when it comes to the salawat of the angels, it is them supporting the servants in their orientation towards Allah and the Prophet, confirming their words and actions, and asking for forgiveness for them …

The salawat of the servant is them turning towards Allah such as praying to Allah, repentance, and glorification …

We, for example, deem saying salawats to our Prophet as just repeating the invocations using words. However, as you can also see, the word salah which also means "to support" refers to inclining to our Prophet's summon to believers, trying to support his prayers and wishes both through fighting against the ego and spreading knowledge to the extent that is incumbent upon them, and making all the effort to practice and spread the verses that he revealed …

Attahiyyat "was salawatu lillahi," all our sincere supplications are to Allah.

In Salli and Barik, there is a supplication to Allah for Him to turn towards, support, and forgive Muhammed (PBUH) and his people as well as a promise for the performance of the obligations for this prayer to be accepted in this way.

"Salah is the ascension of the believer," said our Prophet.

In the Quran, we are told about a state represented as reaching Allah five times a day but is actually called "constant in salah," and originally referring to "constantly reaching" and the purpose of being with Allah in every moment even if we do not understand …

It is said that friends of Allah sit, eat, and live in decency because they are with Him at any time even when they are all alone …

The topic of salah will become more interesting in the oncoming chapters, inshallah, and now let's return to our topic. It is necessary to discuss and contemplate not only on each verse but also on each word of Surah Baqarah, but now I will talk about another matter in the essence of this surah…

The word Baqarah means "cow, cattle, calf." I was deeply affected by a scene from the worldwide phenomenon series called Fringe, where a genius professor brought a cow into his laboratory and said that the cow's DNA has ingenious things for human beings.

Seeing how the scientific expressions in the series have correspondences in the Quran urged me to investigate this topic.

The most important thing is that the existence of a surah in the Quran called "al-Baqarah" and, named after a "cow" (or a type of cattle), understanding that this surah has many depths based on the statement of our Prophet, and symbolizing a dervish with the words and expressions like "cow, bull, calf" spurred me to research this topic further.

It did not take me long to comprehend the ability and the meaning of a dervish on the path of Allah to offer their flesh, milk, children, strength, and hide to the service of humanity is symbolic of a cow or bull.

When I comprehended this description, we were at a farm with my aunt … We saw a cow and its calf. That calf's glance to its mother… It is an indefinable and a great pain for a mother to lose her child. I know this since my grandmother lost two of her children… We looked at that cow and calf. Our eyes were filled with tears. Now, you may say "it is just a cow!" but remember, even the Quran has indicated that some humans are at a consciousness lower than animals … The verse "…They are like cattle, but they are worse for they are heedless" (Surah al-A'raf, Verse 179) is not for humiliating them … It is said that some of them who are of human appearance are even below the animal consciousness… Apart from that, Allah values animals so much that He calls them, "my silent servants…"

As for cows, what magnificent animals they are… This creation that is satiated from a blade of grass serves humanity with all its being.

We said surah means "image." What is an image? Meanings that are embodied. Bodies. And the verse means expressions, symbols, and signs related to the contents of these bodies.

As we say, "One of my friends has called me, it must be a sign." Here, Allah gives such signs through images that it is impossible to not be amazed by the infinite richness of meanings...

Then, one of our Prophet's hadiths came to my mind: "The world is on the ox (bull) and the fish…"

There are numerous accounts related to this hadith that it was explained in some chronicles about the Pisces and Taurus cycles, and I am sure that there are many other explanations…

The "ox and bull" terms in the depiction of the world by our Prophet, of course, evoked thoughts of Surah al-Baqarah.

The cow had already attracted my attention as it was deemed to be divine in India too, one of the oldest civilizations.

So, I started to search for the interpretations of cow, bull, and ox in ancient civilizations.

What truly surprised me the most was that bull and cow figures, and bull depictions were extremely in the foreground even in the civilizations dating back ten thousand years ago.

When I saw the bull and cow figures and the divinity ascribed to them in India - even though it is a very old civilization - and in many other civilizations, my excitement and curiosity began to increase more.

The symbol of the bull actually represented "a productive and highly civilized consciousness" both with the concept of the onset of civilization, agricultural beginnings, power that comes along with soil, and in terms of humans.

When I looked more carefully by considering its meaning in Surah al-Baqarah in the Quran, I began to realize that it symbolizes "consciousness in a dervish" and the dervish's comprehension rising and becoming more productive as well as their enlightenment.

And the horned headpieces or crowns used by the rulers in ancient civilizations made me think that they attempted to express the concept of wisdom with the symbol of a horn.

Moreover, when I encountered the bull symbol used in mural paintings and sanctuaries excavated in Çatalhöyük in Central Anatolia which became a residential area nine thousand years ago, and after I saw a cow and a bull as a god and goddess in Ancient Egypt, pieces began to fall into place. To me, the Sun between the horns evoked the meaning of Shams.

The bull was somehow the symbol of a dervish and an enlightened person, a sage in Surah al-Baqarah. Their characteristics on the path of reaching Allah are explained. For example, not to be too much attached to the earth, that is, to the world and properties, "… 'It should have been used neither to till the soil nor water the fields …" (Surah al-Baqarah, Verse 71), and not to be mottled (mixed, far from purity) …

It is stated through cattle that a dervish should come from an understanding that is neither attached to the world nor property, they should neither be too young nor too old, which is, I think, related to the maturing of the comprehension, and they should not run in place and repeat themselves and their consciousness (not like a well pulley) but improve themselves and their consciousness …Now, let's get back to our topic, al-Baqarah…

The holiness attributed to the symbols of the bull and horn symbolized as the gods of Accad, Assyria, and Babel who lived in Mesopotamia, including idolator tribes, is really interesting.

The Torah and the Bible are falsified books but some of the expressions they include and certain statements with limited alterations resemble some statements in the Quran. It is said that the original form of both the Torah and the Bible may be found in the verses that refer to the Torah and the Bible in Quran…

A story related to our subject, al-Baqarah, is narrated in Surah Taha. In verses 90-95 of Surah Taha and the subsequent verses, it is narrated that a person called Samiri makes a sculpture of a calf and the Israelites adopted it as a god despite Harun (Aaron) in the absence of Hazrat Moses (Musa).

There is a similar part in Surah al-Baqarah in the Quran and the Torah. This story about the calf statue, in fact, includes interesting statements. I will refer to its mysteries in one of my works inshallah.

Like a cow, cattle, and bull, a person called Dhul-Quarnayn whose rank cannot be explained is mentioned in the Quran. You have surely heard of the narration about Gog and Magog and that Dhul-Quarnayn locked them in and built a barrier over them...

Here, the subject I want to attract your attention to is that in the Arabic word Dhul-Quarnayn besides the meanings of Dhu, meaning "double, owner, couple", and QUARN, meaning horn (qurun: era, horn; same root as queren), it takes me to the narration of al-Baqarah and with its meaning "double horned," to the hadith of the world being on the cattle, bull, and fish.

Then, I began to search for the other meanings of QUARN. I was really amazed:

Quarn, on the other hand, had meanings such as, "forelock, hill, time, sun, connection between two things, logical unity, match, evidence."

Forelock and sun made me think about the concept of the place from where the existence of Allah's meaning in us simply goes out. As a matter of fact, the expressions like, "the prostration mark on their foreheads, the divine light and we drag them by their forelocks" directed me to investigate the concepts of "horn, sun and light" together.

Now, look at the verse...

Surah al-Alaq verse 15: "No! If he does not desist, we will certainly drag him by the forelock."

Maybe the pineal gland is the center of our life source?

As for Dhul-Quarnayn, this person spoken about in the section in which Gog and Magog are mentioned is a person who is qualified with the word meaning the "owner of two horns" and who is also identified as the owner of two times. Quarnayn means two of the two horns.

Surah al-Kahf, verses 83-84: "And they ask you about Dhul-Quarnayn. Say; I will recite to you something of his account. Indeed, We established (supported) him upon the earth, and We gave him the means to all things."

Here, it is possible to contemplate about duality, however, I will continue for now in order not to wander off the subject.

When I began studying the slightly different narration of the Samiri account in Torah, I came across the word "qaran" which is very similar to and most probably coming from the same root as the word quarn in Dhul-Quarnayn, meaning the "horn."

The root of "qaran"[37] meaning horn in Hebrew comes from the same root "qrn" with the word "qoran," and it means to SHINE, SPARKLE!

The similarities of these words with the word Quran reminded me of those magnificent verses and hadiths…

The word Quran includes the meanings such as "to collect, read, gather, and to recite."

In many Islamic statements, in addition to its many meanings, one

37 I cannot continue without mentioning… For the sake of leaving one more 'sign' in our awareness. By investigating, you may notice the relationship between the words Qaran, Quran, QRN, QARN and the world-famous word Cern (Qrn) and its experiments (this is the abbreviation of French words "Conceil Européen pour la Recherche Nucléaire," meaning European Organization for Nuclear Research on the surface but what a coincidencethat it matches with the word "cern," that is, horn!) and the efforts towards the intentions beyond the surface, those symbolized by the CERNnunnos which is a Celtic god meaning "Horned God" and the two meter statue of the Hindu god Shiva situated in the campus where the experiments are done in CERN as well as their symbolic relationship with scientific experiments …

Questioning what the circles in the CERN logo and bulges on its edge may symbolize and reading the interesting explanations of world-famous hypothetical physics professor Michio Kaku ("Large Hadron Collider may allow us to read the mind of God!") may help us to draw the curtains that shield our eyes even further…

Furthermore, I will ask you to look at the following article, 'They who come from the future protect our World' in the newspaper Posta on 19 October 2019. (http://www.posta.com.tr/dunya/HaberDetay/Gelecekten_gelenler_dünyamızı_koruyor.htm?ArticleID= 4286, in Turkish). The same news has taken place from some of the global media… Yes, is it possible that the ones we deem to be science fiction are not fiction, but the truths? What is going on behind the curtains, behind what is shown… What are we dealing with? Where are we seeking the treasure instead of examining the Treasure before our eyes?

For now, I will mention this much… And I will add; Quran is a magnificent book and a great mystery… Splendid! Instead of virtual arguments, is this not the time for revealing those which the demonic powers became aware through great efforts and which we are not still aware of? Look for what is hidden from you, not those shown to you … (Infinite thanks to Hamza Yardımcıoğlu, Serhat Ahmet Tan, Olgun Aydoğdu for the program of "Passenger of Time" for expansion of comprehension about perception manipulation, and to Erhan Altunay.)

of the Quran's names was declared as NOOR (divine light)! And one of the meanings of noor was the LIGHT that helps to ILLUMINA-TE and see the surroundings. (Ibn Faris, Kitāb al-Mujmal fi al-lugha, (Summary of the Language), 368; Ragib, Mufredat (Syllabus), 508).

The Quran, a guide for us for both worlds, was described as material and spiritual light and even as a lamp that guides humans…"O Humanity! There has come to you conclusive evidence from your Lord. And we have sent down to you a brilliant light." (Surah An-Nisa, Verse 174)

The role of Quran in our enlightenment will be continuous in both universes.

Our Prophet referred to the descending of Quran as a light upon us in eternity as follows: "Whoever learns a verse from the Book of Allah, that verse learned will be a divine light for them on the Judgment Day." (Darimi, 2/244)

Surah an-Nur, Verse 35: "Allah is the Light of the heavens and the earth. The example of His light is like a niche within which there is a lamp, the lamp is within a glass, the glass is as if it were a pearly [white] star lit from [the oil of] a blessed olive tree, neither of the east nor of the west, whose oil would almost glow even if untouched by fire. Light upon light. Allah guides to His light whom He wills. And Allah presents examples for the people, and Allah is Knowing of all things.."

So, this connection between horn, to shine, light and the divine light led to my gradual comprehension. Then, I began to search which word is referred to for the terms of the words "bull", "ox", "Taurus". The word I came across was SEVR. When you investigate the word "Sevr" you encounter very interesting things…

It was the name of the cave and the mountain which was on the same route of our Prophet when he and Hazrat Abu Bakr were emigrating to Madinah, and they hid to evade the idolaters, and whose entry was closed by a spider web and pigeonhole! It consisted of many mountains and hills.

Furthermore, when the spider web and pigeonhole miraculously closed the cave's entry, our Prophet soothed Hazrat Abu Bakr who was anxious for him by saying "O Abu Bakr! If the third of two people is Allah, what do you think would happen?"

The "Ox" being one of the meanings of "Sevr" which also refers to the cave where our Prophet took shelter on the way to Madinah became more interesting with the connections I have just spoken about…

Now, let's get to the main point, this topic has been explained clearly on the Turkish Islamic website, "Sorularla İslamiyet (Islam Through Questions)," and I and I quote that part:

The following meanings may be understood from the words uttered by our Prophet, "The world is on the ox and the fish".

• Allah designates an angel for each being He creates. We call them "muakkill (appointed) angels". The world has two muakkill angels and their names are "Sevr" and "Hud". That is to say, "ox" and "fish". In this instance, the hadith means, "The world is handled by these two angels called ox and fish."

The two most important sources of income were farming and seamanship fourteen centuries ago, when our Prophet and his companions lived. This has remained partly so nowadays. The symbol of agriculture is the ox, and the symbol of seamanship is the fish. Just as the answer is, "It is on the pen and the sword" to the question "What does the state stand on?" So to speak, the continuation of a state depends on "military force, science, and justice". Here, our Prophet has drawn attention to this fact with the hadith, "The world is on the ox and the fish". Therefore, he explicitly named the most important sources of the continuation of the life of the world.

• As it is known, in the olden days, when techniques were underdeveloped, the world was believed to be standing still and the sun was believed to be turning. However, it was understood in time that it was just the opposite. It was not easy to tell this reality directly to those who believed in outdated information. If done so, maybe the people might not have benefited from the divine light of Islam. The Prophet of Allah (PBUH) answered by performing a literary art and he satisfied the people of that age.

That is to say, the world passes imaginary twelve ranges while turning around the Sun. We call them "horoscopes". Two of them are called, 'Ox' and 'Fish'. Our Prophet was asked on different occasions about what the world stood on. In the first instance, he stated that it stood on an 'ox' and in the second instance he stated that it stood on the 'fish'. He declared that the world passes over the horoscopes of Ox and Fish, thus, he spoke about the turning of the world fourteen hundred years ago.

It is an exceptional success to satisfy the interlocutors both in that period and forthcoming ones until Judgement Day by uttering the three great truths and other realities we may not know with a figurative and allusive statement.

As for Hud, that is, the fish, the fish mentioned in the narration about Moses (Musa) and Khidr made me contemplate. On the other hand, when I learned that it is a word connected with clay, the pieces began to click together...

When I thought about the narration of Moses (Musa) and Harun (Aaron) and the calf of Samiri, I began to understand why Michaelangelo, who sculptured the famous statue of Moses (Musa), added two horns to Moses (Musa) on that statue in 1513. Besides its features, this expression had a part in its fame at this degree.

In most verses, it is indicated that the Quran is divine light.

When I thought of the cow which we talk about by referring to Surah al-Baqarah and which is considered holy in India and when I wanted to investigate the meaning of 'horn' in Sanskrit used to write Hindu holy texts, I came across the word 'usya.' Upon studying this word, I discovered that it means both to 'glitter' and to 'shine'. Finding out these thoughts of mine in the Göbeklitepe documentary and the addition of new information on top of these, to say the least, was a validation for me.

I had lightning bolts flashing in my head…

Moreover, mentioning lightning reminded me of our Prophet traveling from Masjid al-Haram (Mecca) to Bayt al-Maqdis (Masjid al-Aqsa, Jerusalem) with Buraq, a heavenly mount resembling a horse, during his Ascension (there are narrations about Masjid Aqsa the farthest masjid, stated as Beyt-i Maqdis) …

In Sufism, Buraq is described as the symbol of love; then what does Buraq mean?

Buraq is derived from the word 'berq,' meaning 'lightning, flash; to glitter, to shine' in Arabic.

Mi'raj also refers to ascension, that is, the elevation (stairs), of our Prophet who returned even before his bed cooled down, and the phenomenon of Mi'raj in Islam represents the meeting of our Prophet and Allah without any intermediaries and at a level with no time, space, and direction.

With every statement I came across, I realized that the raising of the level of consciousness was told to us through various signs by the Quran and the Prophet.

Our Prophet says "Salaah is the mi'raj of the believer…" It is said that his chest was split, his heart was removed and washed with Zamzam water before Mi'raj by the angel Jibril (Gabriel)… It is fairly emphasized that we must cleanse ourselves, be purified with repentance before raising our consciousness during salaah…

However, we have become so shallow that by pertaining each meaning only to a person and things, we resist absorbing the real message delivered to us behind those people and things.

I began to think that the terms baqarah, horn, and bull talk about consciousness and the raising of consciousness as well as divine enlightenment and illumination.

Dervishes, prophets, and wise men were spoken about through these symbols.

My feeling that the Quran has already advised us of this since the beginning through indicative words such as "read, comprehend, use your mind, raise your consciousness, get rid of darkness, reach the divine light, convert your fire into divine light" intensified.

It was light; it was once again light (cosmic light). The divine light; everywhere and everything was divine light and the science of Allah.

Illumination and divine enlightenment are all speaking of this concept. The path to reaching the science of Allah lies in our own consciousness. And so does our Mi'raj, because it seems like the whole universe is hidden in our consciousness layer by layer.

Everything happens in our brain like a dream. It is just like the moment when we wake up and realize that a dream that seemed to last for hours is merely a glimpse.

We were experiencing the dream in this world just like the dream we had during our sleep at night. For this reason, we had to wake up from the sleep of our consciousness. We had to rise in order to reach our truth.

We first had to work to cleanse ourselves, and then be enlightened with divine light. Our Prophet being the pure divine light who had no shadow was telling us about this; the paths to reach salvation with infinite knowledge...

The moires we see in the portraits of Prophet Jesus (Isa), and even those pictured on the heads of the angels in the cartoons... The concept of the hearts that darken... They began to wrap all around my brain.

Messiah Jesus (Isa) whom I saw in a different portrait, who was cleansed and shining with a glowing heart, and who sheds lights on his surrounding ...

And Surah al-Baqarah which is so important.

The advice of our Prophet to read the verses of Rabbana at the end of the surah as much as possible...

And I finally understood that the bull was used to symbolize 'glitter, shine' in all ancient doctrines. Furthermore, in Surah al-Baqarah, there is a description of the baqarah, which is, 'wanted to be found and it should not be mottled and be bright.' The more you cleanse yourself the more you become a mirror to the name of Allah in you...

Being a mirror that shines and reflects by being cleansed. Just like it is said in Sufism.

Surah al-Baqarah, Verse 69: "They said, "Call upon your Lord to show us what is her color." He said, "He says, 'It is a yellow cow, bright in color – pleasing to the observers.'"

Surah al-Baqarah, Verse 71: "He said, He says, 'It is a cow neither trained to plow the earth nor to irrigate the field, one free from fault with no spot upon her.'" They said, "Now you have come with the truth." So they slaughtered her, but they could hardly do it."

In the Quran, each meaning, each letter is certainly indicated with a symbol... Whatever exists in the world, exists in a human being.

With our motto "in a human being," I wanted to study what we have in our bodies, particularly in our brains, that steer our consciousness, and which resembles a horn.

SOOR (the Trumpet) means "to call out; pipe; horn that makes a sound when blown into." The Trumpet is the pipe that will be blown by Israfil (Raphael) to signal the Day of Judgment and to ensure people come to the Gathering Place (mahshar). In a hadith, it is notified that the Trumpet is a pipe and horn that is blown into (Tirmidhi). However, it is not a trumpet whose nature we know...

Surprised by the realization that our inner ear resembles a horn while researching about the Trumpet being blown on the Day of Judgment, prompted me to research the point where the symbol can be identified in the human body in the narrations from then on. With astonishment, I was locked in our pineal and pituitary glands.

Hypothalamus is one of the most important parts of the limbic system which is a neural net, and which does not produce hormones by itself, but constitutes the center of formation. It makes the gland that is called the pituitary gland and whose primary duty is to secrete the required hormones by the instruction of the chemical secretions from the hypothalamus to perform all these functions.

It is impossible not to see the horn shape when you look at the half section of the brain and hypothalamus. Furthermore, when you see the pineal gland like a dot just under it, it is quite possible for the letter B of 'bismillahirrahmanirrahim' to resemble the horn shape and it is possible for the dot under it to indicate the pineal gland.

Moreover, it is impossible not to think that the fish in the expression of our Prophet, "The world is on the ox and the fish" resembles the pineal gland. The pineal gland, which resembles the eye, has the shape of a fish under an ox; this might be indicating that the world is nowhere but in our brains and consciousness.

I want to present this thought by showing how the Quran verses are parallel to scientific evidence.

This secret which Hazrat Ali indicated as, "The secret of the Quran is in Surah al-Fatihah; the secret of al-Fatihah is in Bismillah, and the secret of Bismillah is in the letter Ba. I am the dot under Ba," is explained in many ways through meanings.

In Sufism, one of the meanings of the letter Ba indicates the "grave," that is "our body."

Hazrat Ali describes the nature of a human being by saying "I am the dot under the letter Ba."

We consist of the names of Allah, the Infinite Power, packed in a restrictive structure of flesh and bone.

While each of us bears His beautiful names with different intensities, each of us is a monument of genius and talent as long as we realize our own realities.

Unless we discover what we are, this body is a grave for us, and we remain dead while living.

Therefore, before we die physically, we must wake up with our consciousness, that is, we need to stand, to die by recognizing our non-existence before death, and to attain the secret of being "eternal" with Allah by making our consciousness aware that the existence in us is only the names of Allah.

Being primarily aware of our own reality and the reason for existence in our comprehension means being free.

Otherwise, we remain a slave as mentioned in the Quran. Unless we bring our existence and reality together with our truth, we cannot attain our desires in this world which is a virtual curtain, and we remain slaves of the system.

I continue without deviating from the subject.

If you look at the letter Ba in Basmala written in Arabic, it resembles the shape of a horn. In the statement, "I am the dot under the letter Ba," the letter Ba is the symbol of the horn, that is, Dhul-Quarnayn has a double horn and indicates the dot with its symbol.

We can also think of the double horn as a person who can use both right and left lobes and all neurons … There will be an interesting expansion about this subject in our explanations regarding Dhul-Quarnayn…

There are narrations indicating that this may imply our pineal gland immediately behind the nasal bridge with reference to the hypothalamus and the inner structure of the brain, and the "energy of life and illumination" in all other doctrines are symbolized with this gland.

I will address this subject in the chapter about "Salah." The hypothalamus that resembles a horn in our skull and the pineal gland just behind the nasal bridge which I will try to explain their importance in the chapter about "Salah" are said to refer to the dot under the letter Ba!

I suppose we will understand what kind of position it is when Dhul-Quarnayn's features are described, but now I want to continue without wandering from the subject.

Hazrat Ali says, "I am the dot under the letter Ba." The letter Ba in Basmala is the horn. It is Dhul-Quarnayn, that is, being double horned, and there is a dot under it.

33 is one of the symbolic numbers in the Quran (and in the ancient teachings). I always wondered why we say some dhikrs 33 times after salahs and why we will resurrect at the age of 33 on the Judgement Day.

This must be related to our spine and its electrical system because our spine is divided into 33 segments.

During my studies, when I noticed a section in our spines[38] named the dorsal horn which extends along our bodies and where our spinal cords are formed, everything began to fall into place.

Surely, this is a piece of information that we obtain from unlimited knowledge, and which is even smaller than a droplet. Only Allah knows the truth of everything.

However, as we have indicated in the chapter about 'Sound,' I think that the essence and relationship of sound existing in the universe, the nervous structures and networks activated through the vibration and resonance generated by these are the prescription to allow us to return to our "noor-light bodies," and not "material-physical" bodies by discovering our energy of life, which is generated by the spiritual structures within us, through certain numbers of dhikrs and these words containing specifically selected frequencies, and using it properly.

---

38 Spinal cord: It lies in the spine throughout the body. There are: the ventral root, dorsal root, and side horn in the spinal cord. Ventral root is the place where motor neurons come out and dorsal root is the place where sense neurons come into the spinal cord.

Neurons belonging to the autonomous nervous system come out from the side horn. The spinal cord is the center of the reflex. It conveys the incoming and outgoing impulses to/from the brain.

Autonomous Nervous System: It sends nerves to the internal organs that work involuntarily, and they are unmyelinated. They are controlled by the centers at the spinal cord, spinal bulbs, and hypothalamus. There are sympathetic and parasympathetic nerves working contrary to each other in the autonomous nervous system.

Sympathetic nerves get involved in case the organism is stuck in a difficult situation. Although it decelerates the events related to digestion, it accelerates other events. Parasympathetic nerves decelerate working of the inner organs except the digestive system.

Once we include our spines, hypothalamus, and pineal glands, they constitute the energy of living, that is, the energy of life. This energy, used for the "consciousness" which is our means for salvation, has also been noticed by the people looking for increasing the vibration of the conscious which is like a snake sleeping on the spinal root.

"I am the prayer of my father Hazrat Ibrahim (Abraham), evangelist of my brother Hazrat Isa (Jesus), and the dream of my mother. When she was pregnant with me, she had seen that a divine light enlightening the palaces of Damascus was coming out of her …" (Hz Muhammad [PBUH])

When I recognized and searched the development of ALFA "a" beginning of the alphabet, and when I read it I couldn't help but weep.

I did not know how ignorant I was…

Aleph means ox. Both the words "alif" and alpha are derived from it. As for ox, OK-US (in Turkish) means 'the man of Allah,' that is to say, "the prophet". For this reason, features of a dervish in Surah al-Baqarah were explained using these symbols and examples. Furthermore, the word Oghuz in 'Oghuz Turks' was the rounded form of Ok-Us.

Each word was a sign and a symbol on its own. So, the magnificent al-kalam attribute of Allah and the pen, and the universe that He granted His divine light mention and speak of Allah with everything they have from letter to word: "Each item has become a letter/Both a case and an enclosure/The science of Ajam has been consumed/A dot has become a thousand words…" (Hilmi Dedebaba). "So he [i.e., Moses] threw his staff, and suddenly it was a serpent, manifest" (Surah Al-A'raf, Verse 107)

"Then he drew his hand out of his collar and it was shining white for all to see…" (Surah Al-A'raf, Verse 108)

"Then he drew his hand 'out of his collar' and it was 'shining' white for all to see…" (Surah Ash-Shu'ara, Verse 33)

Maybe the metaphor of Moses's (Musa) rod thrown on the floor turning into a big serpent and eating the wizards' rods that were turned into serpents indicates the symbol of alanin being a part that comes from the spinal cord in the spine must rise, awaken in order to enlighten us.

If I say one of the meanings of the word universe is 'big serpent' maybe something may occur in us too.

Allah called Moses (Musa) "Kalimullah" because he addressed Him unmediated … He was the one who heard Allah's word.

Moses (Musa) made pharaoh and the oracles watch the virtual realities being swallowed and becoming void by the rising of the true consciousness with the knowledge, awakening, and speech granted by Allah …

"Then Moses threw his staff, and at once it devoured what they falsified." (Surah Al-Shuarah Verse 45)

Is it possible that the verse talking about the rod turning into a serpent and the verse mentioning his hand turning into white divine light follow each other to give us the signs of illumination?

Is it possible to contemplate that the more we are fed from this universe and earth where Allah spread His divine light, that is, from the "main transformer," the more we will radiate and illuminate and the more our network will expand?

The statement that our Prophet – who is completely divine light- has no shadow may arise from his being pure divine light.

Messiah Jesus (Isa), meaning "the purified …"

Zakat and tazkiya, meaning "to purify."

Our Prophet, whose chest was opened several times (Surah ash-Sharh), turning into divine light in his purest state and spreading the light he took from Allah to the universe …

"Have We not uplifted your heart and relieved of your burden?" (Surah Ash-Sharh, Verses 1 and 2)

Symbolization of the meaning of Allah (the divine truth) with the Sun (Shams) and our Prophet with the Moon, that is, al-Qamar, since he takes his divine light from Him, and he reflects the divine light of

Allah and his light to us shows us the connection of all these concepts …

In the division of Allah's divine light told in the hadith above and also indicated in the Quran, our Prophet depicts the divine light of perception, that is, the divine light of the third eye, the divine light of faith, the divine light of the heart …All these show that we are actually beings that have particles of light (cosmic) and the more we convert our light mixed with fire, our energy into DIVINE LIGHT, that is, KNOWLEDGE, and the more we increase it we will return to our Allah, who is the main source, faster and safer. Is it possible that it tells us that unless we are pure light and divine light, we will need to pass through a procedure to convert fire, which is our egoic side, into divine light, and we can only then return to the main source, which is pure light and divine light and where we came from, by passing the painful path called sirat to the extent and in the time that we are cleansed following that painful procedure?

Is it again a coincidence that the Mountain Hira where our Prophet contemplated a great deal and spent his nights is also called Harra and Jabal al-Nour?

Allah created our Prophet from His divine light. He created us from our Prophet's noor (divine light) and light.

Each of us is that photon. We are all one even if we think we have been separated by distance or space… We are affected by each other, and we affect each other. So, unless we love each other we cannot reach our heaven and peace.

We fell into the darkness from the divine light from which we split. Before we are called back and reunite with our light which fell into the mud, we need to strive to become cleansed and enlightened.

Our aim is to remember where we came from and the existence of the truth within ourselves.

We came from light, and we were mixed with fire. You came from the light, which is your origin, then you have to turn back to that light that is confined to the body.

You must feel the suffering of others and you must be pleased with the joys of others. Because even though you think you are confined to your body, you are in fact affected by this.

Allah has created the universe for our Prophet whom He calls "My Beloved." And, He has created us from our Prophet's divine light. That is to say; the universe was created for the sake of love, not for the cause of rivalry.

The key is to help each other, not to fight. Because the one who hurts and the one who is hurt are the same.

The energy of love was the light. Everybody will reach it ultimately.

Firstly, we must all understand ourselves, and thus, the Creator, the source of our existence ...

We came from the same source. From the Oneness...

So, unless we all love each other, we will not have real faith...

The aim of creation is returning to the light, the Oneness you have come from with your moral beauties.

He was called the Creator... It was said He created us...

As for the etymology of the word to 'create', it captivated me after my research.

So to say, it sums up all narratives in a word by confirming them: do you know the real meaning of the word to 'create'?

"To shine, sparkle."

TAWHID, MATRIX, AND THE PHYSICISTS

The world is a mountain
Our actions are the voice.
The voice echoes
It comes back to us.

-Rumi

Max Planck, a German physicist, and Nobel Prize winner, says, "The source, truth, and existence of all matters is based on a superior power that vibrates the atom particles and keeps them together like a tiny solar system ... We must admit that there is an intellect with a great consciousness and intelligence behind this power. And this intellect is the matrix of all the matters ..."

At the same time, Planck indicates that matter does not exist 'in the form we see it'.

This expression unbelievably corresponds with the information in Quran...

How?

The scientifically proven reality is that we don't see "objects" in their "true" state. Our brain "reads," in other words, perceives that object through its perception with its own "interpretation."

This is what Planck and most physicists now tell us. We interpret the object by the shape we perceive and see it in that way. But the truth of the material is not in that shape.

For instance, for our brains to perceive that what we are seeing is an apple, there first needs to be a perception of the appearance and shape of an apple. On the outside, our brain matches the energetic state of an object with the apple data in its own database and it generates the apple image in the brain.

We perceive everything like this. Do you know that we cannot even see the whole image of a person and our brain identifies this image?

Now, I will relate Planck's explanation with the following:

In Sufism, it is said that Allah's name the Most Merciful (ar-RAH-MAN) is the name where the true states of Allah's beautiful names are present.

This expression is the same as Planck's because we deal with the states of objects that emerge from the name "the Most Compassionate (ar-Rahim)".

This is similar to the situation when we look in the mirror. Although we are three-dimensional, the reflection is us, but that reflection is not our "essence," is it? It won't feel even if we touch it … It has no warmth nor softness, etc.

But it is the reflection of our being.

That is to say, when we look in the mirror, we think that we see ourselves, but our true selves are not reflections in the mirror, what we see is just a reflection…

Think of a reflection in another mirror and add another reflection over it… Here, that second reflection is the visions we deal with in the world.

This world is the reflection of echoes and duplicates. We deal with the "shadows of shadows" of the objects, not with the originals.

Hence, the description of 'shadow' is commonly used in Sufism.

The "essence, self, core, source, existence out of mind" of everything is called "ayn," that is, the truth of an object in Turkish. The plural form of this word is "ayan," meaning evident, clear.

The concept of "the firmly evident (a'yan-i sabite)" is qualified as the shadows of the beautiful names of Allah, the divine names. So, the shadow of the firmly evident is the object.

"Ayn" means eye in Arabic … This world referred to as a mirror is AY-NA (mirror), meaning "we saw." Since "ayn" is eye and to see, and "na" is the suffix for "we" in Arabic, when we say this world is a mirror, we kind of say we "saw" the world…

"You are not made up of this object, you consist of "eye." If you see the spirit, you give up the object" (Mathnawi, VI, 811)

A human being is actually like an eye in the cosmos consisting of a small universe and a big universe… Look at the picture above…

It is so excellent, isn't it?

So, if we consider an object, the origins of the objects we deal with as "images" come from the knowledge and beautiful names of Allah.

Consider an apple. It may be the shadow of Allah's names constituting the true nature of that object, for example, the shadow of Allah's name Munim (the Grantor). If there is an artwork, it is seen through the name as-Sani (the Artist, He who creates with infinite beauty). Although they appear in the shape of an apple, a tree, or a bird, the essence and the truth of every object consists of Allah's names.

Being merciful covers the rank formed by the true faces of the names and attributes.

As for the name ar-Raheem (the Most Compassionate), it is the state where the manifestations come to the light in the unitary sense. It is just like a baby that came out of the womb.

We "unitarily" appear in the world of existence by being a shadow of the shadow through the name ar-Raheem (the Most Compassionate), and when we match this with Planck's words, we see that he provides an exact scientific explanation of what is already explained in the Quran... Planck says, "We do not see the objects as they are (their essences, that is, true states are in mercifulness), but the source behind the revelation of all substances is the matrix of the universe..."

In order to understand the concept expressed with the term "matrix of the universe," I am providing you with the lexical meanings without comment:

Matrix (plural): mold, womb, base, and RAHEEM.

This scientific definition precisely describes the attribute of Allah ar-Raheem!

At the same time, we have previously shared that the "numeric sequence" might be the knowledge of the formation of every being in the universe.

The definition of the matrix that Planck has described actually matches the Islamic description of reality. In a unitary sense, the revelation of the beings, that is, their revelation to the world of existence occurs with the name ar-Raheem.

And this intellect is the matrix, that is the "womb," as Planck says!

The name and attribute of Allah that reveals the names of Allah to the world of existence.

The word matrix means "mater," that is, "mother" and "womb." Moreover, in medicine, matrix describes the energy that gives life in the human body which is a copy of the universe...

This consciousness behind all beings is the name ar-Raheem. Allah who calls all of us "My Family" qualifies Himself with the name ar-Raheem, loves and wraps us up with a mother's compassion...

We swam in His womb just like a fetus swimming in the mother's womb… We were surrounded by these names and attributes, and even if we were unaware, He was protecting us like a mother, and like a baby who is not aware of this, we seem to maintain our existence without taking notice...

Planck was tolerant of alternative opinions and religions. He criticized atheists as they mock symbols. Because some symbols were too important for the extremely religious people, and he emphasized their importance. Max Planck uttered these words in 1944: "I, as a person having devoted his life to science, can say, after extensive research about atoms, that, there is no matter as such. We must accept the presence of a conscious and wise being behind matter." Planck is accepted as a believing scientist with a strong imagination. The belief here is similar to the "study on the hypothesis." For instance, the causality principle is right or wrong; there was an action of belief there. He also said these words: "Belief in God may be necessary in religion and in science. God is the beginning for the believers. And for the physicists, He is at the end." It is said that Planck observed God's existence and he was a deist and according to hearsay, Planck declared that he was Catholic six months before his death.

When you read what is written by the world's physicists and researchers and if you have a little bit of information about the Quran and Sufi narrations, you see new discoveries regarding how matter or energy correspond to the knowledge of truth.

For example, one of the narrations that deeply affected me is from Wheeler, who is also a physicist.

John Archibald Wheeler who is an American theoretical physicist, one of the builders of the nuclear fusion theory, and having given his name to black holes, says that the universe is 'incomplete' based on the information he gathered from his experiments and since we are "observing" the universe and we are constantly interacting with our surroundings, we generate the reality that we see, and thus, we are contributors to this formation.

T.E. Bearden and other scientific philosophers emphasize the importance of our mind, consciousness, and intention in the formation of reality. He draws attention to the power of intention. So, these narrations correspond with Islam which is also referred to as "the religion of intention."

Allah, who creates the actions, looks at our intentions... And our intentions lead to our destiny ... And this becomes our 'reality'...

Realities related to scientific areas are constituted by the choices made in the dimensions like entwined labyrinths...

The explanations belonging to the scientists stated above have greatly influenced me.

Because the truth pointed out in the 27th verse of Surah al-Fath was confirmed by a scientist...

"Laqad sadaqallahu rasulahur ru'ya bil-haqq ..."

"Certainly has Allah showed to His Messenger the vision in truth ..." "People are asleep, they wake up when they die." (Hazrat Muhammad [PBUH])

"The worldly life is made up of a dream. Acquiring wealth in the world is similar to finding a treasure in a dream. Worldly wealth is transformed from generation to generation, but it always stays in the world." (Rumi)

And the reality declared by scientists, especially by physicists, in recent times:

"The material (physical) world is an illusion, and life is a dream..." Now, let's come back to the 27th verse of Surah al-Fath. It says that the Messenger of Allah [PBUH] was foretold the conquest in a dream he had before the conquest of Mecca (before reaching Hudaybiyyah).

Of course, this is the first apparent meaning of this verse ... Now, let's see the hidden meaning given in that period by looking at the word "ru'yah (dream)" and the expression "bil haqq" with scientific data ... Let's start with the roots of the word "ru'yah."

Ar ray:

1.View, sight.

2.Idea; ar ra, saw, perceived, adopted an idea.

The Arabic word is the infinitive of the verb "saw, perceived, adopted an idea."

When we look at an etymology dictionary, imagination: ar, fantasy, mental vision, spirit departed from the body, dreamed…

Ru'yah (dream) comes from the same root as Ru'yat. However, there is a distinction between them; "ru'yah" is said to be like seeing spiritually. (Sleep as well as some states similar to it) As for the "ru'yat," it means "to be awake and to witness at this time," that is, to observe. There are expressions in Sufism that a true dream is to see what is happening in the Preserved Slate (Lawh al-Mahfooz) in the mirror of our hearts.

While telling this, remember that when our Prophet was asked, "What is the dream we see while sleeping at night, then?", he replied, "It is a dream in a dream."In the first apparent narration, this explanation comes as the dream the Messenger of Allah [PBUH] saw when he slept.

However, when we pursue the hidden narration going down to the roots, we also see the following:

"I swear that Allah verified the view of His Messenger [PBUH] …" Yes, our Prophet was the first person and prophet in humanity who said this world is actually a dream.

Think of it this way: While we are sleeping and dreaming, how real everything is, isn't it? We get excited, we cry, or we laugh. The people that we see, it feels like they are really there in the flesh. We can never understand this while experiencing it.

This world's life is not different from this. We see one in our brain at night, and we see the other in the daytime while we deem ourselves to be awake. Everybody and everything is so real…

But, as you know, the human brain has a structure that can have effects on the body that occur as a result of running, thinking that it is running or that can feel a burning sensation in the body when it thinks it's in pain. Each incident that we attribute reality to is actually a dream just like a spirit separated from the body.

While all other prophets spoke about the world's material existence and reality, we can see that our Prophet, through the truth, expressed his opinion that everything that we see is actually a dream, an imagination and this has recently been discovered by science and that the truth of "bil haqq" is this.

"I was a hidden treasure, and I wished to be known, so I created a creation (humankind), then I made them love My blessings. Thus, they knew Me." (Hadith Qudsi, Ajluni))

By the embodiment of His Names, His seeing and observing this state just for a MOMENT was enough for the existence of this infinite realm and billions of years of time zones…

If you pay attention to the word imagination, it means "the spirit separated from the body" … So?

We are the formation of the Exhalation of the Most Merciful. He beautifully explains it to us with expressions such as, "I breathed of My spirit, a spirit from my sight …" that our "perception" of spirit separating from the body from the oneness which is like a single body as in the narration above …

We are the souls who think that they are separated from the body. However, this is a dream…

This entire universe is Allah's seeing and watching everything that happens with a momentary overflowing of His hidden treasure.

Physicists, who say the universe is present as an "observer," have detailed this verse…

If we turn back to Wheeler:

He said based on the information resulting from his experiments that the universe is incomplete and since we are observing the universe and we are constantly interacting with our surroundings, we generate the reality that we see, and thus, we are contributors to this formation.

Think of it this way: if an apple falls from a tree and if we don't see or hear it because we aren't there, then this event has never happened according to us, right? So, the narration of incidents existing with an observer is like this ...

Now, let's get to the point where we conclude the topic.

Said Nursi says "Eyes are the windows of the spirit ..." Yes.

Now, as we explained in the chapter called "the Lord," we know that the one who sees through us is a being that is not beyond the names of Allah ...Yes again ......

That is to say, the seeing spirit belongs to Allah. Here, the matter is the state of dreaming momentarily. Otherwise, the interpretation of a dream about Allah is related to seeing beyond sleeping... Everything occurs with the momentary observation of the spirit supposing it has departed from the body...

The embodiment of that spirit is Adam... Each of us is a part of Adam. All of us are "one" person in total...

"That is why We ordained for the Children of Israel that whoever takes a life—unless as a punishment for murder or mischief in the land—it will be as if they killed all of humanity; and whoever saves a life, it will be as if they saved all of humanity. 'Although' Our messengers already came to them with clear proofs, many of them still transgressed afterwards through the land.." (Surah al-Ma'idah, Verse 32)

This verse affirms us.

Now, let's look at what a human also contains in this context...

We have shared a few meanings of the word human under the topics related to relevant subjects.

And let's look at another meaning of the word "human" ...

Do you know what I did when I learned that one of the meanings of "human" in Arabic is "the pupil of the eye"?

I wept... And I wept...

What could be done in the face of such knowledge and glory?

Insan al-ayn ...

Look at the perfection of the description. This describes and more-over reveals both the love of Allah towards us like a mother's affection and His treatment of us with kid gloves and His watching the universe through us ... There is an 'I' within me, deeper than I ...

It must be the profound meaning underlying the statement, "apple of the universe's eye" used by almost all sages to describe the human ...

What joy it is, my Allah!

Allah sees His beautiful names through us. We were perceiving Allah's beautiful names like an apple of the eye...

The universe is shaped by the participation of the observers. And since they are also the creators, the observers, in a sense, contribute to the creation. The participants are Allah's beautiful names within us. They are the ones who see through us. They are the ones who contribute to the creation. As a result, they are the instruments of the One...

The meaning that Allah's beautiful names see through us was so striking... Allah sees and investigates through humans, and this fits the principle and custom of serving the purpose with His Names.

Hazrat Said-i Nursi Bediüzzaman stated the importance of the eye by saying "The eye is such a sense that the spirit watches this world through that window."

To sum up, the expression, "Allah created our Prophet from His own divine light and He created us from his divine light" supported Einstein's theory of relativity. It was once again expressed with this physical explanation told as a summary of Wheeler's career.

Wheeler explained his career by dividing it into 3 points:

• Everything was a particle; basic particles like neutrons, protons... (We are all scattered divine lights, remember the explanation that we are photons as given above)

• Everything is an area (areas brought into existence by these particles)

• Everything is knowledge...

Here, when I saw the third point, I felt fanah. We sometimes say we feel 'fanah in Turkish, especially when dealing with the knowledge of Allah. One day, when I pondered the meaning of this expression which I was inspired to say, I noticed that a person moves towards "fanah," that is, the "non-existence" even by understanding a small segment from the knowledge of Allah.

Allah compelled our Prophet to summarize this situation as follows:

"Allah created His Messenger (PBUH) from His own divine light, and the whole universe was created from his divine light. The divine light is "ilmullah," that is, the knowledge of Allah.

This was the same as Wheeler's expression culminating from his lengthy studies.

"We are participants for bringing into existence not only here and near but also far and before."

"He is the First and the Last, the Ascendant and the Intimate, and He is, of all things, Knowing." (Surah al-Hadid, Verse 3)

"Why do we need more for an explanation of what happened in the distant past if we are participating in bringing something belonging to the universe from the distant past?"

After an interview with Wheeler, Martin Redfernsa expressed his thoughts as follows:

"If Wheeler is right, we and other consciousnesses observe the universe and create in this way, or at least we reveal the creator who created the universe…"

Wheeler: "Everything is knowledge…"

"Allah created seven heavens in layers and likewise for the earth. For us to know that Allah is the All-Powerful and He surrounds everything with His knowledge, the orders constantly descend between the heavens and the earth."

Printed in Great Britain
by Amazon

30965460R00193